Community Action for School Reform

Community Action for School Reform

Howell S. Baum

State University of New York Press

Published by
State University of New York Press, Albany

Printed in the United States of America

For information, address State University of New York Press,
90 State Street, Suite 700, Albany, NY 12207

Production by Michael Haggett
Marketing by Anne M. Valentine

Library of Congress Cataloging in Publication Data

Baum, Howell S.
Community action for school reform / Howell S. Baum.
p. cm.
Includes bibliographical references and index.
ISBN 0-7914-5759-1 (alk. paper) — ISBN 0-7914-5760-5 (pbk.: alk. paper)
1. Community and school—Maryland—Baltimore—Case studies. 2. School improvement programs—Maryland—Baltimore—Case studies. 3. Education, Urban—Maryland—Baltimore—Case studies. I. Title.

LC221.3 B35B38 2003
371.19'09752'6—dc21

2003057267

10 9 8 7 6 5 4 3 2 1

DEDICATION

To the memory of my father, Irving Baum,
who believed in civic action
and hoped it would make a difference,
and
to Bobby English,
who impressed him with her dauntless spirit
and taught me with her actions

Contents

Preface

This book chronicles a journey. In 1994, a few Southeast Baltimore community activists and I decided to see what a community group could do to improve schools. And there is no other way to say it: we had next to no idea what we would do. Nine years later, the Southeast Education Task Force has organized parents, developed and begun implementing a community plan on education, helped an overcrowded school get an addition, influenced the Empowerment Zone's education initiative, aided an elementary school in becoming a full-service community school, lobbied successfully for a new K–8 school, and much else. At least as important as these specifics, the Task Force has convinced ordinary citizens that they can do something about education, and it has established the principle that parents and other community members should participate in the school system.

The handful of activists who set this in motion met the two challenges of community action. One is to attach individuals and organizations to create a network capable of acting. The other is to develop and use tested knowledge in deciding what to do and doing it. They spent their first two years mostly talking, trying to learn enough about education, the school system, and their own capacities to act. They identified other community members, some education activists, and a few in the school system who were interested in going ahead. They took tentative first steps, learned richly from the results, and continued moving. They elaborated a university-community partnership and developed some community-school partnerships.

One might be struck by the informality and looseness of their efforts, particularly at the start. These were not education reformers implementing a clearly articulated model of school improvement. Yet that is one of this book's central points. Most school reform, like most schooling, is a top-down affair, the province of professionals. Ordinary people, though the constituency, clients, and intended beneficiaries of schooling, are assumed to know little that matters for setting directions, deciding on strategies, or evaluating results. Yet there are strong arguments for community involvement in education. First, it is a democratic right. Second, research shows that parental involvement contributes to academic achievement. And, third, community activism is necessary to prod schools to change and to implement change.

There are few models of a community approach to school improvement, particularly in the cities, to complement other efforts. The Southeast Education Task Force has experimented with creating one that works. Readers should examine this book in that spirit. Those looking for blockbuster success in changing a school system or even a school will be disappointed. However, the truth be told, they will find few examples of that anywhere. That, too, is one of this book's central points. School systems are complex and open to their environments. Professional ideologies, bureaucratic politics, and garden-variety organizational dynamics influence what goes on in classrooms. Moreover, children's learning, as we all know, has to do with both what goes on in classrooms and what goes on in homes and on the streets. The school is always in the community, and the community is always in the school.

This book looks at how organizational dynamics and family and community life influence schooling, how both often constrain change, and how, to get to the bottom line, educational improvement depends on organizational change and social reform. The stories realistically describe the organizational and community interests, uncertainties, ambiguities, and anxieties that any reform must come to terms with. Case studies often suppress these discouraging details, but there is no way around them.

For reformers who spend most of their time in schools, this book shines useful light on urban communities. In many educators' cognitive maps, the community is terra incognita, more likely sinister than friendly, amorphous, populated by undifferentiated families or else by a few families and local businesses somehow situated amid broad empty spaces. This book shows what community members look and sound like and how they act when they try to work with schools to improve them. Another of this book's main points is that these community members want to work with schools to help them educate children. Community activism disrupts schooling's normal routines (though many of these, as educators recognize, do not accomplish much), but it offers resources and, yes, knowledge for stronger, collaborative action. One need not romanticize community action or exaggerate its accomplishments to appreciate its potential.

This book's lessons might be summarized in three statements. The first is that a small community organization can accomplish some things of significance in improving education. Part of the explanation is that there is a lot of empty space in the education domain, part is that even a small entity can organize powerful networks, and part is that communities have many useful resources.

The second lesson is that community action could accomplish a great deal more if school systems recognized community groups and were willing to collaborate. One of the severest limitations on the community approach is that school systems try to close communities out of the action. Central to this impulse is a predicament that educators have perversely brought on themselves. As professionals, they have long claimed to be society's sole experts on everything related to children's education. In the meantime, however, society has heaped numerous ambiguous, conflicting, and often unrealistic expectations on the schools. The educators, still claiming to do it all, inevitably fail, to public blame and their own shame. Then they become wary of outsiders, only increasing their chances of failing at what they want to accomplish.

The final lesson is that even if community groups and school systems worked well together, much that influences urban children's education lies outside of their grasp. Social policies and institutions governing housing, employment, social welfare, public safety, health, transportation, and race relations, for example, affect adults' ability to form families, model success for their children, introduce them to the larger world, and convince them that school matters. Social reform is central to educational reform.

Part of the journey recounted in this book is my own. After teaching community planning for many years, serendipitously I had the opportunity to join a group of activists in shaping this initiative. I was a participant throughout, though I have directly mentioned my efforts in only a few places. Even so, this book's tone undoubtedly betrays my ongoing involvement. Chapter 16, on organizing practice, gives voice to my experience of tensions between academic work, which emphasizes knowledge, and community work, which emphasizes attachment. Concretely, academic research normally is well-bounded activity, in which one can control what and when one reads, how and when one analyzes the information, and what and when one writes. In contrast, community work is unbounded, nearly out-of-control activity, where one must constantly be available to make and keep connections, whatever else.

In that context, I must express my deepest respect for those who make community work their calling. I have had the privilege of working with selfless, committed, smart people who have unstintingly invested themselves in community service. Foremost, I have the greatest admiration for Bobby English, with whom I have worked in her dual role as chair of the Education Task Force and director of the Julie Community Center. She sees nothing outside her responsibilities to children and families. As an academic who studies action, I have learned from her a great deal about the possibilities of acting (see, in the text, her recipe for stone soup). I also have had the opportunity to learn from community leaders Ken Strong and Ed Rutkowski. Other participants who have reflected with me on the project have been Mae Kastor, Judy Free, Jack Bovaird, Tru Ginsburg, Jerry Baum, Laura Weeldreyer, and Decatur Miller.

Colleagues in the University of Maryland's College of Education helped out intellectually and instrumentally. My greatest appreciation goes to Sylvia

Rosenfield, who taught me a lot about schools while, among other things, consulting to a school on student discipline. William Strein, Meryl Sirmans, and David McFadden were stimulating partners on that project. Barbara Finkelstein, Patricia Alexander, Kathryn Wentzel, and Sheri Meisel also contributed time and insight. Urban Studies and Planning Program colleagues Sidney Brower, Alex Chen, Jim Cohen, and Marie Howland shared many hours of discussion about community work, university-community partnerships, Southeast Baltimore, and the education project. Others who helped make sense of what went on were Dick Cook, Michael Diamond, Daniel Frank, Bob Giloth, Larry Hirschhorn, Sanda Kaufman, Peter Marris, Dennis Shirley, Paula Singer, and Stanley Wenocur. John Forester and Charles Hoch, as always, provided good ideas and warm encouragement.

Many graduate students advanced this initiative, with some organizing, a lot of research and analysis, some planning, and a goodly amount of committee staffing. Debby Volk served in several capacities helping the Task Force get started, and Julie Herlands and Elin Zurbrigg made focused contributions in the later, more robust years. In between, Jessica Hanson, Becky Himlin, Kristen Forsyth, Bill Jeffries, Angela Frusciante, Polly Peterson, Christine Melekian, and Monika Graves each contributed essential assistance.

Initial support for the project and my participation came in a grant from the U. S. Department of Education's Urban Community Service Program to the University of Maryland's Urban Studies and Planning Program. The Planning Program funded some of my time and that of some of the graduate assistants. A grant from the France-Merrick Foundation to the Southeast Education Task Force made it possible for me to continue. Invaluable support for the time to write this book came from a Wilson H. Elkins Professorship at the University of Maryland during the 2000–01 school year. I am indebted to Dean Steven Hurtt for nominating me for the honor.

More than 1,000 persons have participated in Task Force activities. Parents, teachers, principals, community activists, students, the local school system board and staff, state and federal education officials, academics, elected officials, pastors and lay leaders, service agency staff, education experts, foundation staff, and others—all have been important in shaping this community approach to educational improvement and in learning from it. Without them, this book would have been impossible, and unwarranted.

My wife, Madelyn, and our daughters, Elena and Maya, supported my involvement in this work by tolerating meetings that intruded into family time and helped think about education by talking about their own schooling.

Acknowledgments

Parts of chapter 10 previously were published in "Education and the Empowerment Zone: Ad Hoc Development of an Inter-Organizational Domain," *Journal of Urban Affairs* 21:3 (1999): 289–307, reprinted in agreement with Blackwell Publishing. Parts of chapter 14 previously were published in "Fantasies and Realities of University-Community Partnerships," *Journal of Planning Education and Research*, 20:2 (winter 2000): 234–46, reprinted in agreement with Sage Publications. Parts of chapter 17 previously were published in "How Should We Evaluate Community Initiatives?" *Journal of the American Planning Association*, 67:2 (spring 2001): 147–58, reprinted in agreement with the American Planning Association.

Part 1

Introduction

Chapter 1

School Reform and Educational Improvement
Challenges and Responses

Urban schools enroll one-fourth of American students who represent one-third of all low-income students and 43 percent of minority students.[1] Three-fourths of central city students are African American or Hispanic, and 42 percent are eligible for lunch subsidies. Poor and minority students are the majority in many American cities. Moreover, poverty is concentrated: those who are poor live together, apart from others who are better off, and the concentrated poor are particularly likely to be black. Black children represent 15 percent of the children in the country but make up 63 percent of children in extremely poor neighborhoods (where at least 40 percent of residents are poor) in the seventy-five largest American cities. Just over half of urban students attend schools in high-poverty neighborhoods, while less than one-fourth of students elsewhere do so.

Although city schools face especially challenging students, on average, urban districts spend about 90 percent of what other districts do per pupil. Two-thirds of central city school buildings have structural inadequacies, compared to a little over half in suburban and rural areas. Urban school districts have more difficulty attracting qualified teachers than other districts, and they are more likely to have unfilled positions. One result is that urban students are especially likely to encounter teachers who are not fully licensed. Urban teachers are much more likely than their counterparts to stay away from school. For example, 12 percent of urban eighth graders attend schools where officials consider teacher absenteeism a problem, compared to only 5 percent elsewhere. Urban students often encounter unchallenging curricula. Many classes emphasize low-level material and rote learning. Urban schools have far fewer advanced courses than other schools.

Urban schools are larger, on average, than suburban and rural schools. Physical violence is high and considerably higher than in nonurban schools. In New York, Pennsylvania, New Jersey, and Ohio, for instance, 60 to 70 percent of teachers in urban districts characterized physical conflicts as being moderate or serious problems, compared to about 25 percent in other districts. Urban students often miss class. For example, nearly one-third of urban eighth graders attend schools where officials consider their absenteeism a problem, compared to less than one fourth of eighth graders elsewhere.

Students who attend city schools do not do as well on standardized tests as other students. Only about 40 percent of urban students score at the "basic" level on reading, mathematics, and science tests in the U. S. Department of Education's National Assessment of Educational Progress, compared to about 65 percent of nonurban students. Urban students attending schools where the majority of students are poor do even worse compared to nonurban students in high-poverty schools. Only about 25 to 30 percent of the urban students perform at "basic" levels, compared to twice as many of their counterparts. In a number of states, the "urban effect" is greater. In Maryland, for example, about 10 percent of urban students perform at a "basic" level in eighth-grade mathematics or science, compared to approximately 60 percent of nonurban students.

A simple summary is this: American urban schools are not educating their students, who, by and large, are children of the nation's poor and racial and ethnic minorities. These conditions help keep many African Americans and Hispanics poor, and they help make poverty hereditary. They make it impossible for American cities to reproduce themselves intellectually.

The consequences are numbingly familiar. Many children who live in the cities do not learn what they must know to be productive, satisfied, well-paid workers. They lack the reading, mathematics, and communication skills necessary for jobs that others value and that bring self-respect. They do not look forward to work, because they do not expect much of it. There is little place for them in the postindustrial service economy, and they know it.

They are unprepared for civic activity. They learn little about current events, and they care little about events beyond their immediate surroundings. They lack the skills for deliberating and making decisions in public meetings or developing community organizations. They learn from their conditions and the lives of the adults around them that the larger forces that move society are unlikely to respond to their efforts. They find it hard to see how voting would move them out of poverty, get them decent housing, or provide schools where they really learn. They do not expect to exercise political power.

These children are even unprepared to become parents, as many will be before they graduate from high school. While most have parents who struggle to raise them well, many do not see their parents as successful models to imitate, have the confidence that they can be good parents, or possess the skills needed for the constant effort and trying moments of raising children. Poor children, when they become parents, will have to do what their parents could not in order to help their children find better positions than their own.

Of course, there are exceptions—resilient children and families who overcome the obstacles of poverty (Hrabowski, Maton, and Greif 1998; Maton, Greene, Hrabowski, and Greif 2002; Nettles and Pleck 1994). They know and do more than many from more fortunate circumstances. They are inspiring and deserve recognition. And, yet, they are the exceptions.

This is an educational crisis, but it is not just a problem of the schools. The schools cannot be blamed for all of this, nor can they fix it all. For that matter, the urban crisis is not caused by cities, and it too cannot be solved by cities alone. If we look broadly at the field of education, to take note of everything that significantly influences whether children are ready and motivated to learn, whether they are taught well, whether they learn, and whether their learning brings fitting rewards, we see far more than schools. Whether a young child in an inner-city neighborhood grows up well educated depends, for example, on the economy and labor market, the housing market, race relations, the political culture, tax policy, public transportation, the police and the criminal justice system, and medical care and insurance.

To recite this list is not to let schools or families off the hook for children's educational success, but if we consider how these institutions automatically work well for the middle class, not to mention those better off, we glimpse how much must be done to improve educational opportunities for children growing up in the cities. Improving education is not just a matter of reforming schools. That effort alone can only fail, because it defines the problem so that it cannot be solved. Improving education depends on changing these other institutions as well.

What is discouraging about this diagnosis is that so many of the institutions that matter are geographically and politically distant from the cities. School systems alone can do little about them, but defining the challenge in that way is a step toward addressing it: those who govern the schools must make common cause with allies who can offer leverage with other institutions.

This book examines possibilities for action in this larger territory, which we will call the "education field." Any interventions that significantly improve children's educational opportunities, achievements, or rewards will be subsumed under the heading "educational improvement." Educational improvement includes "school reform," a phrase that we will use more or less conventionally to refer to accomplishments in making teaching and learning at school more fruitful. The term does not imply that schools are terrible, nor does it mean that intervention must be dramatic. It does not require that changes "restructure" schools, or that they be "schoolwide," but only that they bring about some improvement of significance.

Approaches to Reform

Two Functions of School Systems

We can distinguish two, related functions of school systems.[2] One, which may be called "technical," includes the activities concerned with teaching and learning. Focused on the classroom, it consists of actions intended to draw on knowledge about teaching, learning, and specific subjects in order to stimulate and enable children to develop their intellectual capacities, to become curious, to master subjects, and to act knowledgeably. We sometimes simplistically characterize this process as the transmission of knowledge, but we should speak of the communication, construction, and reconstruction of knowledge, with attention to the social relations in which this effort takes place. The technical function of schooling is directed toward individual students, who gain the ability to use knowledge.

The general public and organizations in the larger society want assurance that the schools are succeeding in their technical functions, transforming young children into knowledgeable near-adults. Managing relations with these constituents is school systems' second function, which can be called "institutional." Because few outsiders see, and fewer understand, the technical work in classrooms, most rely instead on symbolic indications that teachers are teaching and children are learning. In place of direct observation of the process and accomplishments of education, schools offer the public a ritual classification of people, places, and activities in education and then present signs that students move appropriately through the classifications.

To take familiar examples: schools classify grades and levels of instruction, along with discrete subject matters, so that it is conventional to speak of "third-grade mathematics" or "high school English." Schools also classify students not only by grade but also by abilities, from variations within a normal range to the "gifted and talented" and those with "learning disabilities." Schools classify students in terms of their apparent interests and aims, from the college bound to those in "general," "vocational," "business," or other tracks. Schools classify teachers in terms of qualifications to teach subjects, grades, and students. Schools certify progress quantitatively in terms of "units" and qualitatively in terms of grades and test scores.

When schools certify their graduates credibly, the larger society is satisfied that teachers have taught students the requisite knowledge. Significantly, while the technical activities of schooling vary from classroom to classroom, the institutional activities are uniform across the nation. What matters with the institutional activities is whether outsiders believe that a school system is organized in such a way as to produce educated graduates, not—to state the contrast extremely—whether students actually learn anything in classrooms.

Two Approaches to Reform

Technical Approaches and Instruction

Most current proposals for school reform focus on one of these two functions. Some target school systems' technical activities, with an emphasis on introducing new knowledge into the schools. They focus on curriculum and pedagogy, but they include other practices and means of organizing schools or classrooms that may influence teachers' teaching or children's behavior or learning. Because of the specialized understanding of the educational processes required, these proposals usually originate with professional educators, most often in universities.

Examples include the Accelerated Schools that enrich offerings for at-risk youth, the Coalition for Essential Schools' principles for active learning, tightly scripted Direct Instruction in reading, and Success for All's highly structured reading curriculum. Those who take this approach speak of "best practices," programs that appear effective elsewhere that could be implemented with good results locally (e.g., National Diffusion Network 1994). Some researchers add that a good instructional program must be supported by school leadership and a collaborative climate. They characterize schools that succeed in this way as "effective schools" (e.g., Edmonds 1979; Purkey and Smith 1983). Whether focusing on instruction or climate, this group of reformers is interested in "replicating" proven programs.

These proposals aim to improve education by introducing more good knowledge into use. The proposals build on four assumptions. The first is that education is essentially a process by which teachers help students gain knowledge. For many reformers, social relations and classroom milieu, as well as students' family and community ties, matter far less than classroom cognitive conditions. The second assumption is that teachers are interested primarily in putting the best available knowledge to use in teaching their students—and that school systems are organized to encourage and permit teachers to discover and use good knowledge. The third assumption is that virtually any teacher, perhaps with some coaching, can readily make use of new knowledge, implementing it in his or her practice. The fourth assumption, crucial to these proposals, is that there is universally, or at least widely, applicable knowledge that, if teachers adopted it, they could use to teach most, if not all, of their students considerably better than at present.

This approach has produced useful innovations (e.g., Herman et al. 1999), but the clearest lesson of limited evaluation is that context matters. What works in one classroom or school does not necessarily work elsewhere. These reformers tend to explain their limited success in three ways. First, central system administrations bureaucratically constrain principals and teachers from innovating and implementing reforms. Second, pressures for "accountability" force teachers to abandon reform practices that do not lead to higher test scores. Third, schools lack the resources to implement reforms properly. These explanations carry weight, but they downplay questions about whether programs fit students, whether school staff are invested in a particular model, and whether teachers have the ability to carry out a specific reform.

Institutional Approaches and Structure

In contrast to this focus on the technical activities of classrooms, a second set of reform proposals emphasizes the institutional structure of school systems. They give less specific attention to classrooms and teachers and implicitly trust educators less. By and large, these are the work of people who are not trained educators and who have a limited understanding of teaching and learning; most of these reformers treat classrooms as black boxes. They assume that by manipulating relationships between schools and managers or constituencies they can influence children's learning or, perhaps the next closest thing, parental and public satisfaction with the schools. That is the essence of the institutional function of schools.

One variant of this approach is managerial, articulated, for example, by those from the corporate sector who talk about "managing school systems better." They prefer a bureaucratic model of organization, manifested in the addition of responsibilities, lines of accountability, and managers to existing central administrations, with a focus on explicit "production goals," in the form of test scores. Although some school boards adopt specific instructional models as the prescribed "production process," others do not, largely because they have little educational expertise. The main assumption of the managerial approach is that principals and teachers already have the knowledge, ability, and resources to educate students, that what they need to do more and better is clear expectations, monitoring, and sanctions. Thus periodic testing accompanies test score goals, and school administrations, often at the state level, threaten to take over or to otherwise punish schools that fail to meet goals.

In contrast to the centralizing impulse in the managerial reforms, another variant of the institutional approach proposes setting schools loose to face myriad parents who would have a "choice" of schools in a "market" (e.g., Chubb and Moe 1990; Henig 1994; Peterson and Hassel 1998; Rasell and Rothstein 1993). Although some managerial reformers may impose instructional programs on schools, the market approach is not concerned with the details of instruction; they are a matter of "consumer satisfaction," left to parents in choosing schools. The common principle in choice proposals is to create or tighten connections between schools and parents and to loosen or sever ties between schools and system boards and administrators. Closest to current school arrangements is "public schools of choice," of which magnet schools are an example, where parents can choose among public schools (Clinchy 2000; Fantini 1973; Meier 1995). Charter schools operate with greater autonomy from system rules (Finn, Manno, and Vanourek 2000; Sarason 1998). Private schools round off the continuum.

The central assumption is that schools that are "accountable" to families through a "market" will educate children well, because the alternative is to lose "customers" and go out of existence. This assumption depends on others. The first is that parents have real choices—not only do they find alternative programs that meet their standards for their children's education, but also there is room for their children in these programs, and they can afford to send them. This assumption is mingled with a second, that parents have adequate knowledge about particular schools, their children's learning needs, and education to make reasonable choices about what suits their children. Gaining this knowledge requires that parents have the expertise and time to gather and analyze new information. It depends as well on schools' revealing sophisticated information about their programs' successes and failures and students' performances. These assumptions require a third, that school staff can balance parental preferences with educational standards in a way that allows them to change their schools to respond to new preferences. Fourth, some reformers assume that parents who choose their children's schools will have incentives and opportunities to involve themselves in the schools to know what the school is doing and to make sure it serves their children. Such involvement depends on parents' discretionary time and formal education, as well as on teachers' willingness to open up their classrooms.

Under "market" arrangements, there is no single standard of educational success. Different schools may pursue different goals, and different parents may evaluate the same school in different terms. Although some parents measure schools in terms of test scores, others base their "market choices" on other criteria. The scant research on choice approaches reinforces the research on instructional reforms: context matters. Choice per se does not produce educational improvement for all participating students (Henig 1994). Even so, many parents are happier than when their children were in assigned public schools. That is a measure of the reforms' success in terms of schools' institutional functions.

Community Approaches

A third group of reform proposals, which we will call "community approaches," consists of hybrids. What they have in common is an emphasis on connecting schools and communities and, for the most part, proponents' grassroots ties. Because they focus on relationships and structure, community approaches might be considered a variant of the institutional approach. They superficially resemble choice proposals in tying schools to families.

However, most community proposals differ from many choice proposals in four ways. First, rather than portraying individual families as the relevant actors, they are concerned with communities, at least communities of parents. Second, rather than considering schooling a "good" that a "consumer" "chooses" in the "market," this approach regards a school as an institution that is part of a community as a social, cultural, and political entity. One implication is that the relationship entails more commitment of the parties to one another than does a market transaction. Another is that community approaches expect schools not only to educate individual children but also to help develop communities, for example, by attracting families with children and preparing a skilled workforce. Third, most community advocates can be comfortable with the public schools, as long as they are connected to the community. Small, community-based public schools would satisfy proponents of both the community approach and the choice approach (e.g., Bryk et al. 1998; Clinchy 2000; Meier 1995). Fourth, because public school staff may resist community involvement, some community approaches take an oppositional stance toward schools, or at least are wary of them, whereas the choice rhetoric emphasizes compatibility of school and parental interests.

Some community approaches differ from most, if not all, choice proposals in a basic way, by recognizing parents as children's ongoing teachers, along with such others as youth workers, coaches, and clergy, in addition to professional educators. These reformers are interested in organizing formal and informal teachers to teach children academic, social, cultural, and other knowledge and skills (Honig, Kahne, and McLaughlin 2001).

Further, some community approaches fundamentally differ from institutional approaches generally, as well as technical approaches, by aiming to do more than change schools or family relations with schools; they want to improve community conditions that affect families, children, and schools. They assume that educators can teach more effectively when communities are secure, when families have resources to raise children and prepare them for schooling, and when children can foresee successful adult roles. Advocates of this approach are interested, for example, in providing social, psychological, and financial support for families, helping parents raise children, finding good housing for families, and getting parents employment. This approach can be seen as part of general social reform, with a focus on supporting child development and education.

Community approaches focus on schools' institutional functions by assuming that parents actively involved with a school will help and push it to operate in ways that give them the confidence that their children are learning.

In addition, some of these reformers emphasize schools' technical functions, assuming that active collaboration between parents and professional educators will help teach more effectively. James Comer's School Development Program, which gives parents active planning and decision-making roles, is a community approach that centers on teaching and learning.

Community approaches share some assumptions of choice approaches. They assume that parents have the time and skill to get the knowledge to make reasonable judgments about school quality, and they assume that schools are willing, or can be persuaded, to inform parents about programs and students. In addition, they assume that parents have the time and skill to take active roles at school—not just volunteering for nonprofessional tasks but also participating in planning and decision making, and even teaching children—and that schools are willing, or can be prodded, to allow parents to do so. Crucially, community approaches assume that parents have the time and skill to organize and persuade school staff to work with them. To draw a clear contrast, choice approaches assume that parents can make informed individual choices, whereas community approaches assume that parents can take knowledgeable, collective action.

When aiming for educational improvement through community change, these approaches make additional assumptions. They assume that parents can be persuaded and helped to improve the ways they raise children. They assume that organized parents can persuade local institutions to join forces with them, to help develop social programs, and to form partnerships with schools. Thus they assume that businesses, churches, and social agencies can be interested in helping families and children or in working with schools. Fundamentally, they assume that parents at home or in alliance with others can have an impact on the conditions that influence children's development and education.

There is no systematic research on such wide-ranging community approaches. However, a "new generation of evidence" shows that parental involvement in children's education is associated with improvements in students' behavior and academic performance (Henderson and Berla 1994; Honig, Kahne, and McLaughlin 2001). Evaluations of child and family programs provide evidence of "social programs that work" (Crane 1998; Schorr 1989, 1997).

A Case of the Community Approach

This book examines the Southeast Education Task Force, a Baltimore project that takes the community approach to reforming schools and improving children's education. As school reform, the initiative is a hybrid of institutional and technical approaches, whereby parents and community activists have organized to help neighborhood schools teach their children better. As we will see, parents and community activists find it much easier to establish external relationships with schools and the school system than to influence instruction directly. Moreover, despite skepticism about the validity of test scores, most are willing to accept these institutional markers of success in lieu of more sophisticated, but less accessible, knowledge of children's learning.

At the same time, the project aims to change community conditions to give more support for children's education and growth. The initiative develops resources for parents to raise their children and prepare them for school, and for children to deal with problems that get in the way of learning. The project encourages partnerships between schools and local institutions, not just to assist the schools but also to connect them more closely to the community and to change educators' views of their mission. As we will see, so many constantly changing conditions affect children that even well-planned and executed programs have limited impact on their development.

The Task Force began as a partnership of community activists and university faculty to find ways to improve schools sufficiently to revitalize a declining blue-collar neighborhood. With little precedent, they set out to create a community-based organization that would organize and plan with schools to improve children's education. While teachers and principals tried to improve instruction in school, the Task Force would aid families and improve community conditions.

From the start, they faced two challenges. The first, which we will call "attachment," was whether they could assemble enough community members interested in the schools to form an organization capable of action and, then, whether this group could form working alliances with schools and the system administration. The second challenge, of knowledge, was whether the organization could learn enough about schools and education to plan and implement projects that might realistically improve conditions. They had to prove that community members who were not professional educators could do anything that mattered to improve the schools or to improve children's education. How could they affect the conditions described at the beginning of this chapter?

Part 1 identifies the issues, sets the stage, and introduces the cast of characters. Following this chapter on school reform and educational improvement, chapter 2 presents a conceptual framework for thinking about attachment and knowledge. Chapter 3 focuses on a crucial type of attachment, parental involvement in schools and education, while chapter 4 describes the Baltimore setting and Task Force origins.

Parts 2 through 5 organize the Task Force's history in terms of a sequence of themes. Chapter 5 in part 2 describes how a core group started by conducting research on people and issues before setting up an organization.

Part 3 turns to activities for generating and sustaining participation. Chapter 6 examines efforts to recruit and keep members for the new Task Force, chapter 7 discusses how the Task Force tried to engage the school system, and chapter 8 describes activities to extend community involvement by organizing parents and forming church-school partnerships.

Part 4 explains how the Task Force then turned to action. Chapter 9 describes projects that resulted from early interests in doing something, and chapter 10 examines a sophisticated interorganizational network that influenced Baltimore's Empowerment Zone education initiative.

Part 5 presents the Task Force's return to research to improve action. Chapter 11 looks at how participants learned about education, the school system, and community intervention from their activities and how they used this knowledge to develop an education plan, while chapter 12 describes research projects used for planning with the school system.

Chapter 13 in part 6 discusses the money needed for community action and the implications of financial dependency for a community organization.

Part 7 analyzes tensions between attachment and knowledge in different contexts. Chapter 14 looks at the challenges faced by university-community partnerships, chapter 15 examines the difficulty of connecting communities and schools, and chapter 16 describes the tensions in the roles of individuals who form the personal connections between organizations in networks.

Part 8 draws lessons and conclusions from the case. Chapter 17 discusses the difficulty of evaluating community action and assesses the Task Force, while chapter 18 draws conclusions regarding the potential for community action to reform schools or to improve education.

Chapter 2

Attachment and Knowledge

A simple way of describing education reformers' aims is to say that they want teachers, administrators, parents, and the others who influence children's learning to act on better knowledge. Teachers should incorporate tested models in their practice. Administrators should adapt sophisticated management methods in operating schools and school systems. Parents should raise children with an understanding of their biological and psychological needs.

However, using new knowledge, with which few would disagree in principle, means not just endorsing abstract ideas but recognizing that past practices have not worked, giving up comfortable habits, and acting experimentally—for example, teaching reading, managing a classroom, supervising staff, rewarding and disciplining children at home, or dealing with family conflict in different ways. Any parent, manager, or teacher knows how hard it is to change, even when customary practices do not work.

Psychologist Kurt Lewin (1951) observed that people are most likely to make and follow through on decisions to change when they can discuss problems and possibilities with others in similar circumstances. "Professional development" or "parenting classes," for example, accomplish little unless teachers, administrators, or parents feel that they are in the same boat with others, are struggling similarly with difficult problems, and have support to try new things. In other words, people adopt—or resist—knowledge in the context of their attachments. They want colleagues, friends, or associates to think of them as acting knowledgeably, and they look to others for affirmation of their beliefs and practices. They act on knowledge not just because it is reasonable or tested but because doing so makes them part of a group. The group may be others they see day in and day out, or it may be people they identify with, such as experts or leaders. Teaching, managing, or parenting differently may entail giving up old attachments and forming new ones. Thus school reform and educational improvement are not merely efforts to change the knowledge that people use but ambitions to redefine and reorganize people's attachments.

This book describes an effort to create new attachments to influence the use of knowledge. The formation of the Southeast Education Task Force would depend on developing one set of attachments. The Task Force's work with the school system would require developing others. These attachments would support community members, parents, teachers, administrators, and others in examining the reasonableness of current knowledge and considering alternatives. This book is concerned with a general question about attachment and knowledge: What attachments make it likely that people will act on realistic knowledge? This chapter elaborates on the question by looking more closely at attachment and knowledge. Because knowledge rests on attachments, we begin with attachment, proceed to knowledge, and conclude with implications for educational improvement.

Attachment

The Societal Context: Turbulence

Societal changes in the past half century have fundamentally altered the conditions in which community members form organizations, superintendents manage school systems, schools develop partnerships with businesses, churches, or universities, and myriad other organizations connect. Fred Emery and Eric Trist (1973) made note of these changes in terms of a paradox. As organizations grew in size to control more of their environments, they eventually lost the power to act independently. Two developments changed the context for action. First, organizations became so large and their actions had such strong, far-reaching effects that any intentional action set other, autonomous processes into motion in their environments. Second, the development of such large entities in many sectors of the society populated each organization's environment with others like it. Each came to depend on others to get its work done, though neither the terms of the interdependence nor its consequences were clear. Thus any organization encounters increased uncertainty about the effects of its actions and reduced ability to control those effects. Self-interested action requires collaboration.

Organizations began to pay attention to their environment because they could neither take it for granted nor dominate it (Trist 1977). Put differently, organizations have become inseparable from their environments, and increasingly it is the overall field, rather than discrete organizations within it, that has the capacity to act. Those who have examined these changes have used various terms to characterize these environments, such as "inter-organizational domains" (Trist 1983), "interorganizational fields" (Warren 1967, 1971), and "functional systems" (Schön 1971). Emery and Trist (1973) characterized the new conditions as "turbulence."

The words "domain," "field," and "system" have dual meanings. On the one hand, they are descriptive, referring to the ways in which the aggregate actions of institutions with interests in similar or overlapping problems create a social system. Thus one can speak of a "medical field," "land use field," or "education field": these are made up of the entities whose actions somehow influence policy and practice in these areas, even if the actors are only loosely organized or unaware of one another. Entities may try to control things on their own. Several may try to accomplish similar goals but in diverse, and even divergent, ways. They end up influencing one another but not completely or fully predictably, and actions may have uncertain, ambiguous outcomes. Hence, the second usage of these words is prescriptive, suggesting that if organizations cooperated to develop agreed-upon roles, relationships, and rules to define and govern their shared field, then they could create a system that is, in fact, functional, where intentional action could be efficacious.

Long (1958) made similar observations in analyzing how public business was carried out in communities, when he called attention to "ecologies of games." Actors, such as elected officials, community groups, unions, schools, businesses, city agencies, nonprofit organizations, and the media, operating in an environment that is more or less beyond their control, construct ad hoc arenas that allow them to advance some interests. He wrote:

> Within the game the players can be rational in the varying degrees that the structure permits. . . . Sharing a common territorial field and collaborating for different and particular ends in the achievement of over-all social functions, the players in one game make use of the players in another and are, in turn, made use of by them. (253)

These arrangements fall short of producing a government that can easily carry out a wide range of public purposes, but they make it possible for players in temporary "games" to cooperate in implementing specific projects.

Acting under these conditions requires inventing new games and new rules. The key is getting more players together on the same field. Observers, investigating fields from political elites to social service coordination to local planning, have called such games "interorganizational collaboration" (Gray 1985, 1989), "interorganizational connections" (Perrucci and Pilisuk 1970), "networks" (Friend, Power, and Yewlett 1974), "resource networks" (Perrucci and Pilisuk 1970), and "resource exchange networks" (Sarason et al. 1977, 1979, 1998).

These conditions complicate the challenge of governing a city, and they pose the question of what kinds of games, or arrangements, make it possible for elected officials or anyone to do so. Stone (1993) defines the task in terms of creating "regimes." "Society," he writes, "is more appropriately thought of as a loosely coupled network of interactions than as a cohesive unit bound together by common beliefs." Hence, "coalition-building [is] an integral part of the governing process." "Urban regime theory assumes that the effectiveness of local government depends greatly on the cooperation of nongovernmental actors and on the combination of state capacity with nongovernmental resources" (1, 6).

Observers of American urban education fields have found, consistently, that local reformers have influenced school policies and programs when they have managed to assemble working educational regimes. Thus Gittell (1994) and Smith (1997) explain relative success in Chicago and Charlotte and failure in New York. At the same time, however, education seems to be a field in which there are few broad, citywide regimes. Stone and his colleagues, studying the politics of urban school reform in eleven U. S. cities, typically find disparate actors who do not trust one another sufficiently to work together (Henig, Hula, Orr, and Pedescleaux 1999; Orr 1999; Portz, Stein, and Jones 1999; Stone 1998; Stone, Henig, Jones, and Pierannunzi 2001). Stone frames the challenge as "building civic capacity" to change and manage schools for the better.

Interorganizational relationships that create civic capacity depend on two conditions. The first, emphasized by those who call these arrangements "resource exchange networks," involves exchanges of goods and especially of services. Individuals or organizations will participate in networks when everyone gets something in the bargain. Networks have advantages over simple two-party alliances in creating pools to which many parties contribute benefits from which members may draw. One participant, for example, may get something from a second, who gets something from a third, until a participant dozens later gets something from the first, without any direct exchange between them.

Yet even though this sounds simply like everyday rational political behavior in a new environment, the complexity of networks means that not all possible benefits may be apparent until a network is formed and members imagine what they might give to and get from one another. Thus Trist (1985), in considering what contributes to newly "negotiated order," emphasized the importance of creating a "learning network" through which parties can find new ways of interpreting, as well as forming, relationships. He and Emery saw remedies for turbulence in new "values that have overriding significance for all members of the field" (Emery and Trist 1965, 28). Warren, Rose, and Bergunder (1971) similarly saw networks bound by an "institutionalized thought structure," or shared assumptions about problems, strategies, and authority. Parties must develop a culture that encourages creativity and provides psychological support for taking risks. Put differently, relationships based on what retrospectively look like rational exchanges may not be possible until parties can see themselves as sharing purposes, a field, and a future.

Forming Networks, Groups, and Other Attachments: Lessons from Experience

Turbulent environments are new, but forming attachments is not. We will look at research specifically on interorganizational collaboration and then consider what other experience can tell us about conditions for interorganizational and interpersonal connection.

Interorganizational Collaboration

Gray (1985) observes of "conditions facilitating interorganizational collaboration" that cooperation typically proceeds through three stages. First, those who think they are concerned about related problems and could benefit from working together engage in *problem-setting*. They identify entities that have the stakes, right, and/or power to be included in collaborative efforts to address issues at hand. Decisions to participate depend on how organizations see their mission, the issues under consideration, their relations with other organizations, those organizations' purposes and legitimacy, and likely outcomes of joint activity.

If organizations agree that they have reasons to work together, they move on to *direction-setting*. Now committed to acting together, they must define their aims. As they calculate individual and collective interests, they narrow general issues into a specific agenda. This phase concludes when parties are satisfied that they have sufficient power to affect the collective program and can get something of value.

At last, organizations can move to *structuring*, detailed planning and organizing to support the collaborative agenda. They must set specific goals, define tasks, assign roles, and secure necessary financial, political, and physical resources. Then they can work together.

Group Development

Tuckman (1965; Tuckman and Jensen 1977), observing group development, found stages similar to what Gray observed in interorganizational networks. Thus Tuckman provides a general framework for anticipating what may transpire when individuals start a community organization or when that organization tries to create a network with other institutions.

Groups—any attachments—begin by *forming*. Parties have general ideas about what they might do together but want to figure out first whether it is reasonable to do anything together. They want to see who is interested in what, how people act, what power relationships might be, and what resources would be available. They calculate what they want a group to do and with whom they want to work. This stage is one of tentative, hypothetical commitment.

Once parties decide to be part of a collective entity, they stake out positions on its purposes, division of labor, and leadership, and each challenges others to go along. Now that they care about what the entity will do, they argue, often heatedly, in *storming*, to try to get things to their advantage. They test whether the new entity will still allow them to be independent.

Should participants convince one another that they are prepared to work together, they can get on with *norming*, elaborating ground rules, roles, and relationships. They define issues, identify knowledge to use in interpreting problems and crafting and evaluating possible solutions, and set an agenda. The group takes a distinct identity, and participants become members who are comfortably interdependent.

At last, they are ready for *performing*. They plan and implement action.

They may continue performing for as long as they have work to do and succeed at it. Satisfied with their efforts, they may voluntarily *adjourn*. Or, frustrated by the possibilities of continuing, they may dissolve. Alternatively, if they run into external obstacles or find that internal agreements or arrangements break down, they may revisit earlier stages of development. For example, they may "storm" again to settle emergent conflicts and then settle on new norms and go on to perform in different directions.

The main ideas about attachment can be summarized simply. Turbulent societal conditions require creating new types of connections. Human ambivalence about forming attachments makes that process disjointed when it occurs. Individuals and organizations give priority to working out social and emotional relationships over using valid knowledge. Stable attachments are a precondition for careful attention to knowledge, but people use knowledge in ways that promote and secure their attachments. In order to form a group, an organization, or a network capable of collective action, individuals or organizations must address three questions:

1. *Participation*: Who is entitled to participate in what ways, and with what authority?
2. *Research*: What is valid knowledge for identifying individual and collective interests and for resolving disagreements?
3. *Action*: What do participants do together?

We now look at knowledge and the ways that people use it in collective action.

Knowledge

School reform and educational improvement encourage teachers, administrators, parents, and the public to act on tested knowledge about children, education, and institutional change. For example, Theodore Sizer, a long-time reformer who put forth "essential" principles of schooling, argues for the importance of "planning backwards" (McDonald 1992, 1993; Podl et al. 1992). Educators should start with a vision of specific activities representing satisfactory student learning and then reason back through a sequence of practices, programs, and policies that would make those accomplishments possible.

This is just one variant of a general argument for planning. When people are bothered by conditions, they should think about what would be an ideal, or at least a preferable, situation and then set that as a goal for action. They should consider what interventions might make that condition probable, or at least more likely than if they did nothing. Weighing these strategic alternatives in terms of their potential benefits and the probability of implementation, they should choose the course that best fits their requirements, and they should carry it out.

Research enters in several places. First, it is necessary to collect information about conditions to ascertain whether they are problematic and, if so, how and for whom. Once a problem is defined, it is possible to consider what would be preferable—reasoning toward and about hypothetical futures to determine which might significantly improve people's lives. After selecting one as a goal, it is necessary to identify strategies with some probability of enacting the desired conditions. Analysis of experience and deductions from social theory help inform the choice among hypothetical future actions. Thus research and reasoning help improve conditions.

And yet things are not so simple. Problem solving is not just a matter of reducing uncertainty—collecting information to understand current and future conditions well. It is also a matter of resolving ambiguity—making judgments about the meanings of conditions, events, and actions that can be seen and valued in various ways. People may disagree about whether conditions constitute a problem, what the problem is, what would be preferable, and how a remedy should be brought about. Some disagreements express conflicts of interest, but many reflect different assumptions, interpretations, and desires. To take familiar examples: some see issues in terms of race, while others look at class; some view education through teachers' eyes, whereas others see as students—or parents, or taxpayers. Simply collecting information does not resolve differences when people view information through different lenses.

Reducing uncertainty and resolving ambiguity both must be collective activities. The reason with respect to uncertainty is simply that many people have information, and bringing them together is necessary to discover, assemble, and analyze what they know. For example, researchers working with formal information systems can get abstract, quantitative measures, such as student test scores, attendance, and referrals for behavioral problems. However, understanding what goes on in classrooms and how those activities influence student behavior, attendance, and academic performance—not to mention how family and community events matter—depends on talking with teachers, students, administrators, parents, and others. They can be interviewed separately, but only if they meet and talk with one another will they recognize particular knowledge they have that a researcher might not ask about, or that they themselves might not consider important in talking with a researcher. Group discussion is more than a means of delivering preexistent knowledge; it is also a way of discovering knowledge.

For resolving ambiguity, group work is essential. When people talk about how they see things and why they see them differently, they have an opportunity to come to agreement about how to interpret conditions and their alternatives, or they may agree to accept plural perspectives. Reaching agreement may be a matter of examining assumptions, seeing where information may help clarify their reasonableness, and looking at the action implications of one premise over another. These understandings create what participants take to be new knowledge. Alternatively, especially if parties decide that they are less concerned about defining situations unambiguously than about protecting their interests, dispute resolution methods can help settle or allocate differences in stakes.

Nevertheless, Chris Argyris's and Donald Schön's studies of professionals in many fields found that most prefer polite, even if noncommittal, talk to heated argument (1974, 1978; Argyris 1982; Argyris, Putnam, and Smith 1985; Schön 1983). Anxiety about ignorance and uncertainty leads people to defend their starting positions instead of looking for knowledge and exploring alternatives. This research highlights the importance of creating conditions for potential collaborators to disagree securely, so that they can join together solidly and work knowledgeably.

Community Action

Collective action generates tensions between attachment and knowledge. For example, 1960s community action programs, landmark efforts to form interinstitutional networks to improve community conditions, suggest what we might anticipate with the Education Task Force. We noted that groups and networks must answer questions of participation, research, and action. Peter Marris and Martin Rein (1982), in analyzing community action programs, found that participation, research, and action follow divergent intellectual, psychological, and political logics. Each has different implications for developing and using knowledge.

Participation

The logic of participation, focused on who may become attached to others in a collectivity, is concerned with the process of making decisions about action. In community initiatives, the normative answer is that anyone who wants to take part may do so: "the people" decide what to do. This position is consistent with the democratic view that those with interests in an issue have the right to decide it (Barber 1984). The analysis of turbulence reinforces this position on epistemological grounds: when problems are fuzzy and there are no clear procedures for addressing them, all who have interests should come together to determine what they have in common, how they see things, and what they should do. Principles of group development add psychological and sociological arguments. Community groups, especially those with little power, take this position for practical political reasons.

And yet, as those Marris and Rein observed found, there are no simple definitions of "the people" or their interests. People disagree about who has stakes and who should take part in acting. Issues of participation quickly move to questions of representation: if not everyone with interests should—or at least can—participate in deciding what to do, what are fair, reasonable principles for identifying representatives for them or their interests? Representation is related to the question of leadership: who may legitimately speak for others? Even among activists there is a division of labor, where a few give direction to and act for many. When leaders act in others' name, what are acceptable bases for their authority? These questions elude easy consensus, and people forming a collectivity often disagree about answers.

Practically, participation is difficult, even for the interested and motivated. It takes time. It requires complex interpersonal and cognitive skills—from running a meeting to speaking in public to crafting decisions from disagreement—and confidence in one's skills and appearance. These resources are more common among well-educated, middle-class professionals than the poor. However, in any community, participation centers on a few who have more resources—especially time—than others. Around this core group, others come and go with fluctuations in their interests and opportunities.

The less active and inactive may authorize the core group to act for them, or they may not even know of it. However things started out, with time, a core group often identifies iteself with the issues at hand and takes proprietary interests in action. It may see itself as being most experienced and best qualified to make decisions. In any case, as events move ahead—as a group forms and proceeds to storm over action—the potential returns on action increase. Some who espoused broad participation earlier may position themselves to get the most of what might come, now pushing others aside (Cnaan 1991).

Along the way, a group may encounter parties that want to restrict its participation—because they do not believe in or want democracy. Organizations running programs often expect clients to accept services without participating in designing, producing, or managing them. Under these conditions, participation is a matter of contention.

The logic of participation typically proceeds from a normative position of support for broad participation when stakes are low to a practical position of narrow, contested participation when stakes rise. This process may produce an elite group that can efficiently get certain things done. However, restricted participation, beyond challenging democracy, presents practical risks in jeopardizing attachments that favor discovery and use of knowledge. A small, narrow, autonomous, and self-satisfied group may be unable to bring a collectivity together around it. If it forms a network with other elites, it may be unable to bring knowledge or commitment from the constituency for whom it speaks. Because it may see conditions narrowly and have access to limited resources from its constituency, what it can do efficiently may not be significant.

On the surface, the logic of participation is concerned with *who* takes part in collective action, not *how they think* about what they are doing. The tacit nexus, with which the logic is not directly concerned, is that people are expected to make judgments about their interests and actions to serve them. What knowledge they turn to and how they use it are open questions.

Research

The logic of research, also concerned with the process of deciding on action, deals with the knowledge used to solve problems. The discussion of "planning backwards" described a logic of research that professional researchers or planners would advocate: people should systematically collect and analyze a lot of information to identify their interests and ways of serving them. Planners would argue that self-interest requires such research. In this way, they link the logic of research to the logic of participation.

Marris and Rein (1982) found broad endorsements of such research but few besides professional researchers engaging in it. The explanation is not that community organizations decide on action ignorantly, but that they conduct research within constraints. One limitation involves capacity: few community members, particularly those with little formal education, have the training or skills to conceptualize and carry out the research that the professionals advocate. A second, powerful constraint is time: ordinary citizens have little time for collecting and analyzing information.

External deadlines do not allow time for proper reflection and research. Moreover, when people give scarce time to a collectivity, they want a rapid return on their investment. Hence, participants often must move quickly, and imperfectly, through the stages of forming an entity for action, storming over purposes, deciding on aims, and choosing actions. They use readily available information, drawing on their experiences, talking with a few others, and perhaps reading a little—and try to move toward action. This point is central: the aim of participation is action.[1] Participants subordinate research to that imperative. Hence, a typical logic of research is to search and reflect expediently, sometimes disjointedly, and rarely systematically.

Action

Whereas the logics of participation and research are concerned with process, the logic of action focuses on outcome: after some people come together and somehow think about things, what do they do? Marris and Rein (1982) observed, however, that relations between process and outcome often are fuzzy. Participants want to *do something* and typically engage in formal and tacit research until they find something that they can do. Rather than systematically analyzing the external world, they concentrate within, reckoning their own desires and capacities.

This orientation does not inherently lead to different conclusions than planning backwards, nor does it necessarily lead to ineffective action, but it proceeds differently, toward finding agreement among participants on some action. This aim may lead participants to choose an intervention because it maximizes internal support, regardless of its theoretical basis. They may "smooth out" or ignore certain analyses and strategies to shape an action that does not offend anyone. They may choose multiple, and even inconsistent, programs to satisfy various constituencies, without determining what is most realistic or setting priorities. To believe that success is likely, participants may minimize or overlook constraints, make facile assumptions about change, or inflate possible outcomes. In these ways attachment works against knowledge.

Marris and Rein (1982) adopt Lindblom's (1965) description of public decision making as "partisan mutual adjustment" in characterizing this typical logic of action. Cohen, March, and Olsen (1988) have offered the more picturesque, if less flattering, metaphor of the "garbage can" to characterize common decision procedures. The process of settling on action, rather than a moment when people engage in research and draw on findings to design strategic intervention, is often a receptacle for problem definitions, programs or actions that might be solutions, and participants with interests and resources. People throw in things that they want a decision to include—favorite programs, possible alliances, problems that ought to be solved—and then mix and match them in ways that offer, perhaps, the appearance of rationality, but, certainly, possibilities of power, status, and connection. Cohen, March, and Olsen (1988) could be describing community action when they refer to

> a collection of choices looking for problems, issues and feelings looking for decision situations in which they might be aired, solutions

> looking for issues to which they might be the answer, and decision-makers looking for work. (296)

Thus the logic of action, even when participants start out espousing rational, strategic decision making, leads pragmatically toward agreement on action that is good enough in three respects. First, the small group who succeed in influencing action can comfortably assume that the action will have desired effects. Second, agreement on the action builds or sustains a coalition. And, third, those deciding believe that they have sufficient resources to carry out the action.

What Marris and Rein (1982) found with community action is not so much that participants opposed the professionals' logic of research, as that this research opposed action. Professional researchers set such exacting conditions for designing action that no real intervention of any breadth or significance could pass. Common research language illuminates the difficulty. Researchers often speak of analyzing data by "holding X constant" or "controlling for Y." The turbulent environment in which social action intervenes opposes control and constancy. Daniel Patrick Moynihan drew the researcher's conclusion in another context when he counseled "benign neglect" regarding poorly understood problems. Community activists, in contrast, still want to do whatever seems possible.

Implications, Anticipations, and Possibilities

Reformers want schools, families, and communities to use new knowledge in educating children; yet attachments and anxieties about forming them can produce resistance to developing or using knowledge, and turbulent environments make attachments tenuous. Numerous entities influence children's educational opportunities and accomplishments, but they largely do so independently, in opposition to each other, and even without knowledge of one another. Improving education depends on organizing the field.

Improving education in Southeast Baltimore depends on organizing a network that extends far enough to give purchase on children's learning there. That is a tall order for anyone, particularly a community organization. At the same time, turbulent settings, because they are extensive, are sparsely populated; they contain much empty space. Thus there is room for initiative, the costs of creating some new relationships are low, and even small entities may exercise influence by building partnerships.

Still, the processes of forming groups and networks are complicated and disjointed. Recognizing differences and working through conflicts are necessary and normal. Moreover, no group or network is ever finished. The norms that fit one set of conditions, issues, or members do not fit others, and as these change, participants must form and storm again to get back to performing. That challenge, too, is an opportunity. Groups and organizations can recreate themselves if they do not get it right or no longer have it right.

That accomplishment is crucial: otherwise there is no attached collectivity to develop and use knowledge. Paradoxically, people have psychological and political cause for sacrificing knowledge to attachment, if knowledge threatens the formation or continuity of an entity or its optimism about action. These latter concerns shape a logic of research that competes with planning backwards. The reason is not anti-intellectualism or rigidity, so much as a lack of resources and opportunity. The challenge of knowledge is to build these intellectual resources into the action network. The university is a candidate in the case of the Task Force.

These conditions frame the test of community action in the education field.

Chapter 3

Building the Education Field
Getting Parents, Schools, and Communities Together

In small-town, rural America of the mid-nineteenth century, the education field was tightly linked. Communities established schools, hired and closely watched teachers, and employed graduates. A great deal changed in education and elsewhere by the time Emery and Trist (1965) remarked on turbulence and the necessity of building interinstitutional networks. Some contemporary education reformers, particularly those taking an institutional or a community approach, advocate making new connections to improve schooling. They commonly describe their priorities in terms of "parent involvement" and "school-family-community partnerships."

This language and the aims associated with it marked out a space in which Southeast activists could try to form attachments to schools, community institutions, and others. The framework offered models for relationships and, up to a point, authorized efforts to develop a network. We begin examining possible connections among schools, parents, and communities by reviewing the professionalization of education that separated schools from other institutions. We move on to identify basic types of involvement and partnership. We then examine arguments for these connections based on the logics of participation, research, and action. We conclude with implications for the Southeast effort.

Schools without Parents

Today the government sets standards for schooling, requires children's attendance, and funds schools. Professional teachers, trained in accredited programs, teach prescribed curricula to children organized in classrooms, by age, from kindergarten through grade twelve. Schools are organized into districts corresponding to geopolitical jurisdictions, so that some, particularly in or around central cities, are huge. Professional superintendents manage the systems that regulate facilities, resources, and teachers' practices. The schools we take for granted today as what schools are were created by late-nineteenth- and early-twentieth-century reformers.

The familiar urban school systems represent the political success of progressive education reformers in replacing one-room rural schoolhouses and small urban district schools with standardized, unified programs. The reformers regarded the "common school" as a remedy for the diversity and parochialism of educational practices. Scattered rural communities made idiosyncratic decisions about which children would attend school and who would teach them what. Meanwhile, as cities swelled with immigrants, many children went to work rather than school, and those who attended school encountered various curricula. Reformers resolved to establish schooling that would not only teach reading, writing, and arithmetic but would also impose a common culture and, in the process, create a dutiful labor force and loyal citizenry.

The school reformers of the mid- to late-nineteenth century emphasized curriculum. In particular, they promoted a Protestant moralism that sprang from their small-town origins, and religious and educational missionaries intermingled in spreading a pietistic curriculum. The main lines of resistance were ethnic and religious, and the success of the common school evangelists stimulated the creation of Catholic schools. As a loose network of reformers spread over America, growing numbers of small towns and cities adopted this curriculum. Local community leaders took part in overseeing the schools.

A second generation of reformers took over at the turn of the century. Attached to the small-town moralism with which they had grown up, these reformers were taken as well by a new faith in science. They would take scientific management from business in adding organizational structure to curriculum. The acceleration of immigration, particularly from Southern and Eastern Europe, increased the size and diversity of city populations. Centralizing control seemed as rational in education as it did in business, where, similarly, the goal was to create a uniform product.

Along with centralization, these administrative reformers introduced science. They believed that students could be assessed scientifically, that pedagogy was a science, that teachers could be trained scientifically, and that superintendents could and should scientifically manage it all. They created normal schools and university schools of education to prepare teachers and administrators for their new professions. At the same time, they moved to "take schools out of politics"—practically, to wrest control from elected officials and party bosses representing new immigrants to put it in the hands of blue-ribbon boards, which would, in turn, put full trust in professional superintendents. All of this, they believed, served the interest of making good Americans out of millions of youths needing guidance (Katz 1975; Tyack and Hansot 1982).

The progressives created systems that limited parents' involvement in education. These reformers assumed that ordinary people could not understand what children should learn and how they should be taught. They did not oppose democracy; they were simply in favor of a rational approach to society's problems. In this respect, as Tyack and Hansot note, they were in step with their progressive counterparts in other domains: "The decline of lay participation in school governance—creating buffers between the people and their schools—was part of a much larger transformation in the way Americans conducted their public business" (1982, 108).

In particular, two principles of the common school system oppose parental involvement. The first is the professionalization of teaching. It rests on the dual assumptions that a science of education can identify the best curriculum and pedagogy, and that specially trained teachers understand this science in ways that laypersons cannot. The second principle is bureaucracy. At first glance, it may seem incidental to the common school, just a culturally favored expedient for managing many teachers and students. And yet the intellectual assumption that there is one right way to teach and that some people, by combined ability and training, know more and better about teaching than others easily supports the political assumption that those who know more and better should dictate to and control those who know less and worse.

These coupled premises justify most bureaucracies (Weber 1967), yet they wield particular force in education, where they take power from the image of the classroom. That is where those who know much give direction to those who know little. The classroom is not merely a culturally transmitted idea but also an indelible personal experience. Everyone knows the classroom as a place where he or she encountered a series of teachers who knew and could do more than their charges. Most children learn to read, calculate, and much else, but they leave school having experienced and subsequently assuming a hierarchy of knowledge and knowers.

The common school reformers took for granted a distinction between those who know and those who do not in structuring relations between teachers and students. They incorporated the assumption of gradations of knowledge into hierarchical relations between expert educators and rank-and-file teachers. They carried it over into building a wall between the teachers in the school and the parents outside the school, who, regardless of what they know, do not know about education. Further, the parents, even though they are adults, best know schools from their experience of them as children, and that humbling memory, coupled with their doubt that they could teach third-grade arithmetic or much else, encourages them to think of themselves, in fact, as people who do not know something that matters. This emotional assumption affects efforts to connect families or communities and schools.

School systems institutionalize these premises in structures and practices. Principals are schools' gatekeepers. When they admit parents, they meet them in offices but rarely let them into classrooms. Classrooms are normally closed to parents, except for occasions when students are not present and teachers are not teaching. In some schools, parents may volunteer in classrooms, where they assist teachers, or elsewhere in the school, where they perform duties that teachers do not want. Principals decide on policies and practices, sometimes with teacher participation, but rarely with parental involvement. A local school system's central offices are not only physically distant from most neighborhoods but terra incognita to parents. Administrators make and implement policies with little public engagement or scrutiny. School boards meet in public, but few publicize agendas or circulate information, and, in any case, much more often than not, discussions ask for comments on completed proposals rather than ideas to go into them.

Urban systems commonly resemble this sketch. Now many parents and some educators talk of reconnecting families and schools. Some want to shore up the system, others want to tinker with it slightly, and still others mean to change it.

Models of Parent Involvement and Partnerships

"Parent involvement" and "school-family-community partnerships" both refer to attachments between schools and family members, neighborhood residents, local businesses, community associations, churches, nonprofit organizations, and the like. The phrases lack precise meanings and often are used similarly, but they carry different connotations. Epstein's (1995) catalogue of types of parent involvement helps identify different emphases among a variety of connections. Her six types of involvement can be grouped into three types of partnerships between schools and parents or other community members.

The first are tacit partnerships, in which parents and teachers engage in parallel, complementary activities without contact. Parents or other adults can contribute to children's education by raising them lovingly and consistently, providing a secure home, feeding and clothing them, and attending to their health and development (Epstein's type 1 parent involvement). These actions prepare students for teachers' efforts at school. In addition, parents can assist children with schoolwork (type 4). In doing so, parents not only help children learn what teachers teach, but they show children parents who value learning and know things that matter at school. These partnerships do not depend on a formal agreement between teachers and parents, though discussion can enhance the efforts of both.

In a second type of partnership, individual parents meet, talk, and make formal arrangements with individual staff members. Parents and staff can communicate about school policies and activities, educational goals, assignments, and children's progress (type 2). They can discuss what a child should learn, how teachers and parents can help, and how the child is getting ahead. In addition, parents can volunteer (type 3). Besides helping instrumentally, volunteering shows teachers and students that parents share responsibility for education.

These two types of partnerships, more often called "parent involvement" than "partnerships," occupy familiar ground. They are formed on the school's terms, with parents supporting school programs. Parents, educators, and school reformers readily endorse such cooperation. A third type of partnership, actively involving parents or community members in school practices and decision making, stakes out largely new ground. A group of parents or an organization may take authoritative, influential roles with schools, with arrangements outlined in explicit and elaborate agreements.

One subtype puts parents in school decision-making roles (type 5). They can participate in entities established by school, from PTAs to advisory committees to site-based management teams. These may be concerned with policy, personnel, budget, or curriculum. Some school systems have advisory or decision roles for parents. In addition, parents can create organizations to express their concerns, set their own agendas, and advocate for policies or programs at schools or in the system. Thus parents can introduce practices that improve children's learning. In addition, they show their children that they care about education and model adults who take leadership. Significantly, in exercising power, parents may challenge teachers or administrators.

The other subtype extends beyond parents' roles as parents to their roles as community members and includes other individual and institutional community members. Epstein emphasizes how communities can give schools resources for programs (type 6), largely an extension of volunteering. These relationships may be purely altruistic, or community partners may get something in return. For example, businesses, churches, or nonprofit organizations can give schools resources and gain customers, members, or publicity. Service agencies can join with schools to form full-service schools; while helping schools educate children better, agencies get more clients (Dryfoos 1994). Business staff can mentor school administrators or students and improve the local labor force.

However, in addition to giving schools community resources, other relationships of this subtype get community actors influence over the school or gain resources for community use. Schools can include community members in advisory committees or site management teams. Community members can organize to improve schools and invite staff to participate. Community members can teach students in the school or the community. Further, schools can provide services to community groups, neighborhoods, or institutions, from cleanups to fund-raising. Whatever the formalities, opening school boundaries to outsiders creates a potential to change school practices, depending on actors' interests, resources, and relations with the school.

Educators rarely think of this last type of partnership as "parent involvement." Often they reserve "partnership" for relations with community donors. Parents and community members speak of "involvement" in decision making, and they are especially likely to think of "partnership" as a means of influencing the school for their children's benefit and that of the community.

Thus the three types of partnership vary in explicitness, membership, purpose, member obligations, and power and status relations. They range from occasional parental or community assistance to a school to ongoing powerful collaboration between staff and parents or community members. One could plead for these partnerships as a means of constructing a coherent education field in a turbulent environment, but advocates put forth more immediate justification. We focus here on community expectations and arguments for connecting with schools.

THE LOGICS OF PARENT INVOLVEMENT AND COMMUNITY PARTNERSHIP

The Logic of Participation

Some argue for parent involvement in schools and partnerships between families and schools with the logic of participation: because parents want them, they should have them. Generally, they frame their position in terms of democracy. Schools are public institutions; their actions affect children's well-being; children, their families, and their communities have rights to influence educational policies and programs (Barber 1984). Parents bolster these claims with appeals to parental rights to influence children's development. If asked to justify assertions of such prerogatives, parents point to their knowledge of their children.

Polling data give indications of parents' opinions on the subject. In 1999, Gallup conducted a national survey on school problems, remedies, and strategies for improvement (Rose and Gallup 1999). Public school parents emphasized controlling students' behavior and increasing contact between teachers and students (in that order), but parent involvement also was on the radar screen. Asked to identify the biggest problems with which community public schools must cope, 5 percent mentioned parents' lack of support or interest. This was the sixth most significant problem, following lack of discipline (15 percent), fighting, violence, and gangs (12 percent), overcrowding (12 percent), lack of funding (9 percent), and drugs (6 percent). Significantly, interest in parent involvement increased from the preceding year, while concerns about violence, funding, and drugs declined. Asked about the one thing they would change to improve community public schools, 4 percent mentioned increasing parent involvement, behind increasing teachers and reducing class size (14 percent), increasing discipline (9 percent), getting better teachers (5 percent), and increasing security (5 percent).

Notably, even though parents considered student behavior and teacher-student contact more important influences on education than parent involvement, many saw parent involvement as a necessary means for getting action on those issues. Thus asked who or what is the main obstacle to improving community public schools, parents mentioned parents and their lack of involvement (12 percent), right next to funding (13 percent).

In a Milwaukee survey, parents testified to their impact on their children's school achievement. Asked to assess the relative influence of parent involvement, teaching, and school programs, 38 percent said that parent involvement is most important, and nearly all the rest (60 percent) said parents are as important as teachers or school programs (White 1999). These statements testify to parents' confident interest in having roles in their children's schools.

The Logic of Research

Parents often justify their involvement on the grounds that they know what their children need and can motivate them. Consistently, "a new generation of evidence" finds that parent involvement contributes to children's academic achievement (Henderson and Berla 1994). Some evidence comes from comparisons of parental practices in families of high- and low-achieving students; various types of parental involvement with the students doing better appear to contribute to their success. Other evidence comes from evaluations of interventions designed to increase parents' involvement in their children's education; these studies find that increased academic achievement and school success accompany increased parent involvement.

The findings are important, because they point to rarely considered interventions that can improve students' learning. They are particularly encouraging, because they show that familiar associations between student achievement and families' socioeconomic status are not an inherent result of parents' income or education but a product of specific ways parents are involved in their children's education—practices that improve low-income students' academic achievement when parents adopt them. Henderson and Berla summarize the research as follows:

> [T]he most accurate predictor of a student's achievement in school is not income or social status, but the extent to which the student's family is able to:
>
> 1. Create a home environment that encourages learning
> 2. Express high (but not unrealistic) expectations for their children's achievement and future careers.
> 3. Become involved in their children's education at school and in the community.
>
> . . . when schools support families to develop these three conditions, children from low-income families and diverse cultural backgrounds approach the grades and test scores expected for middle class children.
>
> The studies have documented these benefits for students:
>
> - Higher grades and test scores
> - Better attendance and more homework done
> - Fewer placements in special education
> - More positive attitudes and behavior
> - Higher graduation rates
> - Greater enrollment in post secondary education
>
> . . . The teachers they work with have higher opinions of them as parents and higher expectations of their children. As a result, parents develop more confidence not only about helping their children learn at home, but about themselves as parents.
>
> . . . Schools that work well with families have:
>
> - Improved teacher morale
> - Higher ratings of teachers by parents
> - More support from families
> - Higher student achievement
> - Better reputations in the community. (1994, 1)

Parents who involve themselves in their children's education in one way are likely to involve themselves in several ways, and the general attitude that leads to involvement, as well as the family relationship it expresses, is more important than any specific action. Thus it is artificial to isolate the effects of one type of involvement without considering the context of parents' relations with their children and with the school. Even so, each type of involvement rests on a theory of change (see Epstein 1995).

Good parenting benefits children directly when parents provide adequate food, clothing, and shelter and ensure a secure home setting, so that children go to school rested, fed, and able to concentrate on their work. When parents understand children's developmental needs, they can stimulate growth, avoid conflicts based on unrealistic expectations, and reinforce teachers' guidance. Children feel understood, take satisfaction from accomplishments, find consistency between home and school, and want to attend school, behave appropriately there, and learn.

Parental actions to *encourage learning at home* reinforce and supplement teachers' efforts. Some activities have direct academic results, as when parents help with homework. Generally, parents' efforts to teach or assist with schoolwork demonstrate that they want children to work hard at school, and they reward children for their efforts. As a result, children are more likely to try to learn at school. Teachers, for their part, work harder when they believe that parents invest in their children and are active partners at home.

Communication among parents, students, and teachers shares perceptions and expectations. It makes it possible to discuss and resolve disagreements. Parents can better understand school policies and practices. Teachers can better understand parents' thinking about school and child rearing, as well as how family and community conditions affect students' development and behavior. Parents and teachers can pool their knowledge about children and their authority over them to impart realistic common expectations. Students can get more open, consistent evaluations of their work, as well as clearer guidance from teachers. Students and teachers both work better when they assume that they have consistent authorization from parents.

Volunteering offers some direct educational results, as when a parent tutors a child. Parents can contribute skills and experiences from which children can learn. They can assist teachers by taking responsibilities that free up teachers to plan or to concentrate on students who need help. At least as significant in terms of children's motivation, parent volunteering reinforces and contributes to a school climate that respects students' parents and home lives. Children see a parent at school as a role model and as a sign that parents and teachers both value learning. This sense of partnership and consistency encourages children to learn.

Parental participation in *making decisions about school* policies or programs can directly affect children's learning by contributing knowledge, influence, and resources to practices that realistically match children's needs. Students, feeling that teachers understand them, are motivated to respond. Indirectly, parental involvement in decision making reflects and contributes to a school climate where teachers value parents and each respects the other. When children see parents acting powerfully at school, they respect parents more, see them as potent role models, and think of themselves also as strong. Students work hard, with the assumption that effort leads to attractive adult possibilities.

Collaboration among teachers, parents, and community institutions directly aids children when community members or organizations help teach students or provide resources for teachers. Indirectly, cooperation between community groups and a school affirms to parents and students that the school values the community, that community concerns have a place in the school, and that both the community and the school want students to learn. School recognition of community entities assures students that they can bring all of themselves to school—that teachers understand that what goes on outside affects them and will try to accommodate difficulties as well as play to strengths. Generally, community partnerships with schools join two sources of authority in motivating children to study.

Although professional reformers are most likely to articulate these theories in support of parent involvement and community partnership, many parents tacitly take them as conclusions from their own "research" with their children.

The Logic of Action

Democratic premises justify parent and community involvement in education, and research shows the potential efficacy of these efforts. The logic of action simply urges doing something that might matter. Stone and his colleagues (Stone et al. 2001) find little systematic school policy innovation and little parent involvement. Their research is consistent with the proposition that community activism is necessary, even if not sufficient, for school reform. If community groups got into the garbage can of educational decision making, they would introduce new interests, preferences, and resources to be taken into account. Two cases offer stronger, positive evidence.

Chicago school reform created local school councils including parents that would make personnel, budget, and policy decisions. Bryk and his associates (Bryk 1999; Bryk et al. 1998) observe that alliances between active parents and strong, creative principals were central to change in schools that innovated. Cooperation made it possible for staff and parents to reflect on schools' purposes and programs and for staff to consider changes with families' support. Organized parents expanded the local mandate for change well beyond school councils' and principals' formal authority. The researchers suggest that these changes improved students' learning, but they do not have systematic data.

In Texas, in the mid-1980s, the Industrial Areas Foundation began organizing parents to improve local schools. Over the next decade and a half, it changed individual schools, helped reorganize the San Antonio system, and created more than 100 Alliance Schools. The institutional changes seem to have contributed to students' improved state test scores (Shirley 1997; Warren 2001), though there is evidence that teachers just taught students to take the test (Klein, Hamilton, McCaffrey, and Stecher 2000). The Alliance Schools, developed with parent participation and attention to research, show that when community organizations take a role in school decision making, action can be effective and innovative.

Implications

A national survey on parent involvement in education finds a lot of the first two types of family-school partnerships (National Center for Education Statistics 2001, table 25). Three-fourths of parents report helping children with homework at least once a week, with more than one-third (38 percent) assisting at least three or four times a week. Two-thirds or more report attending a child's class event (66 percent), a parent-teacher conference (71 percent), or a general school meeting (76 percent). More than one-third (40 percent) volunteer at school. However, variations suggest conditions that influence whether parents get involved.

Parents with less formal education and income report spending more time helping children with homework than parents with more education and income, while the latter engage more in activities at their children's schools. (Non-Hispanic blacks and Hispanics help more with homework, and non-Hispanic whites spend more time at school.) The first finding testifies to low-income parents' commitment to their children's education, as well as, perhaps, their children's greater need for homework assistance. The second points to better educated, wealthier parents' comfort in going to school and their opportunities to do so. Their intellectual skills and social status make it easier to talk with teachers, and their jobs and child care arrangements give them the flexibility to do so. Parents with little education often lack the skills or confidence to interact with school staff. Single parents have trouble making arrangements to go to school. Those whose native language is not English may have difficulty talking with teachers.

All parents are most likely to involve themselves in their children's education when they are in elementary school, less likely in middle school, and least likely in high school. Both home and school involvement drop off sharply over the years. The percentage of parents helping with homework less than once a week rises from 16 percecnt to 52 percent from elementary (K–8) to secondary school. The percentage of parents attending a teacher conference drops from 80 percent to 48 percent. Part of the explanation is that elementary schools are neighborhood schools, near students' homes, whereas middle and high schools draw from progressively larger areas, with facilities farther away. Elementary school parents can most easily get to children's schools. In addition, elementary school teachers have full responsibility for relatively few students, whom they can get to know, while secondary school teachers normally have partial responsibility for many, about whom they know little. Thus elementary school parents can find that their children's teachers share interest in and knowledge about their children, whereas it often is hard to find a staff member who knows how a child is doing overall in middle school or high school. Teachers who know children well are more likely to encourage parents to work with them.

Elementary school children are less formed than older children. Adults see the young with a sense of possibilities rather than constraints. Younger children want parents involved in their lives. This is the easiest and often the most rewarding time for parents to participate in children's education. In middle school, young adolescents insist on independence. At the same time, some begin to encounter academic or social difficulties that seem to limit their life or educational possibilities. Misreading children's assertions of autonomy or putting great weight on these other signs, parents may conclude that their children's fates are sealed, that parents matter less than earlier, and that others have more influence on their children.

For all parents, a school's encouragement of participation greatly affects whether and how parents are involved in education, at least at school (Epstein 2001). Principals and teachers are most likely to suggest the first two types of partnership, where parents support school programs, rather than active involvement in teaching or decision making.

These conditions shaped possibilities for Southeast Baltimore activists who set out to involve parents and other community members in improving schools. Most parents had modest incomes, many were single, some were unemployed, many had not graduated from high school, and a small but growing number were Spanish-speaking immigrants. Few were comfortable in schools, few volunteered there, and for many school seemed an alien institution. Few schools unambiguously welcomed parents. The question of how these parents should be involved in education was a strategic one for the activists—the answer depended on what they wanted to accomplish. Even so, there was no good argument against any type of involvement. At the same time, they could expect that the very effort to create a community organization to influence schools, regardless of the arguments advanced for parent involvement and regardless of specific stances taken, would demand extraordinary energy from parents and arouse resistance in schools.

Chapter 4

Baltimore, the Schools, and the Southeast Education Task Force

The City

Baltimore was once one of America's largest cities. Though the population is declining, it was still 736,000 in 1990.[1] Yet even when 1 million people lived there in 1950, it had the feel of a small, working-class town.

The city rose with industry. It anchored the Baltimore and Ohio Railroad. Bethlehem Steel's Sparrows Point plant, across the city's eastern boundary, was once the world's largest steel refinery. Shipbuilding, railroading, copper and brass work, oil refining, canning, garment manufacturing, brewing, tin can production, cotton milling, meat packing, automobile manufacturing, and many more industries grew in Baltimore. Western Electric, General Motors, American Standard, Lever Brothers, Crown Cork and Seal, Crosse and Blackwell, Amoco, Crown Petroleum, Standard Oil, London Fog, and many other firms started or set up plants there.

Beginning in the mid-nineteenth century and accelerating around the turn of the century, Europeans came to Baltimore for industrial jobs. Whatever the harsh realities of factory work, economic opportunities presented a credible version of the American Dream. Immigrants strove to buy houses and thus to mark their arrival in America. Home ownership also signaled honest work, self-reliance, and discipline and thus gave moral force to a secular version of the Protestant Ethic.

These premises shaped Baltimore as a small town. Even today, many people from all classes stay in their neighborhoods of origin. Individuals, families, neighborhoods, and the city regard themselves as self-sufficient. An outsider who has lived in the city for years mused that sons or daughters who leave for jobs elsewhere are considered failures. Civic leaders see little reason to look beyond city boundaries for help. They assume that they know what there is to know.

Baltimore is a border city in a Southern state. Federal troops briefly occupied the city during the Civil War. Only President Lincoln's political maneuvering kept Maryland in the Union. These experiences linger in the civic mind as a sense of isolation and suspicion of the federal government. President Kennedy once quipped that Baltimore is south of Washington. The remark captures the city's persistent Southern character but misses its Northern elements and their complicated admixture.[2] A number of Baltimore's early settlers were Quaker merchants who moved from Philadelphia when the Revolutionary War disrupted their lives. As the Civil War approached, abolitionist Quakers shared local society with pro-slavery Southerners, while Baltimore was home to the nation's largest free black population. Nine-tenths of the city's blacks were free at the time of the Civil War.

Slavery created relations where calculations of race filled the tiniest corners of everyday life. Thus even though the mass of contemporary Baltimoreans descend from mid-nineteenth to early-twentieth-century immigrants who went to factories and were not party to slavery or its debates, their ancestors easily took what dignity they could from assuming their superiority to the blacks around them. However, the antebellum civic elites' interests in maintaining civility across the chasm that separated them on slavery shaped public discourse in a way that continues to the present: while race permeates public and private life, it may not be discussed.

By occupation, Baltimore is no longer a working-class city. Industry has been leaving since the 1970s. Now, only one-fourth of the city's workers hold blue-collar jobs. Unlike Berkeley, Ann Arbor, or Cambridge, Baltimore does not come readily to mind as a university town, but, in fact, Johns Hopkins is the city's largest employer, long since replacing Bethlehem Steel. Baltimore Gas and Electric and the Baltimore City Public School System are the next two largest, the three together testifying to the postindustrialization of Baltimore.

In the old days, it was not necessary to add that the city's blue-collar workers were white. "Working class" and "white ethnic" were more or less synonymous. Yet by mid-century, ethnic communities lost their distinctiveness with the third and fourth generations, and immigrants' descendants began moving to the suburbs. While whites left the city, African Americans moved in and increased their numbers. In 1960, a majority of public school students were black. In the mid-1970s, Baltimore became a majority African-American city. The city made Kurt Schmoke its first elected black mayor in 1987. In 1990, the population was 59 percent African American.[3]

The Schools

While white and colored schools educated children separately and unequally, beyond that basic injustice they went about their business uneventfully in the late nineteenth and first half of the twentieth centuries.[4] When in 1954 the U. S. Supreme Court handed down *Brown v. Board of Education,* argued by Thurgood Marshall, who graduated from Baltimore's colored schools, in a week city schools were formally desegregated. The U. S. Civil Rights Commission stated in 1961 that Baltimore was the only Southern city that had responded satisfactorily to the Court decision, but residential segregation, a declining white population, and the school system's preference for "free choice" in enrollment over mandatory reassignment of students limited racial mixing in schools.

While the makeup of the student population was changing, enrollment continued to grow, peaking at 190,000 in 1970. Hence, while superintendents tried to balance racial composition, they also hurried to renovate old buildings, particularly in what had been colored schools, and to build many new ones. The swelling enrollment and staff that accompanied it pushed superintendents to bring efficient management to the system. At the same time, superintendents and school boards faced the challenge of improving teaching, particularly for black students, whose test scores stayed below whites'.

Placidity was a condition of the past. One of two competing teacher unions called the city's first teachers' strike in 1967, to push for collective bargaining. The mayor stepped in to grant bargaining rights, but at the same time, the rival union persuaded the National Education Association to impose sanctions on the city, urging its members not to take jobs in schools that were "so extremely deficient that many children . . . are being denied the minimum level of educational opportunity" (quoted in Bowler 1991, 10).

De jure desegregation legitimated black complaints about schools and claims on the system, while growing interracial contact among students created tensions. Violence and protests marked the spring of 1970. The city hired its first black superintendent in 1971, and the school board became majority black during his tenure. While public criticism of the schools' safety and effectiveness grew, the *Baltimore Sun* ran stories about racial conflict in the schools. Though whites had been leaving the city for a number of years, the stories added to fears that the schools could not educate children.

Two 1974 events dealt blows to the system. In February, the Public School Teachers Association, ignoring a court injunction, struck for higher salaries and benefits. Most teachers and students stayed home, and police escorted the few who crossed picket lines. A growing number of black teachers saw the strike as a matter of racial justice. Mayor William Donald Schaefer calculated the issues as a choice between raising property taxes to pay higher salaries for teachers, and eventually other city employees, and holding onto middle-class, largely white parents whom higher taxes would push into the suburbs. After federal mediation, the union settled for about half of what it had asked.

In the middle of the strike, the Nixon Justice Department notified Baltimore that under the Civil Rights Act of 1964, city schools would lose $23 million in funding if the system did not act to desegregate schools entirely. Whites voiced anxieties at public meetings and railed against the specter of "busing." Students demonstrated against changing school zones. The school board finally settled on a feeder plan for junior high schools that ended students' free choice of junior and senior high schools. The decline in white enrollment accelerated the next year.

At that time, two-thirds of 190,000 students were African American, and school staff were increasingly black. To keep his hold on a black-majority city, Mayor Schaefer used the school system as a source of patronage to reward black supporters, making appointments from administrators to teachers to janitors to secretaries. Thus African Americans dominated the school system, but in loyalty to the mayor. Yet at some point, Schaefer found that he could no longer control the system that he had helped create, and he turned away from the schools. He concentrated on renewing downtown and on developing the Inner Harbor.

Racial change reflected or coincided with other developments that made it hard for city schools to succeed. The departure of middle-class, white (and, later, black) families left the city with a higher proportion of residents dependent on public services, reduced the tax base for funding services, and removed from classrooms students who were prepared to succeed and who could encourage and help others who were not. Black students came disproportionately from lower-income families, often headed by single mothers and, increasingly over the years, racked by drugs. Regardless of race, children required extraordinary teacher effort and supportive services, and the city had less and less money for schools.

As a series of superintendents tried to take charge of the school system in the 1970s and 1980s, two themes dominated public views of the Baltimore schools. One was that, by any measure, student achievement was worse there than nearly anywhere in the state. The suburban counties between Baltimore and Washington were conspicuously better. These judgments were formalized when the Maryland State Department of Education instituted the Maryland School Performance Program and high stakes testing in 1991. Baltimore's lower scores were consistent with long-standing national associations between test scores and socioeconomic status, but Baltimore schools stood out in the public mind as black schools, and that shorthand seemed explanation enough for many, though it was unclear what it was about race that affected test scores.

While Baltimore pleaded with suburban counties for higher state funding for city schools, suburbanites and some city leaders responded that the system was so poorly managed that money could not help until the schools were under control. Associated Black Charities commissioned a study that criticized the system's structure and management and made 101 recommendations for improvement (Towers Perrin/Cresap 1992).

The system was out of control at the top. Far from the professional system that progressive reformers envisioned a century earlier, the schools were deeply embedded in politics. In 1984, parents of special education students had sued for more services for their children. Four years later, the city signed a consent decree to spend additional money. Plaintiffs resumed litigation in the early 1990s when the system failed to comply with the consent decree. By this time, 18,000 of the city's 113,000 students were in special education—16 percent of the enrollment, in contrast to 12 percent statewide and nationally (Thompson 1995; Siegel 1997). The system's administration worried that satisfying the consent decree would make it impossible to spend sufficient money on the rest of the students. Approximately one-fourth of the city's school budget went to special education (Siegel 1997).

Along just those lines, in 1994, the American Civil Liberties Union (ACLU) sued the State Board of Education on behalf of Baltimore parents and schoolchildren, arguing that the state failed to provide adequate funding for city students. The state, in turn, sued the city, putting responsibility for poor performance on poor management. The city responded by suing the state on the funding issue. In 1995, the suits were joined before a federal and state judge, who would hear the cases together.

Meanwhile, the city was struggling to do something right with the schools. Mayor Schmoke forced out his embattled, hand-picked superintendent, Richard Hunter, in 1991, and he selected Walter Amprey as his successor. While urging Amprey to seize the system's reins, Schmoke pushed him to contract with Educational Alternatives, Incorporated (EAI), a private firm, to run nine schools. Three years later, in the face of union and parent opposition, after EAI had failed to produce, the city fired the company.

Test scores in most city schools remained low. In spring, 1994, on the reading section of the Maryland School Performance Assessment Program (MSPAP) test, 9 percent of third graders, 10 percent of fifth graders, and 5 percent of eighth graders performed at a "satisfactory" level. Scores in other subjects were a little higher, but far from nearby Howard County's percentages in the 40s, 50s, and 60s, or even those statewide in the 30s and 40s. Baltimore girls outperformed boys, scoring twice as high in the eighth grade. Whites did better than African Americans, more than twice as well by the eighth grade. On the nationally normed Comprehensive Test of Basic Skills (CTBS), median Baltimore third graders were in the 39th percentile on reading, with fifth graders in the 32nd and eighth graders in the 38th. Language and mathematics scores were similar. Again, girls outperformed boys, and whites did better than blacks. Howard County means were around the 70th percentile, and the state's were around the 50th (Baltimore City Public Schools 1994a; Maryland State Department of Education 1994).

The State Department of Education began designating low-performance schools eligible for "reconstitution," or state takeover. In February 1995, it named the first three reconstitution-eligible Baltimore schools, it added thirty-five more the next year, and the list grew annually. After the first list was named, Amprey ordered twenty-seven principals demoted and transferred.

As litigation heated up, Amprey could not satisfy the special education plaintiffs. In 1995, Mayor Schmoke, following a federal court ruling, appointed a school administrator with responsibility for special education. Because most schools had some special education students, the position essentially was that of a second superintendent.

The courts crafted a settlement with parents, the ACLU, the city, and the state in early 1997. The agreement was framed in terms of a plan for restructuring the Baltimore City Public Schools (renamed the Baltimore City Public School System [BCPSS]), with the superintendent replaced by a CEO, who would be supported by a chief academic officer and a chief financial officer. A New Baltimore City Board of School Commissioners would be jointly appointed by the governor and the mayor. The board was expected to develop and start implementing a master plan for reform in short order. The agreement depended on an endorsement by the Maryland General Assembly and, specifically, an allocation of $254 million to the Baltimore schools over the next five years. The legislature acted favorably in its 1997 session.

This chronology moves past late 1994, when a handful of Southeast Baltimore activists decided to organize to improve their schools, but it portrays a system that was not educating students, was poorly funded, was poorly managed, was highly politicized, and was subject to so many parties' influence that it was out of anyone's control. The field was turbulent.

Southeast Baltimore

Much of what has been said about Baltimore generally is true of Southeast Baltimore. After all, that was where most of the city's immigrants first settled. English, Irish, and Germans arrived in the early and middle nineteenth century, followed by Polish, Italians, Greeks, and Russians at century's end. Southeast Baltimore also was the center of the city's industrial development. Thus as late as the 1950s, an observer could see residents there living separately by ethnicity and religion but working together in the factories.

Few became wealthy, but many gained the security of home ownership. The Catholic majority, as well as the Protestants, Jews, and Orthodox, lived by a version of the Protestant Ethic. They measured themselves against simple standards of honesty and Golden Rule morality. Of necessity and choice, they were self-reliant. People assumed that they were solely responsible for what they accomplished. Not trusting outsiders, communities helped their own.[5]

Residents drew distinctions among themselves, most prominently between home owners and renters. Those who owned could claim to have been thrifty and could display their house as a sign of grace. Owners looked down on others who rented and associated renters' streets with the worst of social pathology. By and large, renters accepted the norms that condemned them.

Race did not divide the community, for in 1950, Baltimore was three-fourths white, and Southeast Baltimore remained the whitest section of the city. In 1970, when the city was only 53 percent white, 88 percent of Southeast Baltimore's 98,000 residents were white. When the city was recorded as majority black in 1980, Southeast Baltimore was still 77 percent white. Even when African Americans grew to 59 percent of the city's population in 1990, 70 percent of Southeast Baltimore's 78,000 residents were white.

Still, these gradual racial changes accompanied other trends. Middle-class Southeast families joined other whites moving to the suburbs. They left family homes with realtors, who sold them to people who saw the area as a housing market, not a community. As families with resources moved out and as strangers moved in, local merchants lost customers, and vacant stores cropped up. These joined empty factories left behind as manufacturers closed or moved.

Many who stayed lost the economic security once guaranteed by the factories. Many of the families moving in had marginal incomes. Blacks, who lived just north of Southeast Baltimore, moved south into traditionally white areas. By increments, Southeast Baltimore was becoming poorer and blacker. A few statistics summarize these changes. During the 1980s, Canton, Southeast Baltimore's industrial center, lost 49 percent of its jobs. One in nine housing units was vacant in 1990. One-fourth of adults were functionally illiterate in 1990. At that time, median household incomes in sixteen of the twenty-six Southeast Baltimore Census tracts were below the modest city median of $24,045, and seven were below $20,000. Only 82 percent of children were in public schools.[6]

And yet Southeast Baltimore had assets. Good highway, rail, and water links existed for commerce and commuting. It had vacant land for economic development. Housing was far cheaper than in Washington and within easy commuting distance of the capital, as well as downtown Baltimore. And Southeast Baltimore sat on the waterfront, with magnificent views of the harbor.

In 1966, the city and state had joined forces to extend the Interstate Highway System through Southeast Baltimore. A new leg would provide easy transit through the city—as soon as several hundred Southeast Baltimore houses were leveled and construction proceeded. Demolition began, but a coalition of working-class residents and middle-class "urban pioneers" organized to halt further destruction. They prevailed against "the Road," and neighborhoods were saved. The activists found other problems to work on, and in 1971, they formally established the South East Community Organization (SECO).[7]

The victory against "the Road" saved Southeast Baltimore's waterfront residential character. In the 1980s developers discovered the land where homes had been leveled, next to vacant factories, and began building upscale housing. Working-class residents took umbrage. The new housing blocked their water views and access. Expensive housing raised tax assessments. Perhaps most disturbing, new upper-middle-class residents wanted nothing to do with the old-timers. Yet to Baltimore boosters, these developments were only good news. Southeast Baltimore, which had not only cheap housing but also stunning views and a seemingly securely white population, was one of the few areas that attracted middle-class home buyers.

The Southeast Planning Process

Ironically, defeating the demolition of working-class homes led to gentrification. However, another result was the birth of grassroots organizing in Southeast Baltimore. SECO became one of the city's premier community organizations. It encouraged and helped form neighborhood associations and alliances. Southeast Baltimore grew thick with organizations, and community meetings became part of the culture. As upscale development accelerated, residents organized to curtail development and limit property taxes.

In 1989, SECO director Robert Giloth helped activists form the Southeast Linkage Group to promote policies to exact community benefits from development (Giloth 1993). The group drafted a City Council bill to assess impact fees. It did not pass, but the council urged Southeast Baltimore residents to prepare a community plan to articulate their interests. Giloth began talking about a planning process and in 1992 had a grant for organizing and staffing.

A Southeast Planning Council of fifty individuals and organizational representatives, leading participation of about 300 community members, produced the *Southeast Community Plan* in December 1993 (Southeast Planning Council 1993). The plan included recommendations for revitalizing the local economy, regenerating housing, providing services to support youth, families, and the elderly, and improving transportation. The Planning Council presented it to the cabinet of the mayor, who urged department heads to help implement recommendations. The Planning Commission endorsed the plan as a basis for assessing zoning and development proposals, as well as the city's capital improvement program.

In early 1994, once the planning process was over, the Planning Council disbanded, transferring authority to a coordinating committee of ten, who continued to meet. During this time, Giloth left SECO, and funds for Planning Council staffing ran out. A handful of activists held responsibility for implementing twenty-three recommendations. Some were already engaged in efforts that would implement certain recommendations; in these cases, the plan endorsed what they were doing already. Some extended their reach to other recommendations in areas of interest. Thus coordinating committee members took on, took part in, or kept track of initiatives in housing, economic development, transportation, and social services.

One service recommendation concerned schools. In fact, it was largely an afterthought. When leaders introduced the planning process in 1992, they said that the agenda would focus on physical and economic development. These were areas where community nonprofit organizations had expertise, and the Planning Council thus could credibly and effectively recommend action. As for education, it was beyond any community's influence and had to be tackled citywide.

Perhaps also because few planning participants had school-age children, few said much about education. And yet occasionally someone would insist that community revitalization depended on improving schools. Sister Bobby English, a planning leader who ran a multiservice center with a focus on youth, encouraged these statements, and a slowly growing number of voices spoke up about education. Even so, the draft plan presented to a community assembly in August 1993 did not mention schools. Only after a parent liaison spoke up and insisted on a recommendation about education was anything put into the document.

Still, Recommendation #20 was vague: "Establish a study-action group for schools. Assume responsibility, as citizens of southeast Baltimore, to create opportunities for community control, and to provide channels for community input in schools." The text listed three activities that the study-action group would conduct with the school system:

- Analyze the problems related to quality education in Baltimore City Schools.
- Take steps to improve schools.
- Evaluate the need and potential for new schools, including community-based schools, in order to create more options for quality education.

The plan also listed five activities to be carried out in the community:

- Survey the positive things being done and . . . assess the gaps in services.
- Advance community and School Board awareness about what is being done.
- Act as advocates to strengthen and/or create community-based programs and after school tutorial programs through local School Improvement Teams and through business partnerships.
- Link Senior Citizens and college volunteers to work in the schools through a variety of educational, cultural, recreational, and health oriented programs with children, families, and parents.
- Market quality public and private schools options in southeast Baltimore (Southeast Planning Council 1993, 40).

The recommendation conveyed concern but did not set forth a specific agenda. No one on the Task Force knew much about the schools. As a waning coordinating committee struggled to find ways to implement their plan, education was not one of the areas in which they moved.

Proposing to do Something about Schools

I had been a participant-observer in the Southeast planning process (Baum 1997), and I sat in with the Planning Council's coordinating committee as it wrestled with implementation. Fortuitously, in early 1994, the U. S. Department of Education (USDE) issued a notice of funding availability for its Urban Community Service Program, aimed at supporting universities in working with community groups to solve community problems. Colleagues in the University of Maryland's Urban Studies and Planning faculty decided to submit a proposal. One professor would aid a Palmer Park, Maryland, community group with housing and related neighborhood problems. Three others and I would help the Southeast Planning Council implement recommendations in economic development, housing, recreation and safety, and education.

I developed an education proposal with two coordinating committee members, Bobby English and David Casey. They had just completed a planning process and had extensive organizing experience. They were recognized community leaders and had deep local roots. English had been a teacher and worked with three schools in conjunction with the multiservice center she directed. I had three years of familiarity with Southeast Baltimore and doctoral research experience with schools. Yet none of us was current on education issues, no one knew much about the school system, and we did not even know which schools were in the area.

We had faith in the recent planning process as a model. We envisioned creating an education planning council, consisting of people concerned about schools, who would debate, develop a plan, and implement it. And yet there were no specific models for what we had in mind, and we did not know about the little relevant activity around the country. I took the recent planning process as support for two assumptions. The first was that Southeast Baltimore had many education activists who cared about schools, involved themselves in school policies and practices, and held pet schemes for fixing schools. I had the names of people in PTAs and Parent-Teacher Organizations, SECO's Education Committee, and neighborhood associations. In addition, I assumed that these people, like participants in the planning process, thought of all Southeast Baltimore as their community. I anticipated that a community education planning council would convene them, struggle to reconcile disagreements based on race, class, geography, or ideology, and then craft a plan representing a hard-won area-wide consensus.

The Department of Education's program announcement encouraged lofty aims:

> This program provides grants to urban academic institutions to work with private and civic organizations to devise and *implement solutions to pressing and severe problems* in their urban communities. (*Federal Register* 1994, 15810, emphasis added)

The agency wanted partnerships to involve community members and to conduct research to plan and implement realistic, comprehensive, and cost-effective proposals.

The funder's expectations, community activists' high hopes about the university, and lack of experience with education produced an ambitious proposal. Its aims were reasonable, but it projected swift accomplishment of complicated tasks. The initiative would improve education in an area with eleven elementary schools, four middle schools, and one high school. The effort had four objectives: (1) Establish a community education planning committee that would articulate an active community role in Southeast Baltimore schools; (2) Develop a Southeast Baltimore community plan for education; (3) Create a database on education issues of concern to Southeast Baltimore residents; and (4) Begin to implement interventions recommended in the plan. The proposal anticipated starting implementation within a year.

The Department of Education approved this proposal with the rest of the University of Maryland's plan and began funding the five projects in October 1994.

The Logic of Starting Up

When USDE announced funding, I reported to the Planning Council's coordinating committee and asked who would lead the community's education effort. The coordinating committee had happily endorsed the proposal but had put off any commitments until it came through. Now everyone was busy. Most were not interested in education. At last, Bobby English stepped forward. She and I constituted the university-community partnership.

Practically, the University's proposal bound almost no one. I felt committed to abide by it. English was committed to it in the spirit defined by the *Southeast Community Plan:* to do something to study and take action to improve schools. Those who would participate in the Southeast Education Task Force, even if they understood the project's origins, had no knowledge of the proposal and, in any case, would not feel bound to an agreement to which they were not party. Even though USDE believed that it had funded specific actions, much was up for grabs.

In this context, Southeast Baltimore traditions and English's and my beliefs and styles shaped initial premises about participation, action, and research.

Participation

Community activism is a strong Southeast Baltimore tradition (Crenson 1983; Truelove 1977a, 1977b). Resistance to "the Road" set a pattern. One group of activists were working-class white ethnics, mostly women, who saw themselves defending their families' values and interests. A second group were professionals who had moved into the area and valued its people, architecture, and society. The former had greater legitimacy by their families' longevity, but the latter, even if reproved as "gentrifiers," brought valued time, skills, connections, and ease and competence in dealing with the government and foundation world. Some of the latter staffed nonprofit community organizations, and over time, the groups found ways of working together.

Even so, the groups participate on different issues, for reasons largely related to class. Working-class residents worry more about external dangers and immediate problems, because they face greater threats and have more to lose. Unlike middle-class professionals, who feel able to act on the world, those who are poorer experience the world as acting on them (Gans 1988). Hence, they confine themselves to neighborhood affairs. Working-class or poor residents, racial and ethnic minorities, the elderly, and single mothers, if they participate in any civic activity, are most often found in neighborhood or tenant associations.

Middle-class people are more likely to have cognitive maps that include many people and interests, cognitive skills in conceptualizing relations between the local and immediate and the global and long term, the ability to imagine a decision process that moves from problems to solutions, and the skill to guide or navigate such a process. They see a larger world, because they securely move in one. Many middle-class residents, even if relative newcomers—perhaps especially because they are newcomers, not bound to a specific neighborhood—have geographically more extensive networks than working-class natives. They think of all of Southeast Baltimore as their community, and they confidently plan for it.

In associated ways, the practicalities of participation favor the middle class. Civic activity is an investment of time and effort, competing with family and leisure. It rarely brings immediate returns, and benefits usually are collective, even if individuals share them. Success requires not just cognitive ability but skills and resources. Higher education and professional status enable middle-class people to act comfortably and effectively in public deliberations. Their jobs have flexible schedules, and some, such as those working for nonprofit organizations, may include community work in their professional responsibilities. Adults who do not have children at home have much more time for civic activity than those who do. Adults in two-parent families and families with child care have more freedom than other parents.

These patterns manifested themselves when a few middle-class activists designed the Southeast community planning process in 1991. The core group invited participation broadly, from neighborhood associations, public housing tenant organizations, churches, and other groups. However, those who took part were largely middle class, and often college educated and professional. The group was whiter than Southeast Baltimore overall. Few had children, at least with them at home.

Despite the leaders' good intentions, the narrow participation raised questions about their representativeness. In response, some reply that, through their professional and civic contacts, they have come to know the interests of those who do not participate. They can represent the community's interests, if not its demography. Some activists point to the benefits that they have brought residents, and they note agreement about purposes when the poor, minorities, white ethnics, or elderly do turn out.

The Education Task Force proposal, echoing the ambitions of the planning process, was predicated on securing broad participation, for three reasons. First, only such participation could give the Task Force legitimacy as representative of community preferences. Second, broad participation was necessary to learn about complicated issues and to develop thoughtful proposals. Third, practically, getting work done required a lot of effort.

Bobby English, while endorsing these principles, expected limited participation. As an experienced organizer, she knew that extensive participation required more effort than the Task Force could call on. At the same time, she assumed that initial research in each school would encourage some parents to take an active role.

Action

Southeast community organizations have been among Baltimore's most successful in raising funds, running programs, and organizing residents. SECO and its community development arm, Southeast Development, Inc. (SDI), were among the first, followed by Neighborhood Housing Services, the Julie Community Center, Jubilee Baltimore, the Baltimore American Indian Center, the Patterson Park Neighborhoods Initiative, Centro de la Communidad, and many smaller community and neighborhood organizations.

A few of these organizations have invested in organizing. Programmatically, many have focused in areas tied to the private market, where they act as nonprofit entrepreneurs with government assistance. Housing and economic development are prime examples. Only a few provide social services. One reason is that community organizations find it easier to get funding for housing or economic development. Part of the explanation, in turn, is that even with recent moves toward privatization, public agencies dominate most service fields.

No Southeast community organization has run education programs besides Head Start. The state exercises a near monopoly on education and does not fund others to set up schools. Only financially secure churches or other entities can develop private schools. Maryland does not authorize charter schools. As a result, few outside of the school system have experience with or knowledge about running schools. Hence, even when the Baltimore City Public School System has solicited proposals for charter-like "New Schools," few community organizations have the knowledge, let alone the resources, to consider setting up and operating a school. Hence, SECO's Education Committee, until its dissolution in 1994 the only community entity concerned with education, restricted itself to analyzing public programs.

To start programs, community organizations must obtain funding. Alternatively, they can try to influence other organizations, such as public agencies or private developers. The community planning process typified how Southeast organizations have exploited the second route. Although planning was guided by a general vision of a revitalized Southeast Baltimore, the plan was built "up" from participants' interests rather than "down" from the vision. Recommendations grew by accretion, as leaders added proposals when people advocated for them. When it came time to set priorities, planning leaders moved opportunistically. They recommended initiatives that people already were working on, and they added others that would be easy to start.

As a leader of this process and a longtime activist, Bobby English represented this approach in the education project. Sensitive to the privations of poverty and the paucity of resources, she takes great satisfaction in any improvements in children's or families' lives. Practically, she is an artful chef in making "stone soup." In the fairy tale, a hungry itinerant comes to a hamlet and gets the villagers to feed him by persuading them to help him cook "stone soup." He starts with a stone; if only someone provided a pot with water, he could make the soup. Then, as he boils the water, if only someone had a little onion to add, that would improve the flavor just the right amount. Then, all it would need to make it just so would be a few carrots. And so on, until he has a hearty soup that all declare unsurpassed. English is expert in building programs in this fashion. She took on the education project with high faith in the power of spontaneity: try something, get started, and somehow a worthwhile result will ensue.

Research

The seminal event in Southeast community action was opposition to "the Road." Action was pure and heartfelt; no research was necessary. Some who liked the results of protest created more substantial vehicles for action. Many of these organizations used research in deciding what to do. They studied housing conditions to craft an initiative to turn a block with abandoned buildings into one with home owners. They studied the labor market and surveyed the unemployed to develop a referral service to put people in good jobs. In the 1980s and 1990s, as national clearinghouses and journals circulated accounts of programs, Southeast Baltimore community organizations began to look at programs elsewhere that could be models for local action.

The Southeast community planning process incorporated both types of research. Staff analyzed census data, surveyed land use and building conditions, interviewed community leaders, and elicited the views of community participants. Then leaders invited experts to evaluate local perceptions and findings and to suggest models for action. Recommendations, even if prioritized expediently, were shaped by research.

Three variables distinguish the community organizations that consistently base action on research. First, larger organizations are more likely to have a budget that can pay for research. Second, some activists value research more than others and, even in smaller organizations, are more likely to seek funding for it. Third, some substantive areas have more readily available data and customary methods for analysis than others; for example, community organizations can obtain good housing data more easily than health or education data.

A central purpose of the Urban Community Service Program was to make university research resources available to community organizations. The proposal assumed that planning depended on three types of research. One involved assessing children's educational conditions and defining problems. A second entailed identifying or formulating theories and models of intervention that could improve conditions. A third concerned identifying parents' and community members' beliefs about the first two questions: which problems mattered, and what should be done. Those who joined the education project valued research, but the practical challenge would be to exploit scarce resources to acquire useful knowledge.

In Conclusion, at the Start

Baltimore was losing people and money. The city's schools, with weak leadership and inadequate funding, were struggling to teach challenging children. Southeast Baltimore had suffered the city's losses but sought to redeem itself. A handful of activists decided to try a community approach to improving their schools. The education field was turbulent, and they were hardly part of it. They cared a great deal about schools, but they knew little about them. They wanted to find and use sound knowledge to build connections in the field. They assumed community involvement could be a lever of change. We turn now to the story.

Part 2

Research as a Way of Getting Started

Chapter 5

Getting Started, Getting Bearings

Getting Started

Bobby English decided to chair the education project in order to create the "study-action group for schools." As community and university partners, she and I began to discuss the details in January 1995. We said little about the entity's purpose or goals, beyond improving education. We talked about its first activities. It would interview parents and school staff to assess the schools and to develop an action plan. A coordinating committee would develop and oversee it.

English suggested five members besides herself and me. Two—David Casey and Carolyn Boitnott—had led the Southeast planning process with her. Another—Ed Rutkowski—had become increasingly active in that process as it went on. A fourth—Irona Pope—had participated in planning, and English knew her from several years' assistance to the school where Pope worked. The fifth—Peggy Roth—had not taken part in planning but knew the schools.

Roth and Pope were the only ones whose children were or had been students in the city public schools. They also were the only members who might not be considered middle class. Roth lived in the heart of working-class Canton. She had high aspirations for her two daughters and cared a great deal about their schools. She had recently finished a Volunteers in Service to America (VISTA) assignment staffing a low-key SECO education initiative. She had voluminous notes on school interviews and meetings, definite views of many principals and teachers, and ideas about what would improve the schools. She offered the best direct understanding of the perspective of working-class, white families, and she did not hesitate to offer judgments about schools.

Irona Pope, the only African American in the group, was a parent liaison at City Springs Elementary School. The purpose of her federally funded position was to involve low-income parents in school. She had grown up in one of Southeast Baltimore's first public housing projects but had gone on to buy a house elsewhere in the city. From making her way, she had come to know community activists, politicians, public agency staff, and civic leaders. Her unflagging message to parents was to take responsibility for themselves and their children. She would advocate for almost anything "her parents" needed. She never hesitated to speak her mind, and she minced no words when talking about school problems. Persistently, she would explain how poor and black students did not get what they deserved. In December 2000, *Baltimore Magazine* would include her, along with Ed Rutkowski, among ten of "Baltimore's Best."

Rutkowski was the only other group member who had grown up in Southeast Baltimore. He was unusual among those born there, in going to college and moving away to follow a career in computer programming. He had returned to improve the community. He concentrated on what he came to call the "Patterson Park Urban Transition Zone," an area of racial, economic, and housing transition. With Marcus Pollock, a black activist, he wrote and circulated *The Urban Transition Zone: A Place Worth a Fight* (Pollock and Rutkowski 1998), proposing "a strategy for urban stabilization and revitalization." Rutkowski had an inductive style, taking empirical evidence seriously. Paying keen attention to changes in individual dwelling units, for example, he slowly built up theories of the local housing market and ideas for influencing it. Carefully seeking bold remedies for community problems, he drew the attention of civic leaders, agency staff, and funders who wanted a broad approach for redeeming one of Baltimore's slipping neighborhoods. He was deeply committed to improving schools because of what they meant to community life.

Carolyn Boitnott was one of an early wave of middle-class people to move to Southeast Baltimore from the suburbs. After raising children in Baltimore County, where she had been active in the PTA, she and her husband resettled in Butcher's Hill, a neighborhood of stately, nineteenth-century homes. She became a professional volunteer and devoted her full time to neighborhood and citywide activities. The Citizens Planning and Housing Association gave her its annual award for civic improvement. She believed that society should allocate wealth equitably, and she was committed to a reasoned, well-ordered process of involving community members in planning and acting.

David Casey was a Methodist minister by training and passion, though at this time he had no permanent church and was working with a nonprofit housing developer. He had children but sent them to private school elsewhere in the city. He was a longtime community activist, having been, among other things, a SECO board member and president. He read avidly and liked discussing big-picture views of Southeast Baltimore, the city, and their futures. He had enjoyed leading the Southeast planning process as an opportunity to advocate for community needs with city officials, agency staff, and foundation officers. He thought that Southeast Baltimore parents should create and run a new school. He was confident he knew what Southeast residents needed, and he aggressively took their case to whoever might help.

Bobby English was the only professional educator in the group. She had studied to become a teacher as a Sister of Notre Dame de Namur and had taught for twelve years in K–8 schools. In 1966, she went to Brazil to teach and became involved in community organizing with rural villages and urban barrios. Through contact with Paulo Freire and radical theologians, she developed a faith in popular education as a means of helping people understand and organize to change their conditions. She returned to the United States in 1985 and became director of the Julie Community Center. The storefront center operates youth and health programs, conducts parenting and adult education classes, provides emergency help, and generally is available for community projects. English worked with three neighborhood schools. Nearly all of the children who attended her center's after-school programs were African American. She had become a community fixture, always willing to help solve problems. In 1993, the Neighborhood Design Center recognized her as one of the city's twenty-five top community leaders.

English's views gave early shape to the effort. It would rest on a small core of people who knew one another and could get along. They would involve others beginning with the research. The group would emphasize the positive, both in terms of what schools had done and what the Task Force could do. It would work with schools, not against them. It would proceed incrementally: as a small entity, it would tackle small problems and find accessible remedies.

Getting Bearings

The coordinating committee met often and talked a lot. Members struggled with grasping education issues, understanding the school system, figuring out what a community organization could do to improve education, and creating an instrument for action. They moved between a framework for understanding schools and a process and structure for acting. Free-flowing talk held a place for the specific ideas and plans that they hoped eventually to find.

Constituency, Participation, and Process

Regardless of what the funded proposal said, the Task Force would become what its participants wanted. In any case, the proposal was unclear about both constituency and membership. These questions occupied much early talk, because they mattered for accomplishing the Task Force's purposes, and because they concerned whom else the core group would bring into their project. Central was whether the Task Force would include only parents and community members, or whether it would be open to school staff.

In part, the issue was one of democracy. If schools, parents, and community members shared responsibility for education, and if changing the schools was one strategy for improvement, then it was only right for school staff to have formal roles. No one in the core group would question that principle if it were a matter of including poor people in, say, housing decisions. In addition, the issue was one of expertise, and thus effectiveness. Educators knew about schools and students, and it would be foolish to think about improving education without this knowledge.

In addition, the constituency question was strategic. If the core group were convinced that the schools were so intractable that only an assault from outside could push them into changing, then educators should be excluded, but that conclusion posed the question of whether the Task Force could develop the political muscle to move a school. Alternatively, if the group believed that community members and school staff had to work together to accomplish anything significant—that an interinstitutional network was necessary—then that conclusion posed the question of how to get parents and educators to trust one another sufficiently to collaborate.

When Bobby English opened the first meeting in January 1995 by asking members about their expectations for the project, the constituency question took center stage. After much back and forth, the group reached consensus on first recruiting parents and other residents. However, even taking parents and community members as the first constituency was not uncontroversial. Someone quickly insisted, "only good people." Another disagreed: attracting members would be difficult, and the Task Force should take anyone interested. Yet despite the democracy of the latter view, the first comment voiced some members' persistent hesitation. They wanted enough people for the organization to be effective, but they wanted them to be thoughtful, tolerant of others, and loyal to the core group's aims and vision.

Caution about participation, combined with uncertainty about what the Task Force should do, led the group in March to adopt an eighteen-month process that emphasized research and first brought in participants at two events: a "mini-kickoff" of the Task Force for community members in April and a "maxi-kickoff" that would include educators in the fall. The group launched three committees to conduct research to get bearings for moving ahead: one to collect and analyze school and student data; a second to interview principals, teachers, parents, and students; and a third to search for model programs that could be replicated locally.

The Mini-Kickoff

The purpose of the April Mini-Kickoff was to introduce the Task Force to PTA and parent-teacher organization (PTO) officers, Southeast Baltimore elected officials, and community and education activists, and to encourage them to assist with the research projects. Twenty-five came, counting the core group: mostly, as is common in education, women, two-thirds white, and one-third parents, including one on the school board, as well as a city councilman and two teachers who lived in the neighborhood. English, describing the Task Force, explained that success would require a great deal of effort. She asked people to describe what they wanted to accomplish.

In contrast to English's emphasis on what was good in the schools, many participants catalogued problems. Irona Pope noted that her school, whose students lived in public housing, was an isolated black school that white families successfully kept their children out of. Elizabeth Locklear, a Lumbee Indian leader, observed, "People say Southeast Baltimore has the poorest schools in the city." A Patterson High School parent said that the school lacked safety and order. Ramona Piskor, a parent and a plaintiff in the ACLU's suit against the state on funding adequacy, said that school improvement was essential for the city's survival.

Undaunted, English followed this recital by laying out the plan for three research groups and invited people to take part in the first meeting of one of them for the remainder of the evening. With these modest beginnings, a community education task force was starting out.

When the coordinating committee reviewed the meeting a week later, it was optimistic but sober. David Casey was pleased to have seen so many interested people, including parents, but he noted that it would be hard to attract others who had no previous contact with the core group. Rutkowski simply commented, "What a lot of work we have to do!" English remarked that she was inspired by people's enthusiasm. The group then planned the research projects.

Research

Model Programs

Ed Rutkowski convened the committee on model programs in late April, but it soon pulled up short. It was hard to find people interested in searching for models for Southeast schools. Part of the problem was that few community members knew much about academic programs or had the time to investigate. In addition, the committee came to realize that it made little sense to look for programs to solve school problems without knowing, first, what the problems were. The Data Committee was meeting at the same time and would not make findings for several months. After three meetings, the model programs committee disbanded.

School and Student Data

David Casey got the Data Committee off to a quick start at the end of April. The group included Ramona Piskor; Kate Finston, a resident who taught and became an administrator at schools elsewhere in the city; John Cain, a city councilman; Jerry Baum, who had started the Fund for Educational Excellence, a local education fund, and was interested in community education initiatives; Casey; and me. The meeting's aim was to formulate research questions for my graduate student and me in collecting and analyzing data. The discussion ranged widely, from causes and consequences of student mobility to relations between teacher turnover and student test scores to impacts of race and income on student performance to connections between class size and learning. This broad assignment launched several years of meetings as the university analyzed data and committee members interpreted findings.

Interviews with Principals, Teachers, Parents, and Students

Bobby English recruited volunteers to interview at the sixteen schools. They would talk with the principal, three teachers varying in experience, three parents varying in school involvement, and three students varying in performance. They would ask about schools' strengths, problems, changes needed, and characteristics of an ideal school, with attention to teacher performance, parent involvement, school climate, student spirit, and school-community relations.

The volunteers interviewed all sixteen principals and opportunistic samples of teachers, parents, and students. The interviews may have lacked scientific rigor, but they produced consistent general portraits, in addition to information about individual schools. When a school was successful, people credited committed teachers and an energetic principal, perhaps with the assistance of a few good parent volunteers. The principal might be effective in getting outside resources, and teachers worked well as a team and had good morale. They succeeded in creating an atmosphere that students found caring and safe.

When a school had problems, people typically saw causes in two places. They pointed to communities where drugs, violence, and family problems made it hard for children to learn and challenged teachers' efforts. Or they blamed decision makers for not giving schools enough resources. Classes were large, and books were scarce. Particularly in the face of community problems, limited resources made it hard for teachers to meet students' needs. In short, teachers and principals were doing as well as they could under the circumstances.

People at all school levels generally described similar strengths and concerns, but there were differences, some related to students' ages. For example, while elementary schools seemed caring and safe, schools for older students faced challenges on safety. Although people at all levels felt that parents were not sufficiently involved, parent participation declined from elementary to middle to high school.

The interviews helped the coordinating committee cross a threshold: they gained confidence they knew something about schools and, in particular, had a framework for setting an agenda. They identified four concerns: (1) improving existing school programs and introducing new ones; (2) making schools safer; (3) developing relations between schools and the community; and (4) increasing economic and human resources for schools.

The (Maxi-)Kickoff

With heightened expectations, the coordinating committee prepared for an October 14 Kickoff. They invited principals and teacher and student representatives from the sixteen schools to receive awards for past accomplishments and to join in this effort to make the schools better. They invited community members, elected officials, school officials, and other education activists.

Opening the meeting in a church hall, Bobby English welcomed a crowd of seventy, including principals or delegates from nearly all schools, teachers, parents, and other community members. In a pattern the Task Force would follow other times, the coordinating committee presented its analysis and recommendations and asked community members and educators to comment and concur. In this way, research and participation would be linked in a step toward action.

English described the four issue areas. When she was done, Barbara Moore, a parent who would later join Ramona Piskor as a member of the restructured school system's Parent and Community Advisory Board, zeroed in on parent involvement—why was there so little of it? An assistant principal observed that parents were uncomfortable at school, and, at any rate, schools often had nothing for parents to do. A mother noted that parents dropped out of their children's schools in the second or third grade, thinking that older children could take care of themselves. Another parent added that jobs often kept parents from school. Irona Pope said that Title 1 of the federal Elementary and Secondary Education Act, which funded her work, required parents to take part in children's education, but that parents were insecure about their knowledge.

David Casey introduced Data Committee findings. The Task Force had not yet received data requested from the school system, and it was relying on a few published documents. Casey reported that enrollment in Southeast Baltimore schools had increased to 11,010 during the first half of the 1990s. Attendance in Southeast schools, as elsewhere, had slowly increased since 1990, but Southeast Baltimore's 93 percent was still below Maryland overall. While Southeast elementary school attendance had increased from 92 to 94 percent, and middle school attendance had risen from 78 to 84 percent, high school attendance had dropped from 77 to 69 percent.

Student eligibility for free or reduced-price meals showed high, growing poverty in Southeast Baltimore. Eligibility is based on families' reports of income; those below a federal poverty income level can receive a subsidy. In the first half of the 1990s, the proportion of students in this group increased in Southeast Baltimore, the city, and the state, with Southeast Baltimore highest at 77 percent in 1994, Baltimore at 69 percent, and Maryland at only 30 percent.

Special education, the subject of ongoing litigation, was more common in Southeast Baltimore in 1994 (16 percent of students) than the city as a whole (15 percent) or the state (12 percent). Enrollment in special education is an unreliable indicator of students' abilities, because teachers sometimes use it to get students whose behavior they do not like out of their classrooms. That would help explain why Southeast boys were twice as likely as girls to be in special education, and why middle school students were twice as likely as elementary school students. High school students were in between, probably because many whose behavior did not fit in dropped out of high school.

Student mobility was high in Southeast Baltimore, and higher than in the city or in the state. On average, during the first half of the 1990s, 42 percent of Southeast students entered or left school in the middle of the academic year, compared to 39 percent in Baltimore and only 24 percent in Maryland. In addition, 14 percent of Southeast Baltimore high school students dropped out in 1994, compared to 15 percent in the city and only 5 percent in the state.

A measure of the usefulness of high school education is whether students take courses that enable them to attend college. Southeast Baltimore's Patterson High School students had improved considerably in the early 1990s, but still only 27 percent had courses required for admission to the University of Maryland, compared to 32 percent for Baltimore and 48 percent for Maryland.

Casey had decided not to present state MSPAP scores for individual schools, because they would shine a critical light on many schools, but principals were keenly aware of them. Administered to students in the third, fifth, and eighth grades, the test emphasized active group work rather than multiple-choice questions. Schools were measured in terms of the percentage of students scoring at "satisfactory" or "excellent" levels in each of six subjects. In 1994, the percentages of Maryland third- and fifth-grade students scoring "satisfactory" ranged in the 30s and 40s across subject areas. In Southeast Baltimore, only six of eleven elementary schools had more than 10 percent of students scoring "satisfactory" in even half of the subjects in the third and fifth grades. Only four schools had at least 20 percent "satisfactory" in even one area.

A growing chorus would challenge the test's validity toward the decade's end, and scores seemed to fluctuate annually without obvious pattern or reason. Over time, it would become clear that MSPAP scores, like those on other tests, corresponded to families' socioeconomic status. However, that correlation, while meriting attention, was not unambiguous. It measured a complicated interaction of students' family and community conditions, family and community expectations of boys and girls, teachers' expectations of students, teachers' abilities, school policies and practices, students' abilities, and students' learning and accomplishments. Much of this worked against children whose parents had limited formal education and were poor, and none of it argued against improving teaching, but there was no good news about Southeast children.

Following Casey's presentation and discussion, the audience broke up into groups corresponding to the four issue areas and began their task: elaborating on the issues, suggesting areas for action, and signing up for ongoing work. The school-community relations group continued the discussion of parent involvement started earlier. Teachers, parents, and community members easily agreed on the importance of parents' participating at school but noted obstacles, such as work schedules, family obligations, parents' self-consciousness about their own education, and school opposition. The group recommended studying what parents currently did at schools and creating supports for more parents to take part. It suggested flexible work schedules, adult education, parent training, and development of parent opportunities at schools.

Along these lines, the resources group noted that there were many resources in the community, but that schools knew about little outside of their walls. They suggested cataloguing the resources for schools and recommended training school staff and parents to write grant proposals.

The safety group talked about a lack of safety. Walking to and from school could be dangerous, school buses were crowded and did not always let students on, students got harassed walking or on the buses, and those kept after school could not get home on the buses and got into trouble walking through alien neighborhoods. At school, children encountered students who disrupted class and others who threatened or hurt them. The group suggested community policing and visible parent presence around schools. It recommended conflict-resolution programs for students and families, as well as alternative schools for disruptive children. It urged more communication between staff and parents.

The programs group distinguished two areas of interest: curriculum and social service programs. Participants wanted more systematic professional development for teachers and suggested incorporating services into schools as a means of addressing social problems that interfered with teaching and learning.

A *Baltimore Sun* reporter who attended described the meeting as "Baltimore's most ambitious community-based school-improvement effort in a quarter-century" (Bowler 1995).

The Beginnings

The activities of this first year set the tone for what followed. The Task Force grew out of the Southeast planning process as an agenda item in community revitalization, an approach to community action, and a network of friends. The core group knew that many of the community's children left school with little preparation for adulthood, and they regarded that as a matter of urgency. Still, they moved and extended their number cautiously.

For some, deliberateness reflected a proprietary wish to hold the education initiative to the vision and norms of the planning process. Even so, no one had a clear idea what a community organization could do to improve schools. Hence they called on a few whom they already knew to conduct research to help get their bearings before reaching out to other community members or schools. Yet the group obtained limited information. Published reports gave some measures of students but did not systematically distinguish them by race or income. The Task Force sought to supplement these data with stakeholders' perceptions, but those the volunteers interviewed, like those invited to the kickoffs, represented people who worked or were active in the schools. Parents, especially those who had difficulty taking part in their children's education, were hard to reach. Interviews offered sketches of schools, but with uncertain accuracy. Tacitly, the emphasis on cooperating with schools, recognizing positive achievements, and finding doable projects may have made it hard to hear strong criticisms or to see systemic problems.

Nevertheless, the Task Force took research seriously and started with it. When the core group presented its findings to community members and educators, the audience listened. For one thing, it was reassuring to see a community group trying to act on the basis of knowledge. For another, as the Task Force would repeatedly discover, principals and teachers themselves got so little information that they were grateful for whatever the Task Force could tell them.

For the core group, research preceded participation. The Task Force would conduct research and formulate proposals and then present its ideas to community members and educators. This approach gave intellectual structure to the participation of those who attended public meetings, but it was uncertain whether earlier, broader participation might have produced different analysis or recommendations. Core members' desire to chart a cautious course through a turbulent field encouraged this approach. Limited resources for organizing reinforced it.

Part 3

Participation

Chapter 6

Creating the Southeast Education Task Force

Moving from Research to Participation

The coordinating committee reconvened two weeks later to review the kickoff and to figure out what to do next. People congratulated themselves on a success. They had drawn a good turnout, including principals, and participants had talked earnestly and respectfully. Yet Ed Rutkowski noted that few came from outside of the schools. David Casey argued that the Task Force needed more staff to sustain participation and to follow through. Although the kickoff had endorsed an agenda, the core group struggled to define the parameters of action. Discussion focused on a scarcity of resources, though some of that talk may have been an effort to transform inner uncertainty about what to do into external constraints on doing anything. After the high of the kickoff, people talked hesitantly. Perhaps, some suggested, instead of trying to develop and sustain four work groups that would each study an issue and make proposals, they should just assign projects to ready volunteers.

A month later, English opened the coordinating committee meeting with a design for a planning process that included four work groups, each completing something tangible between January and June, but each also identifying broader interventions that were needed, with findings and recommendations codified in a plan to be released by December 1996. English emphasized that groups should focus opportunistically on projects that were "doable . . . with a little bit of longevity." Established by these accomplishments and armed with accompanying recommendations, the Task Force could then go to funders for staff to organize schools and community members and to implement the proposals. Now the coordinating committee would invite kickoff attendees to join the Task Force and work groups.

The committee scrambled to find four people to convene the groups in January, with the hope that each would lead the group over the following six months. As for staffing, I would work with the school-community relations group, and Debby Volk, my graduate assistant, would aid the safety group. We would do what we could with the resources and programs groups.

At last the Southeast Education Task Force would take form. Participants in the work groups would constitute the general membership, and their convenors would join the core group as an expanded coordinating committee.

Developing Participation

The Contingencies of Participation

Presciently, English had asked about setting snow dates for the work group meetings, but the question got lost in the exigencies of finding convenors. In mid-January, Baltimore's worst blizzard in years canceled the initial meetings of the four groups. When they finally met, school safety and school-community relations each drew fourteen people, resources got eight, and six showed up to discuss programs. Most participants were teachers, community activists, or coordinating committee members; few parents came. The snow was an omen of the odds against organizing.

To begin with, leadership was uneven. The convenors of the programs, resources, and safety groups were coordinating committee members who agreed to call the groups together but had extensive commitments. They lacked the time to recruit participants, keep in touch with members between meetings, or put much into planning or implementing projects. A merchant who had young children volunteered to lead the school-community relations group but soon resigned to put more time into his business.

The experience of the programs group highlighted a second challenge: getting good information. The group started out trying to compile an inventory of programs in the sixteen schools. They found it hard to obtain information from schools and difficult to conceptualize and categorize the functions of programs they had heard about. They foundered on the challenge of making any judgments about programs—whether they were good, whether one was better than another, or even whether in a crude quantitative way they met students' needs. Carolyn Boitnott, the convenor, became increasingly clear about the inadequacies of easily available information, while participation in the group dwindled. Her experience reflected a third challenge.

Participants found that there were no simple problem definitions or answers in education, and that it would take a long time to develop the knowledge to make authoritative proposals. The prospect of spending months in a group without tangible results led a number of people, including some convenors, to other, more attractive opportunities.

The groups encapsulated community organizing predicaments in education. Parents are busy being parents and have little time for meetings, even those serving their interests. The childless often have more time, but they also have commitments, and education is not a pressing issue for them. People who are not professional educators feel intimidated by the intellectual and political complexity of schooling. Even if disgruntled, they doubt that they have much to recommend. Professionals who work with children, particularly those without children of their own at home, are most likely to have the knowledge, confidence, and time for community action on schools.

Even so, participation has opportunity costs: to attend a meeting on education, people must give up something else. They want returns on their time. Most value short-term opportunities to do something tangible far more than a long-term learning process that may lead eventually to action, no matter what its possible impact. Hence, community organization is entropic: people who join are constantly pulled by other attachments. Someone must provide incentives to stay, continually recreating the organization, or it will disintegrate.

While these challenges troubled the safety, programs, and resources groups, the vitality of what came to be the School-Family-Community Relations Work Group provided straightforward lessons. It initially attracted several young teachers and others in education who had time, knowledge, and commitment for work. When the first convenor left to attend to his business, someone volunteered to take over. Members enjoyed one another. As staff, I supported the convenor, kept in touch with people between meetings, recruited new participants, and helped implement decisions. Later, when some teachers moved to schools elsewhere, new people joined, and one led the group toward forming church-school partnerships.

Parent Involvement

While the groups met in the spring, Carolyn Boitnott, reflecting on her earlier PTA activism, called coordinating committee members' attention to the dearth of parents and asked how to bring them in. The committee decided to invite PTA and PTO officers to discuss how the Task Force could help them. Members contacted the sixteen presidents by phone and mail to ask them to a May meeting. At the appointed time, ten from the Task Force arrived with abundant food and a full agenda. Not one parent showed up.

Those present, after sharing their embarrassment, considered the lessons. David Casey took the nonmeeting as conclusive evidence that intensive, full-time, funded organizing was essential to involve parents. Fortuitously, one of those present was Laura Weeldreyer, the education director for the Citizens Planning and Housing Association (CPHA), a citywide civic organization. She reported that she had applied for funds to start organizing parents in two or three schools. If money came, she would work in Southeast Baltimore.

Role and Mission

The purpose of the June coordinating committee meeting was to hear status reports from the work group convenors, to see what they had accomplished in the allotted six months, and to chart the next steps. The failed parent meeting added to uncertainty.

Boitnott reported that the program work group had stopped meeting, its members had no expertise to analyze curriculum, and no parents participated in the group. She recommended closing it down. The ensuing discussion, continuing in the next month's meeting, juxtaposed the value and feasibility of organizing parents and implementing projects. With limited resources, emphasizing the former might create an articulate, active group, but it would not necessarily lead to interventions improving education. The other path would implement programs, but without a parent constituency's participation or knowledge. Debate moved back and forth between assumptions about school change and opportunities for Task Force action.

Commenting on the program group report, Rutkowski said that the Task Force could be community activists supporting and lobbying for schools and principals. Boitnott advocated putting energy, instead, into parent involvement. English argued that the group had a role in networking, or creating relationships among community members and schools. In that context, it could get resources for schools and advocate for actions leading to systemic improvement. For instance, the Task Force could hold resource fairs or take educators to see model programs. Boitnott picked up on the first theme: the Task Force should be creating relationships, such as cheerleading for the schools with businesses. Organizing, she repeated, was crucial.

English took her report on the safety work group as an opportunity to emphasize what the Task Force could do well. She mentioned the School Safety Colloquium, where three schools described programs for disruptive students. Strikingly, teachers and principals expressed their appreciation for a rare opportunity to learn what other schools were doing. Thus the group could promote success stories, could take positions on school safety issues, and could connect nonprofit and community organizations to schools. Yet the group planned no further meetings.

At the same time, English introduced a new project. Sylvia Rosenfield, University of Maryland College of Education professor, was conducting a "safety assessment" in a Southeast Baltimore school. The consultation would examine how school practices affected student behavior and would help implement changes to improve behavior.

For the school-family-community relations group, I reported that members were deciding on fall projects.

The resources group had stopped meeting. David Casey mentioned projects that it had considered and added that the group had suggested convening the principals in the fall to report on Task Force efforts and to get their advice. The suggestion stimulated consideration of various possibilities for a fall meeting, including another effort to connect with parents.

The July meeting began with questions of how, and for what purposes, to recruit parents. Laura Weeldreyer had just received funding to organize parents at two Southeast Baltimore schools. English, supporting parent activism at schools, declared that the Task Force itself could work without more parents. After all, Casey recalled, five or six people did most of the work on the Southeast community plan. Several people noted the difficulty of organizing parents, but Boitnott insisted that parent organizing was the most important thing the Task Force could do. If CPHA did that work, Task Force members should support it, she said, and the Task Force itself might go out of existence. English affirmed that the Task Force was an ad hoc group.

People talked about relations between the parent organizing and the Task Force. CPHA had applied for another parent organizing grant, and if it came through, would give SECO the funds to hire someone to work with Weeldreyer. Ken Strong, SECO's director, a coordinating committee member, pledged that the second organizer would cooperate with the Task Force. People tried to define relations among CPHA, SECO, and the Task Force. Weeldreyer wanted an advisory board with representatives from all three entities.

The only decision was to invite principals to a fall meeting. That was a purpose requiring continuation of the Task Force, as was Weeldreyer's need for a partner. The coordinating committee remained split between emphases on parent involvement and projects. One group argued that parents were the only legitimate constituency and that the Task Force had to involve them so their needs informed its actions and gave it authority. Also, practically, the organization required more hands. A second group did not so much oppose parent involvement as doubt that the Task Force had resources to organize parents. These people wanted to act, and they believed that only projects would improve education. CPHA organizing aided the Task Force with the parent challenge and, in so doing, supported those who wanted to focus on programmatic action.

In the end, coordinating committee members agreed considerably on a Task Force role. Boitnott spoke for all in stating that the group, because they were not educators, had little expertise on curriculum and should concentrate elsewhere. Thus people described ways the Task Force could intervene in the community, in at least tacit partnership with school staff. Even though no one was fully confident about involving parents, much of what people endorsed was organizing—creating a network of community members interested in school change, connecting people and organizations in the community with schools, bringing resources to schools, advocating for parents with schools or for schools with policy makers, and analyzing school issues in terms of parent and community interests. Inexplicitly, committee members drew these ideas from the events of the past year and a half. This consensus, even if not overtly acknowledged, supported impulses to keep going.

Meanwhile, organizing proceeded with informal understandings among CPHA, SECO, and the Task Force. Several persons had roles in two of these organizations, key actors saw one another often, people trusted one another, and ongoing discussion kept organizations informed and gave the organizers guidance. Funders, however, would have trouble comprehending that informal coalitions could be solid bases for organizing or for any other activity.

Legitimacy

At that July meeting, I suggested that a benefit of parents' involvement, besides their ideas and work, was their authority. The Task Force, I said, needed community legitimacy. David Casey replied that he had authority from his activism. More modestly, Bobby English answered that no one on the Task Force had, or required, any special authority, that the group were simply gathering people's opinions, had learned from the efforts, and should, therefore, publish their conclusions. Perhaps because of their personal and professional involvement with community members, most people had little question about the group's authority to speak for parents.

On the other hand, the Task Force had little connection to schools and uncertain authority with them as a community representative. Some members had met the superintendent in a get-acquainted meeting. Volunteers had interviewed principals and teachers. Peggy Roth knew some principals from her VISTA work. English knew three principals from her service to their schools. Ed Rutkowski knew the superintendent, an area assistant superintendent, and a middle school principal. I had met some principals. Many principals had come to the kickoff. Coordinating committee members had met the two area assistant superintendents responsible for Southeast Baltimore schools. Still, these contacts did not add up to an institutional relationship.

Early on, the core group had hesitated to consider school staff a constituency and decided to include them when it became strategic to do so. In part, they doubted that teachers and principals were interested in community concerns. In part, they expected conflict between educators and parents and wanted to get parents' positions first. In addition some did not feel comfortable talking with teachers and principals on topics where they considered the educators to know far more.

In this context, Task Force members grouped principals into three categories. One was a self-sufficient entrepreneur who knew what he wanted and got many grants. At the other end of the continuum, a few principals were unequal to the challenges of running schools. They needed help but could not make use of what the Task Force might offer. In the middle were principals who were talented but overworked. If interested, they could take advantage of assistance.

Coordinating committee members thought most about the last group but were uncertain what they had to offer. The Task Force had no money. It lacked expertise on teaching and learning. It could claim to represent community opinion, but that had no obvious practical value. It might organize some volunteer effort, but not a lot. In short, members had no confident answers about what they could do for the schools that would matter to them.

Thus one thing a fall meeting with principals could accomplish would be to get their approval for the Task Force and their request for, agreement on, or at least acquiescence in certain projects or activities.

Meeting with the Principals

In late November, seven Task Force members met at one of the school system's area offices with ten principals and the two area assistant superintendents, who had urged principals to attend. Sandra Wighton, the Southeast Area Assistant Superintendent, praised the Task Force for "fact-finding, not fault-finding." She and Gary Thrift, her Southern Area counterpart, encouraged the principals to participate actively.

David Casey summarized a report on student data that had been sent to the principals. Principals responded by endorsing the analysis and interpreting puzzling findings. Then Task Force members proposed projects—a grant-writing workshop, a book of best practices, a truancy project, a mentoring-tutoring program, and a campaign for public support of the schools. Principals expressed interest in some ideas and pointed to difficulties with others. In a general concluding discussion, the principals asked the Task Force to support them by publicizing accomplishments, supporting the schools with the central administration, and serving as a liaison between the schools and the State Department of Education. They spoke more warmly of such political support than any of the suggested programs.

Recreating the Southeast Education Task Force

When the coordinating committee reviewed the meeting two weeks later, they were pleased by the turnout and by the principals' and assistant superintendents' desire for community support. They noted individual principals' interests in specific projects as approving encouragement. The meeting had been a success. And yet the committee faced a persistent problem, following up: how to invest limited resources to the best, or any, effect. The meeting clearly framed these questions that had troubled participants from early on. Yet its symbolic meanings helped Task Force members codify good enough answers to move ahead.

Tacitly, the principals' meeting helped coordinating committee members find answers to the questions that troubled them. In a sense, they shifted frames for measuring themselves—from looking at what they could do in comparison to oceanic educational problems to seeing what they were beginning to do in comparison to doing nothing. In terms of group development, after the core group used the first year for forming the Task Force, participants took the second year for storming about its purposes. The principals' meeting enabled them to adopt norms and to move on to performing in the third year.

The Logics of Participation, Action, and Research and the Doldrums

Normally, the logic of participation would lead a group such as those who set out to improve Southeast Baltimore schools to recruit members widely and to encourage all to define problems and advocate solutions. The logic of action would lead them to search for something they could do together. Yet the group did not widely publicize their existence, and they hesitated to act.

Those who regarded school reform as urgent had only general ideas about what would improve education. They felt particularly troubled, because they lived by the logic of action. They were fixers, and education frustrated them. They might have tried to break the stalemate by recruiting newcomers, to add information, interests, and ideas, but they did not.

One reason is that core group members knew one another well, had enjoyed the collegiality of community planning, and thus hesitated to bring in others whose judgments they could not anticipate. A second reason was their belief in the logic of research. They wanted to succeed by acting intelligently, and they had little confidence in their knowledge of education. They hesitated to add others who might have unwarranted faith in their own ideas, who would favor courses of action that would not add up to any measurable school improvement.

The core group set out to educate themselves in the first year. Each time they gained confidence in their knowledge, they brought in participants—at the mini-kickoff, the maxi-kickoff, and the work groups. When an audience apparently accepted their knowledge, the core group invited them to join in and take action. Yet the Task Force lacked the time to follow the logics of both research and action. Some participants, especially in the work groups, sacrificed research for action, while others, particularly in the coordinating committee, postponed action.

People loyally continued to meet, but more of their work was talk, mainly in the service of their learning, than action directed toward improving children's learning. Agendas developed incrementally and opportunistically. Individual interests brought projects forward, and work groups' study of their topics constituted the bulk of research. The failure to convene parent leaders was a blow to hopeful ambitions: the Task Force, a community instrument for studying and taking action on the schools, did not even have parent ties. Doubts about the effort converged in the summer of 1996, when some members of the coordinating committee talked about closing things down. Questions about membership, mission, knowledge, and resources still called for answers, and the Task Force had had little impact on schools.

Tacit Learning

Yet participants were learning from their experience in ways they barely recognized. Their disjointed action was, nevertheless, action research. From formal research, they learned about education and began to talk confidently about schools. Interviews provided information about schools and in identifying issues important to educators and parents gave participants a framework for interpreting what they later encountered. As the school system began to provide data, analysis provided a closer look at how students were doing. Task Force members noted the growing poverty of Southeast Baltimore students and the fact that most students performed similarly on tests in the first grade, before familiar racial and economic differences emerged.

In addition, Task Force members learned from projects they took part in or saw around them. Three who were members of school improvement teams observed school problems and decision making. Participants in the School Safety Colloquium learned from various school practices. During the summer, when some doubted the wisdom of continuing, Sylvia Rosenfield's offer to start a safety assessment in the fall was instrumentally and symbolically important: a university team was conducting research in a school on behalf of the Task Force. Thus the Task Force had knowledge about education.

The CPHA project, which unexpectedly brought two parent organizers to Southeast Baltimore schools, similarly offered answers about the Task Force. First, like the safety assessment, it was a project, something the Task Force was doing to improve education. Second, also like the safety assessment, it represented recognition and approval by a significant outside group. Third, the parent organizing project demonstrated that what the Task Force wanted to do was fundable. Fourth, parent organizing directly addressed the most urgent participation need.

During this time, the Julie Community Center, under Bobby English's direction, was conducting projects for children. For example, the Nurturing Program, following a Parents Anonymous model, helped parents raise children and taught family members conflict resolution skills. Thus families could better support children in learning at school. Significantly, Julie Center projects identified the family and community as domains about which Task Force members knew where action could improve children's education.

Meanwhile, English and I had joined Rosenfield in developing the Ad Hoc Group on Education and the Empowerment Zone, a network including U. S. Department of Education staff, faculty from three universities, and board and staff of the Baltimore Empowerment Zone. That project showed that Task Force work was of interest to federal education officials and that Task Force members had useful community and school knowledge.

These activities tacitly answered questions about Task Force purposes. Projects focused on family and community influences on children's learning. Parent organizing exemplified Task Force action: it would assemble parents and teachers to assess and remedy school problems, get them together with system administrators or elected officials to solve problems, or start church or business partnerships with schools. These relationships would provide new resources. Even if the Task Force had not yet done all of these things, what it had begun offered coherent answers regarding its mission: to connect people and institutions to improve community and family support for children in partnership with educators, who would do their best inside schools.

Thus at the same time that some members of the coordinating committee despaired of getting the Task Force on firm footing, experience provided answers to basic questions. The principals' meeting was important in this turnaround. The Task Force had asked the principals and assistant superintendents to comment on its data report, and the administrators endorsed the analysis: the Task Force knew about education. The Task Force proposed to carry out projects, and the principals expressed interest: the Task Force could do something the schools valued. Moreover, administrators asked the Task Force for political support. The school system affirmed the Task Force's knowledge and mission and gave it a role. Hence, it became easier to focus realistically on what the group should try to accomplish.

Strikingly, after the coordinating committee finished reviewing the principals' meeting, they moved ahead to discuss the Task Force's future. Members talked about its virtues. It had a broader picture of educational issues than any school did. It had greater independence than parents who needed to keep peace with their children's schools. It could help schools with projects, and at the same time it could advocate for all Southeast Baltimore schools. It should publish its data to help parents act more knowledgeably. And it should develop a Southeast Baltimore education plan. English said that she would prepare a menu of funding ideas for meeting a foundation representative.

Renewing the Task Force

The January 1997 meeting, starting the third year, began with a review of current projects. The Ad Hoc Group on Education and the Empowerment Zone was convening national experts on extended school day programs to help Empowerment Zone (EZ) schools develop funding proposals. Parent organizing and the safety assessment were proceeding. The School-Family-Community Relations Work Group was developing a mentoring-tutoring project and planning to draw pastors into partnerships with schools. A wish list for foundation funding was circulated.

English proposed restructuring the Task Force to make the best use of people's time. In place of the two-tier structure, with work groups and a coordinating committee, the latter would become the Task Force as a whole, with participation open to all interested. Work groups would be created—and terminated—on an ad hoc basis. The inactive work groups were thereby closed, and the school-family-community relations group would continue as long as necessary.

Later that month, in preparation for meeting with the foundation representative, English drafted a list of ten proposals, including creating a separate Southeast Baltimore school district, reconfiguring Southeast schools into pre-K–8 schools, limiting school size to 500, and providing extended day programs. That first meeting with a foundation staff member marked the start of funding efforts. Eventually, the list grew into the *Southeast Community Plan on Education.*

Lessons about Organizational Development and Community Action

The Proposal and Reality

The first two years bore little resemblance to the proposal, which called for the formation of an entity, publication of a plan, and start of implementation in one year. The proposal rested on unrealistic assumptions about participation, knowledge, and action. Yet two years may be a reasonable time for a new entity to agree on purposes and to organize participants—though the federal government might not have funded a proposal that said so. Thus the unrealistic proposal served an important purpose. It provided the group with a vision and an agenda, even as they set their own course. The Task Force was the "study-action group for schools," to which core group members felt strongly committed. While they floundered, they could refer to the proposal in delineating their purpose. Eventually the Task Force would prepare a plan and execute projects.

The Logic of Development

We can consider how the unfolding process of creating the Task Force reflected an implicit developmental logic. To get from a "study-action group" on paper to a stable organization, the Task Force had to develop the capacity to act, explicit purposes to guide its actions, and a collective identity to define those purposes. In reverse order, these requirements match the stages of group development and correspond roughly to the logics of collective action.

Forming and Participation

Most of those who started the Task Force were already a group, having worked together in community planning. In a sense, the Task Force began well formed. However, the core group had not developed its identity in terms of education. Thus crucial to creating the Task Force was transforming their identity—unforming the existing group and forming a new one with similar members. This is a general issue: attachments that constitute a new organization must be formed in the context of existing attachments. Those ties constrain a new entity if it requires dissolving or weakening them. Hence, the core group moved cautiously—conducting research, periodically publicizing findings and interpretations, and then recruiting those who endorsed their conclusions.

Storming, Norming, and Research

The coordinating committee's dubbing the kickoff attendees and work group participants members of the Task Force did little to specify what the entity would do. While research shed light on education issues, old and new members together could not draw clear conclusions about action. People argued for organizing and programming against one another.

Research and negotiation regarding aims and tasks has two aspects. Overtly, members survey the field and consider what can be done to improve it. In addition, they examine themselves, to see what they want and what they are capable of, to draw conclusions about themselves as actors. For example, most coordinating committee members probably would have said that schoolwide reforms were necessary, but they lacked confidence in their ability to evaluate such reforms and their power to institute them. Eventually a sequence of activities—such as the safety assessment, parent organizing, and the principals' meeting—served as action research, enabling members to learn about their capacities for action. CPHA's grants provided resources that made it possible to end this storming inclusively: the Task Force would work with community members, organizing them, providing them with programs, and bringing their resources to the schools.

Performing and Action

This agreement made it possible for the Task Force to get down to business, turning espoused purposes into practices. The core group members were seasoned opportunists who rummaged comfortably through the "garbage can" of action possibilities, soon adding a tutoring-mentoring program, church outreach, development of a full-service community school, a General Educational Development (GED) program, and lobbying for a school addition, facility repairs, and a new school. We look next at how the revitalized Task Force created networks for action.

Chapter 7

Organizing Networks for Southeast Education
Engaging the School System

To help parents and community members take active roles in improving education, the Task Force had to build networks that included them, the school system, and other entities. This chapter examines efforts to connect with the school system, and the next focuses on parents and community institutions.

The Task Force and the School System: A Case of Data

When the core group pulled together the Task Force in early 1995, the Baltimore City Public Schools were struggling with low scores on the high-stakes MSPAP test, state designation of three poorly performing schools as eligible for reconstitution, criticism of the system's management, conflict over a federal special education consent decree, community and union protest against imposition of a private vendor in nine schools, an ACLU suit against the state for adequate funding, a state countersuit against the city for poor management, and the city's joining the ACLU suit. Under the most tranquil of conditions, school systems have little interest in community activism. When Bobby English, Ed Rutkowski, Irona Pope, and I went to see Superintendent Walter Amprey to introduce the Task Force in February, he was sorely distracted.

The episode and its sequelae adumbrate the larger context in which much of the rest of this story took place. The school system's 1995 organization chart included forty boxes. The Central Office included the Office of the Superintendent and Divisions of Administration, Instruction, and Management

Services. The latter were divided into approximately 100 departments, offices, and other units. More than 500 people worked in the central administration building, with twenty others in six area offices, and dozens more in facility maintenance shops. A community organization wanting information or access needed a guide or, better yet, a sponsor.

When the four from the Task Force met with Amprey, talk was full of good feeling. English, Rutkowski, and Pope described the project, and Amprey endorsed it with the remark that he believed in centralizing power. He quickly corrected himself to emphasize that he meant decentralizing power to community groups. He offered to make his staff available and to urge assistant superintendents and principals to work with the Task Force. I gave him a list of data the Task Force wanted, and he suggested contacting certain staff members. Later, he sent English a letter of support and enclosed a copy of a memorandum asking staff to aid the Task Force.

Following Amprey's referral, I met in March with Dan Richmond, an analyst in the office of accountability. The Task Force wanted student and teacher data. He suggested that the personnel office would resist sharing the latter information, and we focused on available student data. Taking his suggestions, in early July I wrote to Richard Tate, his boss, asking for certain student files, and I sent Amprey a copy of the letter. The request covered data on student demographics, test scores, grades, and suspensions. In August, Richmond delivered tapes of demographic data.

The data described students but said little about how they were doing in school. They could be characterized by school and grade, race, sex, eligibility for lunch subsidy, attendance, and where they went if they withdrew from school. These were independent—or at least intervening—variables: possible influences on students' academic performance. The other data held the payoff—for example, school, race, sex, grade, or income differences in students' grades or test scores.

In September, I called Richmond to see how the rest of the data were coming, only to hear about problems. Apparently he and Tate had had a falling out. Tate had blocked his computer access. Then Richmond was transferred to another office. As for getting the rest of the data, he had little to offer. He was willing to come in on Saturdays to prepare tapes but would need his current boss's authorization to do so.

I wrote to the director of accountability and Tate, reminding them of the data request and the superintendent's endorsement. Both indicated that they would do what they could, but, particularly now that Richmond was gone, they were short on staff and could not guarantee anything. I regularly contacted Tate, who unfailingly expressed sympathy and a desire to be helpful. As soon as he could, he would have someone prepare the tapes. Richmond suggested, however, that Tate had stakes in not producing the work. He wanted to make a case for more staff, and if he could meet requests with what he had, he would lose out. Perhaps, too, he took pleasure in frustrating someone associated with his former subordinate.

In late 1995, a former school system employee on the Task Force called to offer help. Someone she knew would be meeting with the superintendent the next day. If I called and gave him details of the data situation, he would bring up the matter with the superintendent. I talked to him, but nothing happened. In January 1966, a city councilman offered his help, but nothing came of his efforts.

In February, I called Amprey to remind him of his support, to describe the current situation, and to ask for his help in getting the data. He warmly offered to take action. Richmond, even in his new position, remained the best person to produce the tapes, and I mentioned him. In early March, Richmond prepared tapes with test scores, apparently doing so on a Saturday. When I went to get the tapes, he showed me a note from Tate, thanking him for helping get me the data. The meaning of the note, Richmond said, was that even now, Tate closely monitored Richmond's computer use and wanted him to know that he knew what he had surreptitiously done.

I wrote to Tate to thank him for the data and to alert him to another concern. His staff expert on state test data was leaving. I asked whether she could prepare tapes before going. Meanwhile, I wrote to Amprey commending Tate, emphasizing the necessity of getting the data before the end of the school year and asking for his intervention. The staff member who worked with the state test data left.

At this point, a year after the original request, I called a colleague working on an unrelated project with the school system and asked for advice. She offered the name of an assistant superintendent with whom she worked. I called him, described the situation, acknowledged that he had no responsibilities related to the project, and asked for his help in getting at least the test data. He said that he would see what he could do. A few days later, he called to say that, though he could not give details, he had arranged to have the data put on tapes. Someone had come in on the weekend and done the work. He would leave the tapes for me in the lower right-hand drawer of a desk in an unoccupied office. I found the tapes there.

Network Building in the Education Field

This is not a portrait of a school system interested in working with a community organization. One explanation is quantitative. Many parties demand staff attention. School officials give priority to those who can bring great benefit or harm. Pervasive criticism and litigation added to this sensitivity. Task Force research interests mattered little. In addition, the number of demands made it hard for staff to give continuous attention to anything, including some high-stakes items, as state and special education litigants charged. Thus though sometimes the superintendent seemed to want to give the Task Force data, his attention quickly shifted. His critics charged that he was generally weak on follow-through.

Another explanation is bureaucratic. Even a superintendent's directives to subordinates can be tenuous. They too respond to myriad requests. They have little incentive to recall a low-stakes request, even from the chief executive officer. Still, the school bureaucracy is not a monolith, and lower-level staff have discretion. However, while Richmond devoted time to helping the Task Force, Tate spent time monitoring subordinates' computer use and jockeying for position, apparently more concerned about building his power than serving a constituent.

Part of the explanation is cultural. In a seeming slip, the superintendent defined the organizational culture when he told Task Force representatives that he believed in centralizing power. The Task Force request implicitly challenged that control. Whereas another organizational culture might lead staff to assess data requests on a case-by-case basis, here a release of information could seem like a threat to the school board itself. Organizational culture reinforced a professional culture that assumed that credentialed educators knew everything about schooling and hence should run the system. Parent or community interests in partnerships tacitly challenged that position. In this context, avoiding or resisting community requests did not take thought.

This was the environment in which the Task Force tried to work with Southeast Baltimore schools.

Connecting to Schools: The Challenges of Helping

Although state-mandated school improvement plans included a section on parent involvement, relations with parents or community members played virtually no role in a principal's evaluation. The state judged schools eligible for reconstitution if MSPAP scores stayed low, and test scores were the currency in which parents and taxpayers measured schools. Principals had little incentive to work with community members. Some principals appreciated parent activity as good citizenship, but most were more likely to value community collaboration if a group could give the school resources to meet the goals on which it was judged—academic performance and, secondarily, attendance.

To use community assets well, a principal must be able to plan with teachers and parents, identify potential resources, meet with possible partners and negotiate arrangements, and manage new relationships and resources. In addition, a school needs space and time for new activities. Some principals have time to consider partnerships but limited ability to design ones that would strategically contribute to academic or other goals. Other principals can plan and manage well but lack time to engage new partnerships, because new activities would take time from current ones.

The Task Force decided to focus on principals who had the time, attention, and capacity to take advantage of what it could offer. As we look at efforts to draw schools into a network, one point is crucial: partnerships with schools depend on personal relationships with principals. Often, when a principal leaves a school, partnerships disintegrate. Even when a principal signs a formal agreement, generally the principal can commit the school's participation and resources only for his or her tenure.

The Task Force set out to work in an area with eleven elementary schools, four middle schools, and one high school. Of the sixteen principals in place when it started in January 1995, only two would remain in the fall of 2000. Including interim and acting principals, these schools had forty-five principals during this time. On average, one-third changed each year. Thus as potential partners, schools presented moving targets.

We look here at an early effort to work with a school that illustrates common challenges. Chapter 9 describes an exceptionally successful partnership and it identifies keys to collaboration.

A Consultation on Student Discipline

At many schools, parents and staff worried about students' behavior and safety. Wanting to offer a school something that could start a long-term relationship with the Task Force, I persuaded Sylvia Rosenfield, a school psychology professor in the University of Maryland's College of Education, to conduct a "safety assessment."

Rosenfield viewed student behavior ecologically. She was interested in how the school environment—for example, staff practices, policies, curricular content and organization, the building's layout, and the schedule—influenced children's behavior and contributed to discipline or safety problems. She saw the project as an effort to help staff reflect on how their actions affected students and to redesign programs to improve the likelihood of behavior conducive to learning. She also was interested in developing a model for consulting to a school on these issues.

Meryl Sirmans, a doctoral student, would spend one day a week in the school for one year, observing classrooms and other spaces and interviewing staff and students about student behavior and influences on it. At the end of the year, she would present a report with recommendations. If staff wanted to implement recommendations, Rosenfield, Sirmans, other education faculty and students, and the Task Force would assist. The Task Force publicized the project to Southeast Baltimore schools. Two principals expressed interest, and Rosenfield, after interviewing them, decided on William Paca Elementary School, where a new principal voiced high ambitions for a needy school.

The students were poor. Between 1990 and the fall of 1996, when the consultation started, the proportions eligible for meal subsidies rose from 76 to 90 percent. Racial composition changed from 53 percent black and 39 percent white to 88 percent black and 6 percent white. What had once been a white, working-class neighborhood now had mostly low-income African-American residents. And families were constantly moving: 52 percent of students entered or left during the 1996–1997 school year. One child in six was absent more than four weeks of the year. Scores on the MSPAP test were low, with single-digit percentages of students scoring "satisfactory."

Sirmans quickly started her observations, but Rosenfield and I had difficulty connecting with the principal. We consistently had trouble scheduling meetings, meetings often were canceled at the last minute, and a couple of times the principal simply missed meetings. When we did get together, she frequently left the room to handle a problem of the moment. These incidents epitomized the difficulty of getting the principal's essential active attention, involvement, and support. This pattern continued for much of the project's three years.

The principal did care about the project. She repeatedly said that she valued it. She included it in her school improvement plan as a strategy to improve student behavior, and thus academic work. She testified enthusiastically about it before the school board's school safety committee. Practically, she cared that she had a project provided by the University of Maryland and a community group. She could count them as "partners" and cite the project as a sign that in the face of reconstitution threats she had experts solving problems. At the same time, as all principals, she had numerous problems and faced incessant demands on her attention. As many principals, she responded to issues with discrete programs, each somehow linked to a problem but none evidently linked to one another. She cared about the safety assessment as much as she cared about other programs.

In addition, she saw things like many other principals who had come up through the teaching ranks. Her accustomed focus was on individual students. She reacted empathically when a child had a problem. But by character and training, she had difficulty thinking of the school as an organization, a whole system, rather than as an aggregation of individuals. She could talk about the school concretely when she referred to persons but soared to high abstraction when trying to speak of it as an institution.

This individual orientation influenced both her caring for the project and her understanding of it. One reason she would leave meetings was that she learned a child had a problem and instinctively felt that ministering immediately to the child took priority over analyzing long-term, systemic school influences on the behavior of children as a group. One reason she canceled meetings was partly related. The central administration often summons principals to meetings on short notice—a pressure a new principal heading a school under reconstitution threat feels keenly. It is possible, if difficult, to decline some requests. However, insofar as the principal thought of herself as having a personal obligation to a superordinate calling a meeting, rather than acting as a manager responsible for improving the school as an institution, she would give administrative meetings unquestioned primacy.

The essence of the project was helping staff reflect on their organization's culture and climate. Thus it was concerned with collective thinking and activity in two respects. Substantively, it aimed to look at the cumulative effects of the actions of the school's adults on the school's children. Success in changing what adults did depended on a collaborative staff effort to recognize their role in shaping the school's ecology as an influence on students and to take responsibility for analyzing problems and trying solutions for some. Neither the consultants nor the principal could change the school alone. Success depended on the principal's persuading her staff to reflect on the school and helping them take risks in changing.

Instead, the principal's individualistic orientation, compounded by newness to the school, made it hard to understand the project as Rosenfield designed it. She habitually thought of problems as the products of individual teachers' actions or situations rather than as part of a system. She thought of the project's work as being done primarily by the consultants.

She did little to involve her staff beyond asking them to let Sirmans observe classrooms. Few faculty understood the consultation's purpose. A number of teachers asked Sirmans to help manage their students rather than allowing her to observe. Perhaps this was their way of turning the consultation to their own purpose: to show the consultant how overburdened and needy they were in the hope that she would take that message to the principal and get relief. Perhaps they regarded the school ecology's effects on themselves as more urgent than its effects on students.

The situation was symptomatic of the principal's not developing relationships with other staff. She was new and did not know her colleagues. Spending a lot of time dealing with students or going to meetings left her little time to get to know her staff. Perhaps, beyond that, she was not comfortable directing staff. Perhaps she did not recognize the necessity of doing so.

Enabling staff to reflect on the school's ecology and their roles in it required changing the school culture. As at most schools, it isolated teachers from one another, giving each responsibility for a single classroom, leaving all with little knowledge of anything outside of their room, and asking no one except the principal to take responsibility for the school as a whole. Since everyone's actions influenced students, the consultation could affect the school only if the culture encouraged all to think about and feel shared responsibility for programs and students.

Such a change would depend on the principal's talking differently with staff, offering a collaborative vision, encouraging them to work together, and supporting them accordingly. In short, she would need to think and act like an educational leader and a manager—two different roles difficult for any one person to find the abilities and time for. She needed training and mentoring to take on these unfamiliar dual roles. That development might take a couple of years, an essential part of, but extending beyond, a discipline consultation. However, it was unclear that the principal shared this view, and, at any rate, the school system did not offer such support.

Around the time that Sirmans and Rosenfield were preparing their report, the assistant principal independently started to implement a social skills curriculum. Although the report pointed to the importance of teaching social skills, the new curriculum probably was not the best for the school. Even so, Rosenfield began to assist the principal, in two ways.

She recruited faculty colleagues and doctoral students to help a few teachers interested in the new curriculum learn to use it and monitor its effects on student behavior. In addition, Rosenfield, whose Instructional Consultation model of school psychology was in use at a number of city schools, got the school a full-time school psychologist who would initiate this program, which emphasized a staff team approach to diagnosing and treating student learning problems (Rosenfield and Gravois 1996). To the principal and core staff involved in these programs, the university advisors emphasized the importance of collecting and using appropriate data to assess students' needs, identify problems, and measure interventions' efficacy.

By the second year of implementation, a few teachers effectively taught social skills in new ways. A couple had improved their classroom climates by using Instructional Consultation for behavior problems. However, its team approach to student assessment, which required a group to meet regularly, foundered against competing demands on staff time. Still, the administration and some teachers began to use data more consistently in making decisions about students. Rosenfield believed that the project was taking hold. She assumed that it took a year to build trust with a school before it might be really ready to consider the consultant's help, to take the ideas seriously, and to proceed toward the hard work of reflecting and changing. However, in the middle of the year, family problems took the principal away from the school, and she left at the end of the year. The next principal did not want Instructional Consultation, and the school psychologist left. No one else adopted the social skills curriculum. The consultation ended.

The safety assessment had one concrete result. The school was seriously overcrowded. The state calculated its capacity at 474 students, and enrollment was 929 in the fall of 1996. Moreover, the facility, built in 1975 when open schools were the fashion, had no classroom walls. Portable blackboards, shelves, wardrobes, boxes, and partitions suggested where one room stopped and the next took up. Yet any visitor was immediately struck by the visual stimuli that knew no boundaries and the unceasing buzz of ambient noise. Near the beginning of the consultation, Sylvia Rosenfield asked if the Task Force could help get an addition built to relieve overcrowding. The next chapter tells that story.

Elusive Connection

This school typified the challenges that the Task Force encountered: schools could have used help but could not uncouple ongoing routines to make new strategic connections. Part of the explanation was personality. By temperament, many principals conceptualized their work in terms of personal relationships rather than organizational management. They may have developed interpersonal skills but neglected managerial skills.

Part of the explanation concerned the principal's role. Historically, the principal was a school's lead teacher. As school systems became bureaucratized, principals became middle managers. Nevertheless, advancement paths continued to "move up" individuals who started out teaching into managerial positions for which they were not necessarily qualified.

However, whatever a principal's competence, the role had become more than a full-time job, where educational leadership and organizational management competed for scarce time. The latter typically displaced the former, for two reasons. First, the system rewarded and punished organizational management but not educational leadership. Although system officials wanted high test scores, they gave little attention to how educational leadership could facilitate teaching and learning and offered schools few resources consistent with those responsibilities. Second, because so few principals had managerial skills, they spent extra time on administration.

The systemic emphasis on management created another, chronic role difficulty for principals, seen here. The central administration constantly shifted principals, with the result that a principal often was new at a school and perhaps also as a principal. One reason was simple: the system, offering principals more challenging students, older facilities, and lower wages than the suburbs, could not attract enough people equal to urban principalships and kept shifting candidates around, hoping to find catalytic combinations. Second, sometimes the system operated like sports teams, scapegoating the manager for problems both within and beyond his or her control.

Finally, the central administration constantly ordered principals to solve "crises." One should not be surprised by a crisis atmosphere in a system where nearly every measure of student learning pointed to failure. However, few of the "crises" that interrupted principals' attention to school affairs directly concerned students' education. Most involved keeping or getting something back under control. The system "solved" crises with meetings and paper rather than decisions and innovative action. In these ways, the central administration left principals little time or attention to consider new ways of educating children, including joining forces with parents and community members.

Thus parent organizing could be expected to arouse resistance—not necessarily for opposing school policies but just for taking time and attention.

Chapter 8

Organizing Networks for Southeast Education

Connecting with Parents and Community Institutions

Organizing Parents In and Around Schools

Origins

In the late summer of 1996, around the time the safety assessment was getting started, Laura Weeldreyer notified Southeast Baltimore principals that she had received a grant for parent organizing and wanted to work with interested schools. She heard from a half dozen schools, talked with the principals, and, in consultation with the Task Force, settled on two.

Parent organizing would be a learning experience for Weeldreyer, the Task Force, and schools. Weeldreyer had taught for three years in New Orleans through Teach for America, a program that prepares people without formal education training to teach in urban schools. After coming to Baltimore to teach, she got interested in organizing and policy and became CPHA's education director. The initiative, particularly after CPHA turned over to SECO a grant that let the latter hire an organizer to work with Weeldreyer, produced a novel arrangement for the Task Force. The two organizers reported at Task Force meetings but were not Task Force staff. They had considerable autonomy in an informal network including the Task Force, CPHA, and SECO. The Task Force would have to figure out what organizing could accomplish and how to tie it to Task Force aims. Finally, the project would push principals to accommodate independent organizers preparing parents for active school roles.

CPHA's proposal to the Hazen Foundation set out a theory of change. Organizing would build ties between schools and neighborhoods, and these links would improve communication between home and school, school climate, and class discipline, all of which should contribute to learning. In addition, parent organizing would bring community resources to schools, enabling them to do more, and also make schools resources for the community, which might meet, conduct classes, or carry out other activities in school buildings. Finally, organizing could create a climate in which parents and educators felt comfortable innovating and reforming schools. Organizing strategies would be modeled on the Texas Industrial Areas Foundation (IAF).

Yet ambiguities lay at the core of the Southeast Baltimore organizing effort. The IAF organizes aggressively and confrontationally. Texas organizers, working with low-income, mostly Hispanic parents, actively challenged schools and school systems. Southeast Baltimore has a more collaborative organizing culture. In addition, Bobby English, who served on two school improvement teams and helped several principals, was committed to cooperation. Weeldreyer, while drawing on IAF language, talked of collaborating with principals as she began work.

One framework emphasized organizing and training parents to define issues and carry out their own agenda. The other emphasized organizing and training parents and teachers to collaborate in improving schools. The perspectives converged where parents and staff saw eye to eye but diverged when parents were critical of a school's policies, programs, or staff. Parent organizing might produce negotiation or mediation but also could lead toward open conflict.

In introducing her project to principals, Weeldreyer emphasized that organizing parents would give schools more knowledgeable, effective supporters. As time went on, she sometimes added that conflicts might arise as part of a normal process of parents' and educators' beginning to take one another seriously, but she suggested that the parties could expect to work toward consensus. Still, that said, there remained the question of what the organizer's position would be when parents and staff disagreed about problems, remedies, or priorities.

Initial Organizing: Matters of Principal

Soon after Weeldreyer started, she ran into resistance. The principals regularly heard from complaining parents and feared that those interested in organizing wanted to attack the school. The principals worried about what went on at parent meetings. Meanwhile, activated parents demanded a lot of the principal's time—at best, to discuss how she made decisions; at worst, to battle over policies or priorities.

One principal, Yvonne Garner at Highlandtown Elementary School #237, began to appreciate what parents could offer. She had been made principal in fall of 1994 to close down the school; instead, parents organized to keep it open, and she stayed on with their support. In October 1997, Weeldreyer took her and some parents to Texas to see the Alliance Schools, and Garner returned committed to parent activism. Weeldreyer and her CPHA intern, Tana Paddock, organized a walk where teachers visited families at home, and teachers were surprised to find friendly parents opening up doors to them. Later, parents and teachers met to set an action agenda. Parents made creating a school library a priority. When Weeldreyer left in the spring of 1998, Paddock took over and worked with parents and churches to raise money and collect books for a library.

However, organizing never got that far at the other school. After a year, Weeldreyer helped establish an active PTO there, but the principal grew increasingly uneasy with organizing. Parents criticized the school. They raised budget and personnel matters that she did not want to address. They took time. They could not be controlled. Suspicious of what parents discussed, the principal forbid them from meeting at school but then worried about what they said when they met elsewhere. Weeldreyer saw the principal less often and found herself justifying and pleading for the project when they met. After a year and a half, they agreed to stop.

The two principals exemplified variations that organizers would encounter. The difference was partly one of perspective: Garner recognized what parents could give a school, while the other principal did not. Temperament was central: Garner was more comfortable with the disorder and occasional conflict of parent activism and worked more adeptly with parents. Experience mattered. When organizing started, Garner was in her second year as a principal after having been an assistant elsewhere, while the other principal was in her first year after having been an assistant elsewhere. Garner had longer tenure in the system. Still, she embraced organizing only in her third year at the school, after she knew it and its families and was secure in her role.

Tangible Results: An Addition for an Overcrowded School

Meanwhile, the safety assessment was proceeding at William Paca, and the group that met with the principal and Sylvia Rosenfield saw that overcrowding contributed to discipline and safety problems. Children were pressed in on one another. A student might accidentally brush against another in the hallway, and the second would throw punches to thwart an imagined attack. These conditions vitiated teachers' efforts. And yet, as long as the faculty made do, the problem was theirs. The system administration knew the numbers but did not see the school. Central staff talked about redrawing zone boundaries to reduce overcrowding to "only" 161 percent after five years. Rosenfield asked whether the Task Force could help.

SECO hired Keith Hunt as parent organizer in February 1997. He had IAF training, saw situations clearly, spoke directly, had a good sense of humor, and could bring disparate people together. His first task was to help Paca get an addition. This issue united staff and parents. The principal wanted Hunt to organize parents and community members to take a more aggressive stance toward the central administration than she felt she and her faculty could. She had asked for an addition, instead of rezoning, but the system's facilities department was not moving.

Hunt began working with the handful of parents in the PTO. Meryl Sirmans introduced him to school staff and went with him to meet parents at homes. They persuaded parents to come to PTO meetings. Hunt helped them articulate concerns and make a case. As the meetings grew, parents demanded an addition. They invited school officials and elected officials. The principal's sense of urgency encouraged parents to talk insistently to system administrators. Where faculty felt constrained, parents felt free to be angry. After a PTO meeting with 120 in attendance, the system's administration agreed to build an addition.

In intense summer construction, a new building housing 250 students was erected next to the main building. The school was still crowded, but less so. A significant number of students had classrooms with walls. The crush and distractions in the main building were less.

This textbook organizing case offered lessons about the ingredients of success. First, Hunt was a skilled organizer. Second, staff and parents agreed on a problem and a solution. Third, the issues were concrete and easy for elected officials to understand and act upon. Still, the episode also offered lessons about the fragility of parent organization. Shortly afterward, SECO's grant expired, and Hunt moved on. The parent organization shrank to its earlier size. Part of the reason was that action had achieved its aim, and part was that the organization still depended on Hunt. At the same time, the principal's interest in activism ran out once she got an addition. When a later organizer approached her to pick up Hunt's work, she said that she saw no need.

Organizing Conflict

Between 1996 and 2001, seven organizers worked with the Task Force, at seven of the eleven elementary schools, three of the four middle schools, and the high school. A concentrated two-year effort began in the spring of 1999, when the Task Force had three organizers. One of two new organizers was Dottie Fried, who had worked with the Alliance Schools. The other was

Amber Picou, who had political and labor organizing experience. They were ready to join Tana Paddock, now working for SECO, in assertive organizing that followed an IAF model and took parents' interests as the basis for a school agenda. When Paddock took another job in the fall, Stephanie Lightfoot, a returning Peace Corps volunteer, came on. Though not an organizer by training, her experience had shown her the importance of grassroots initiatives in community development, and she too gave primacy to parent interests.

When they started up, they found that though principals had asked for organizing assistance, most simply wanted help implementing their own programs. They envisioned, for example, more supportive PTAs. They had little time to meet with organizers or parents. None wanted an autonomous parent group. Some vigilantly sought to keep parents as well as staff under control. New principals were especially skittish. In a couple of schools, misunderstandings blossomed, and welcomes soured.

An example shows how an organizer's approach could run afoul of a principal's concerns. In a school where the principal had given easy access, the organizer began working with parents who did not like the principal, and he formalized conditions for her entry. She had dropped in on parents, teachers, and other staff as their schedules allowed. Now he insisted that she make appointments to meet with staff and, in any case, reduce the number of these meetings. He forbid one staff member to meet with her at all. At the fall back-to-school night, he declined to introduce the organizer, who was present, and a parent spoke up and did so. Shortly after, the principal removed one of the organizer's fliers from faculty mailboxes and insisted on reviewing others prior to distribution. Finally, he refused to meet with her and barred her from the school.

By mid-fall 1999, three principals had complained about Task Force organizers to area executive officer Patricia Abernethy, the official responsible for Southeast area schools. In November, she asked to meet with the organizers and Ken Strong, a Task Force member and SECO's director. SECO was the fiscal agent for a Task Force grant for two organizers and employer of the third. It housed the organizers. Strong was their formal supervisor, though Bobby English provided periodic supervision, and the two of them and I shared direction for the organizers. He met with Abernethy for the Task Force. At the meeting, two principals and a representative of a third said that they could not run their schools if organizing continued as it was.

Strong met again with Abernethy, this time with Michael Hamilton, chair of the school board's Parent and Community Advisory Board, Carol Seubert, director of the system's new Office of Parental Involvement and School/Family/Community Connections, and Edwina Green, the system's liaison for PTAs and PTOs. All agreed that parent organizing presented new challenges to the school system and expressed interest in finding common ground and workable procedures.

Organizers Encounter the System

Conflict is inevitable in organizing, for four reasons. First, any outsider entering a system introduces new perspectives and interests. Second, schools, as every organization, already have conflicts—among staff, between staff and parents, or among parents. When organizers support some parents' views, they inevitably side with positions that others oppose. Third, the organizing process of helping staff and parents find common ground requires extraordinary time, attention, and tranquility. False assumptions and misunderstandings easily displace communication and mediation. Hence, fourth, centrally, when a community organization tries to link the community and the schools, organizing is where "the rubber meets the road." An organizer experiences the system's full force as it asserts its identity and defends its boundary.

The impulses in the school system that resist connection oppose organizing. In the safety assessment, for example, the principal's failure to set or keep appointments could be ascribed to personal idiosyncrasies, but it also was an expression of the system that hired, socialized, directed, and made demands upon her. The same is true of the principals who did not get together with parent organizers. If principals were supposed to meet with parents, organizers, or consultants, then the system would help them do so and reward them.

Although principals' preoccupation with organizational maintenance is bureaucratically normal, one of its functions is to prevent outside contact and thus to secure the organization from external influence. The professional culture justifies this isolation by emphasizing that only trained educators know how to teach children. It also is bureaucratically normal for staff to try to control turf. If jockeying for position leads to disorganization, then that condition, too, protects the system from external ties. Where the schools are distinctive is in their extreme wariness toward outsiders and ritualistic obsession with control. Hence, not only is conflict probable when organizers work with parents, but strong political and psychological forces push and toss organizers from the moment they take their roles.

The Dynamics of Organizing

A different organizing approach could have avoided some problems, but normal conflicts between parents and schools create dynamics that make it hard for organizers to analyze issues and mediate among parties.

A parent organizer starts without a role clearly defined or sanctioned by a school or parents. For example, when she enters a school where parents and staff are in conflict, she proceeds without a secure anchor. On the surface, the difficulty is that each party wants the organizer to represent its position—for example, parents want help changing policies, and a principal wants parents reoriented or muted, and it is hard to satisfy both.

However, under such conditions, groups often unconsciously elaborate organizers' ambiguous roles in complex ways. Not only do they expect an organizer to lead or assist them in battling the other side, but they want her to express their anger for them. They may divide the emotional labor of negotiating a solution, delegating the organizer to act aggressively while acting nicely themselves. Thus they can reassure the other side, and themselves, that it is only the organizer who is hostile. After all, parents and staff must get along in the long run.

Yet if an organizer shows signs of being less than fully loyal, she can become the enemy. For a principal who sees an organizer work with parents who challenge school policies, it may be realistic to regard the organizer as an adversary. Even so, the principal, who must coexist with parents, may imagine the parent-organizer alliance in a way that justifies his own policies and exonerates the parents. It may seem that only the organizer opposes the principals and causes conflict; after all, there was no conflict before she arrived; if only she left, the school could be harmonious. In this line of thinking, the organizer becomes the sole enemy.

For their part, parents, even when they get an organizer's primary attachment, also can doubt her loyalty. If they are in conflict with a principal, they may see or imagine that the organizer meets privately with the principal and wonder whether she represents their positions. When things get hot, does the organizer compromise with the principal in order to stay in the school? When things get too hot, some parents, like the principal, may imagine that the organizer is the main cause of conflict. Without the organizer, disagreements could be settled amicably.

Issues' complexity and ambiguity contribute to complications. Usually there are no clear villains or victims but shared responsibility for problems. Both school and home, teachers and family, influence children's learning. Often the parties recognize their responsibility. However, they can avoid feeling guilty by incriminating the organizer. Thus parents, instead of acknowledging how poor child rearing may hinder their children, may choose to see their families purely as victims of insensitive or incompetent teachers. They can do this by denying their own faulty actions and associating them with the organizer. Without consciously thinking of the organizer as an irresponsible parent, they may simply feel negatively about her as they would toward irresponsible parents—even while working with her to influence school policy.

A principal, rather than recognizing, for example, how his poor management hampers teachers, may see staff simply as victims of dysfunctional families. He may deny his administrative shortcomings and fixate on what he considers those of the organizer, such as heavy-handedness, failure to keep meetings, and poor listening. Further, he may act to limit her effectiveness, making her in reality similar to the way he sees himself. Thus a principal's missing a meeting with an organizer may be poor planning, an effort to keep the organizer from planning, or both. Such tactics come naturally when the organizer seems allied with parents against the principal.

Thus parents and staff can find it easier to lock into polarizing denial and blame than to share responsibility for problems. An organizer must anticipate these possibilities, recognize them when they occur, and try to limit them by identifying concerns that motivate them. She must be able to "hold" bad feelings that others cannot bear to keep in themselves and put onto her, and she must be able to "contain" in herself conflicts that make it difficult for parties to get together and work. By managing what is toxic in parent-teacher relations, an organizer can provide the security for groups to get together. To do so, an organizer needs a firm institutional foundation.

Situating Organizing in the Task Force

The Task Force planned to create two structures for organizing in the spring of 1999. A Parent Organizing Advisory Committee, including Task Force and SECO representatives and parents from schools where organizers worked, would provide a strategic community perspective and secure institutional ties. Ken Strong, who had organizing experience, would supervise organizers. Neither structure came to life as planned. Task Force members, SECO board members, and parents lacked time for the committee, and Strong, managing a large community organization, had little time for the organizers. Instead, Strong, English, and I met monthly with the organizers to review work and to set general directions. In the fall, English began giving weekly supervision.

Practically, organizers took supervision from her, Strong, or me—whomever they could find when problems arose. This arrangement did not secure them as they struggled with conflict, and direction could be inconsistent. Monthly meetings provided an ephemeral corrective. When the principals complained about organizing, the six considered how to respond.

Reorienting Organizing

At a December meeting, the organizers talked about how some principals were difficult to work with, and they believed conflict was inevitable under the best conditions. Nevertheless, Strong and English thought, events had taught two lessons. First, new principals usually were not secure enough to work with organizers. Second, school system anxiety and suspicion made principals generally wary of organizing. Hence, organizers should concentrate on more established principals, respect the pressures they faced, and start where administrators and parents had common interests. Strong urged organizers to build ties between principals and parents rather than to ally themselves with either and risk antagonizing the other.

English circulated "Southeast Education Task Force Parent Organizing," which she had given the organizers when they started in the spring. It identified four areas of activity: promoting parent development (helping parents become better parents), getting parents involved in schools, creating parent organizations, and bringing benefits to students. Whatever organizers worked on, she wanted them to start by asking principals how to be of help. Although the document familiarly demarcated a broad organizing domain, the tone had changed. Organizers should avoid issues or actions that antagonized principals.

The document asserted priorities that English would make more explicit over time. She put parent development first and building a parent organization later on. From her work with low-income families, she believed that many parents lacked basic parenting skills and thus hindered children's learning. If parents increased their involvement in education in only one way, that should be raising their children and preparing them for school. Forming a parent organization, though important, did not lead as directly to educational benefits. Later, when she heard foundation staff or others talking about "systemic change," she would declare that developing parents, family by family, was the most potent strategy for changing the system that produced poorly educated adults. For now, her emphasis on parent development would subtly shift the Task Force from organizing to delivering services.

In February, Patricia Abernethy invited English, Strong, and me to join her, three principals unhappy with the organizing, and Carol Seubert to figure out how to proceed. Abernethy wanted organizers to work on what schools needed. English reported on plans to reorient parent organizing and suggested attendance and facility conditions as common interests. A principal endorsed that agenda. Seubert proposed creating policies on parent and community involvement and offering training to help school staff work with parents and community members. The meeting concluded with talk of starting over.

Organizing with Schools

Helping Parents Organize to Solve School Problems

Two examples illustrate the directions that organizing took. The first involved Dottie Fried's work with General Wolfe Elementary School, begun when she started in April 1999. Susan Errichieolo had headed the school only since September 1998, but she was a veteran principal from New Jersey. The Task Force had a long-standing relationship with the school through Bobby English, who served on its school improvement team, placed AmeriCorps tutors there, and ran a Nurturing Program for parents.

Students were poor: 87 percent were eligible for lunch subsidy in 1999. Latin American immigrants had increased: about one-fourth of students were Hispanic, one-fourth African American, and half non-Hispanic white. Family mobility was high: 56 percent of students entered or left during the 1998–99 school year. The school was one of eighteen, including three in Southeast Baltimore, implementing Direct Instruction, a tightly scripted phonics reading curriculum. Under the new principal, single-digit "satisfactory" MSPAP scores, particularly in language usage, would rise noticeably, even if they were still low.

The principal wanted to reach out to the community. With her encouragement, a few parents were trying to organize others. Thus Fried found a supportive principal, parent leaders, and community connections when she arrived. Still, she confronted common challenges. Parents were preoccupied with supporting their families and had little time for meetings. Some had drug problems that took their attention and limited their ability to raise children or take part in school. Many, having had their own difficulties as students, hesitated to speak to teachers or the principal. Even among those whose native language was English, many had trouble reading and could not easily respond to school communications. And yet they cared about their children's education.

Fried got two organizing interns from the University of Maryland School of Social Work to assist Hispanic parents. She contacted the Education-Based Latino Outreach (EBLO) and Pastor Fidel Compres to work with parents and students. A Colombian intern from St. Mary's Seminary translated school material into Spanish and interpreted at school meetings. Parents were interested in learning English to help their children with schoolwork, and EBLO decided to offer adult English classes. Compres, who had taught mathematics, would tutor children in math.

Space was an issue at General Wolfe. Constructed for kindergarten through second grade, the building now housed a full elementary school. Immigration was swelling the school's enrollment. In the spring of 2000, 247 students occupied a facility with a capacity of 229. The building was cramped, and it lacked a gym, an auditorium, and a library. Its playground was small and in disrepair. The principal wanted a portable building.

Fried helped parents organize to do something about space. Their quest picked up steam when the school system launched an initiative to improve facility utilization. The central administration asked each school improvement team to form a subcommittee on school safety and climate, and this group became Wolfe's agent in seeking more space. Mike DiMenna, a SECO organizer, became chair, with Fried and Compres the other community members; three parent leaders—Joe Smith, Sherry Romanowski, and Carrie Frias—and three staff members rounded out the committee. In January, DiMenna, Smith, Romanowski, and Errichieolo put the case for a portable building before Gary Thrift, now the area executive officer responsible for Direct Instruction schools. Thrift, supporting the request, forwarded it to Wilbur Giles, the system's facilities manager, who gave signs spawning cautious optimism at the school.

The subcommittee located unused portable classrooms at other schools and notified Thrift. In April, Errichieolo met with a BCPSS facilities staff member, who assessed the school's condition and talked about requirements for putting a portable building on the playground. On May 1, Pete Dixit, maintenance and operations chief, summarized his conclusions to Giles: the school required at least two additional classrooms and a resource room, and site constraints did not allow a portable building. Instead, enrollments should be cut to make the facility adequate. He sent a copy to Thrift, who asked him about the site's constraints.

Meanwhile, the Task Force began responding to the system's facilities utilization initiative by assessing conditions at all Southeast Baltimore schools, to develop plans for renovations and long-term improvements (described in detail in chapter 12). Fried tied parent organizing at Wolfe to this larger effort. In June, Bobby English and representatives of General Wolfe and other schools presented Task Force findings and recommendations to the school board. They proposed a portable building on the school playground.

Colene Daniel, the board member responsible for facilities, invited the Task Force and schools involved to meet with her, Dixit, and Thrift. A week later, a dozen people assembled at school headquarters. DiMenna made the case for a portable building. Daniel noted that there was not much land at the school; an addition would eliminate the playground. English proposed leasing unused space at a nearby Catholic church. Dixit interjected that the system's attorneys had raised red flags about parent lawsuits over putting children in religious facilities. When Smith returned to the portable idea, Dixit closed off that option, saying that there was not enough space for even the smallest portable building.

Daniel believed that controlling enrollment was the only feasible action. She recommended a moratorium on new enrollments and rezoning to send some students elsewhere. Romanowski objected: this course would send children to school outside of their neighborhood. Daniel offered to take up the church option with the legal department but wanted a commitment that parents would not object to using a Catholic facility. Judy Glasgow, a teacher, asked whether the school could be made into K–3, with fourth and fifth graders sent elsewhere. City Springs, nearby, had space, but Romanowski rejected it: it was far from students' homes, and, though no one said so, white General Wolfe parents did not want their children attending nearly all-black City Springs.

Daniel summarized the options. State money would be spent on resurfacing the playground area. Community leaders would explore church possibilities, while she checked with the lawyers. Staff would look at ways of rezoning the school to limit enrollment.

General Wolfe representatives met again with Daniel in July. She reported that BCPSS would rezone to reduce enrollment. As for students then attending Wolfe but living outside of the zone, fourth and fifth graders could stay to graduate, but younger students would have to go elsewhere. Parents at the meeting reluctantly agreed to this policy, which the system implemented, to protests from parents whose children had to leave.

Working with Parents and Getting Resources

A second case involved a school where the principal was less interested in parent activism and where parents were less organized. Organizing efforts followed the conflicts with principals and reorientation of organizing toward getting resources for schools. As at several Southeast Baltimore schools, students were predominantly African American and poor, mobility was high, and MSPAP scores were low. Two years earlier, the school system had moved a principal from another school to try to improve the school's academic program. Taking over a school eligible for state reconstitution, she wanted active parents to pull in her direction. While meeting with the organizer, she made clear that she was busy and urged her to work with the PTA.

In fact, the PTA was having trouble meeting. The four elected officers of the five-member PTA could not get along. The organizer tried to meet with them individually to size up the situation. She encouraged them to talk with one another and to find ways of resolving differences. Yet officers would arrange meetings with one another or her and not show up.

Explanations were multiple. The president had family problems and did not call regular meetings. Another officer seemed to tangle with her whenever they got together. The principal sometimes gave paid jobs to loyal volunteers; when one of the officers was rewarded in this way, some of the others were resentful. The officer who complained the most about the president nevertheless could not set forth an alternative agenda. He was a trusty lieutenant but did not comfortably take initiative. For some reason, the treasurer gave inconsistent reports on the organization's funds. One of the officers wanted to raise funds for a specific student activity but did not want to discuss or coordinate the effort with the others. At a meeting when the president had to come late, before her arrival the other officers discussed voting her out of office, though they gave the organizer conflicting reports on whether they had told the president the outcome of the vote or whether, in fact, they had taken a vote or merely talked about it. Unsurprisingly, the organizer found that other parents had little interest in the PTA.

The organizer continually tried to reconcile the officers, advised them on running an organization, and coached one in planning and leadership. At the same time, she worked on activities that did not depend on them. She involved parents in a leadership training program. Consistent with the new Task Force orientation, she put her energy into getting services and partnerships for the school. She found a fraternity to run a mentoring program for boys. She arranged with local organizations to sponsor after-school programs that required school attendance as a condition for participation. She brought a counseling service to the school to take referrals for students with behavior problems. And she helped arrange for a national organization to fund a position at the school to match people and organizations with resources to school needs.

Observations: Ambiguous Premises and a Predicament

Parent organizing began with ambiguously mixed purposes: to organize and train parents to set an agenda for school improvement, and to organize and train parents and teachers to work together in improving a school. These aims amounted to the same thing when parents and educators saw things similarly but led to conflict under several normal conditions. In a taut, demanding school system, subject to public criticism and paranoid about outsiders, administrators regarded community members suspiciously. Partnerships risked trouble and, in any case, took time from activities on which staff were evaluated. Moreover, principals and parents were continually changing, so that most encounters involved people who hardly knew one another. Candor was unlikely at least at first, because many parents felt angry about schools but defensive about their limited knowledge of education, and many principals felt defensive about their limited success in educating students. Taking an adversarial stance was easier than taking shared responsibility for problems and solutions.

These conditions framed a predicament. On the one hand, many Task Force members wanted to organize parents to set their own agenda, for two reasons. They believed in grassroots democracy, and they assumed that outside perspectives and pressure were necessary to change schools. On the other hand, in many schools, even where principals requested organizing, this position led to conflict, and principals told organizers to leave. Two responses were possible. One was to organize parents more aggressively, in opposition to school staffs, as the IAF did in Texas. The other was to shift to the second view of organizing, emphasizing common ground.

The group of three overseeing the organizers rejected the first tack for two reasons. As a matter of principle, Bobby English insisted that the Task Force cooperate with schools. Practically, it was doubtful that the organizers could succeed in building independent parent groups that could improve the schools. Hence, organizers were told to look for shared interests and to start by asking principals what they wanted.

Unquestionably, organizers worked on important issues, from space shortage to student behavior problems, but the new stance changed organizing's definition and the Task Force's orientation. Organizers would not go to those schools, which probably were a majority, where principals did not want independently active parents, and they would not touch issues where parents and staff disagreed. This position took organizers out of the action if parents wanted to challenge school practices, and it could lead parents to doubt an organizer's usefulness or loyalty.

The focus on helping principals and avoiding conflict led toward providing services and resources to schools. It was reinforced by English's emphasis on parent development, which could be seen as a long-term approach to activating parents but which in the short term involved educating parents to raise their children better. The organizers would do less to build potent parent organizations and more to get programmatic or financial resources, perhaps involving parents in delivering resources or providing services for which parents were clients.

These changes involved strategic questions of what the Task Force wanted to do and could most effectively do to improve schooling, practical questions of what organizing could accomplish, and political questions of who should authorize parent organizing. Though there were reasonable arguments for the reorientation, it took place inexplicitly. The Task Force built its own relationships with schools but may have foregone possibilities of incorporating more parents into the network.

Building Partnerships with Churches

Though Southeast Baltimore had many needs, Task Force members emphasized community assets. People and organizations had expertise, materials, space, and time that could aid schools. Partnerships between schools and community institutions would help school staff and community members know one another, would reduce schools' isolation, would create a climate conducive to reflection and innovation, and would increasingly produce knowledgeable collaboration.

Whether the Task Force could develop such partnerships depended on whether local institutions had resources to share with schools. That was partly a matter of interpretation. A business or church, for example, might contribute people, facilities, supplies, or money if its leaders knew that a school wanted help and believed it would use resources wisely. For many organizations, however, schools down the street could have been on the moon. Schools never contacted them, and they knew nothing about what went on. If anything, they shared a diffuse sense from newspaper stories, talk shows, and word of mouth that the schools were inept, incapable of using resources well, and a bad investment.

In fact, some schools had partnerships with nearby businesses, though most firms were small and many relationships simply contributed food as a reward for student attendance. Tying schools to community institutions would require teaching both parties how to think about possible relationships and getting them acquainted and started. The Task Force began looking at churches, because a member of the School-Family-Community Relations Work Group had led her congregation in assisting a neighborhood school and wanted to encourage similar efforts.

Starting up with Churches

Judy Free, a longtime work group member, belonged to the Patterson Park Baptist Church, which had aided nearby Hampstead Hill Elementary School and was conducting a study center two afternoons a week. Free liked talking about the low-cost ways her congregation helped the school, such as collecting register receipts from supermarkets that redeemed them for school computers and donating school supplies and winter mittens. She readily explained that this work was an expression of the church's mission, that her congregation did not draw on exceptional wealth in making this commitment, and that all churches easily could—and should—do similarly. A retired high school English teacher, she also was clear that even if a church attracted a Sunday school student or congregant in the process, a relationship with a school focused on education, without reference to religion.

At Free's initiative, the group became the Church Outreach Work Group. Bill Jeffries, a graduate student, identified 100 churches near the schools, ranging from larger, older, mostly white congregations with salaried pastors and occasionally other staff to storefront African-American churches without full-time pastors or, sometimes, even phones. Pastor Jeannie Marsh joined the group to see how her Salem United Methodist Church could work with nearby Highlandtown Elementary School #237.

As the group encouraged and advised Marsh, she, Keith Hunt, and others invited other ministers to attend. Those who came generally were young and new to their congregations. They had energy but did not know their parishioners yet, and they hesitated to ask anything of them. They were interested in the larger community, but they needed to satisfy their congregations first. For example, one minister offered church vans to take schoolchildren to the public library but then quit attending. Others came and talked but had weak ties to congregants and little to deliver. Two events in early 1998 crystallized the challenges.

In February, Laura Weeldreyer and Tana Paddock, organizing parents at Highlandtown, invited pastors to meet faculty and parents and to explore collaboration. Ministers from four churches heard a one-sided discussion of "partnerships." Staff and parents elaborated a long list of what they needed that the churches might get them: recreation space, a library, an auditorium, a cafeteria, books. And there were problems the churches might help with, such as dysfunctional families and the long distances that students had to travel to school. Eventually a minister asked what his church might get from the school in a partnership. No one offered an answer.

Meanwhile, another pastor had received a work group flier about partnerships and went to Holabird Elementary School with a proposal. Meeting with principal Jean Tien and Task Force member Mae Kastor, he described an after-school program with a "spiritual" component. Tien was unsure if this was appropriate, and Kastor brought the issue to the work group. The next meeting discussed whether churches could include religion in school partnership programs.

Three ministers attended. While all agreed that activities in schools should not have a religious content, there was no consensus about programs on church premises. Marsh and Pastor Jeff Snodgrass of Canton Baptist Church had no doubt that they could include religious content, for example, in tutoring reading. Especially if the programs were funded by denominational organizations, they thought it reasonable to include religious material. Churches needed congregants, and that was why the denominations published the material.

The group commenced a long effort to formulate a policy but quickly reached consensus on the realities of partnerships. Principals and pastors would work out details as they went along. Churches would sponsor any programs they wanted, and principals would decide whether to consider them part of a partnership, to endorse them, or to publicize them. Parents would decide whether to send their children. And congregations would draw conclusions from the results. As for the pastor proposing the spiritual after-school program, he disappeared.

The two incidents turned on the same issue. The pastor who asked school staff what they would give his church and those who argued for religious content in after-school programs wanted reciprocal partnerships; they wanted to get as well as to give. Churches might give to schools altruistically, but they too had interests and, especially in the declining neighborhoods they shared with schools, needs. If churches and schools could think creatively about what churches could give schools, they also could imagine what schools could give churches. Churches were more likely to start, and continue, partnerships if they served churches' interests.

By the time the school year ended, Paddock helped Marsh's church do several things for Highlandtown. The church hosted lunch for the fifth-grade graduation. The congregation contributed books for a school library. A couple of years later, however, a new principal lost interest in the partnership. The church then gave another school money for immigrant students to buy uniforms. Marsh planned to start an after-school program at the church in 2002.

Partnership for Projects

The work group decided to recruit churches for specific projects rather than encourage partnerships in general. In October 1998, they assembled representatives of nine schools and six churches. Task Force member Father Dan Sinisi, of St. Elizabeth of Hungary Catholic Church, proposed church-sponsored tutoring. School staff talked at length about tutoring needs, but pastors voiced uncertainty about getting parishioners to volunteer. The group decided to survey schools on how they could use tutors and develop a strategy to recruit volunteers.

Schools readily supplied information on their needs. A handful of pastors came more or less regularly to monthly meetings but reported difficulty enlisting parishioners. Eventually, near the end of the school year, the group made plans for a May meeting of schools and tutoring volunteers to get set for the next fall. When the day came, twenty-six showed up, including staff from seven schools and three pastors. In the end, six persons, counting the pastors, volunteered.

When school reopened in September, Sinisi was the lone tutor, at Patterson High School. He committed himself to building a tutoring program at the school. However, even though a teacher had asked for tutors, Sinisi found that the administration had little interest in a program. He struggled to find students to work with, and he had no success recruiting other tutors. He left Baltimore for another assignment in the summer.

While he was trying to start a tutoring program, Dottie Fried, Amber Picou, and Stephanie Lightfoot began working with churches. In the middle of the 1999–2000 school year, pastors got the idea for an end-of-year Educator Appreciation Day. They would ask students to submit essays describing their favorite teacher, would give prizes for essays, and would recognize teachers' contributions at an assembly and a picnic, where students would read their entries. In May, several hundred principals, teachers, students, and family members came to an event full of celebration and good feeling. The organizers helped repeat the day in May 2001.

Observations

Part of the difficulty of forming church-school partnerships grows from the tenuousness of many churches in low-income neighborhoods. Part stems from school system culture. Educators want to be self-sufficient, regard outsiders warily, and communicate little with community members. They turn to a community mainly when they want something. They need a great deal, but they commonly expect community members to come to them ready to help. School staff think little about how the realities of community life require schools to extend themselves to get the help they want, and they rarely consider what schools could offer individuals or organizations in return for their aid. Though using the language of "partnership," educators more often think of getting specific assistance rather than developing a long-term, reciprocal relationship.

A community organization interested in matchmaking under these conditions must first identify specific individuals in, for example, a church and a school who would be likely to find common interests and form a personal relationship that could bind their organizations. It must teach them about the possibilities and responsibilities of partnerships. It must stay with them for a long time, joining their hands until they can hold together on their own, and it must be prepared to start again if one of the key individuals moves on.

Conclusions about Organizing Networks for Education

Solving problems in turbulent environments depends on organizing networks. The past two chapters have described Task Force efforts to create the Southeast Baltimore education field with the school system administration, schools, parents, and churches. Although the Task Force could not build an encompassing network, it developed some partnerships.

Partnerships and Networks

Partnerships are networks. "Partnerships" often are two-party relationships, while "networks" involve more, but that difference is unimportant. Churches' hesitations about partnerships with schools, for example, concern general challenges in building networks.

Pastors distinguished two bases for relationships, *altruism* and *exchange*. In altruism, one party gives to another for moral reasons and takes recompense from doing good. Many school staff thought of partnerships altruistically. Churches might go along with that for a while, but ministers wanted to reach a fair exchange, where each party got something for its interests. Thus a church might tutor students, and a school might advertise a church youth group. Still, despite this difference between altruism and exchange, both relationships rest on transferring resources.

Those who make the case for interorganizational networks identify two bases. One is exchanging resources. In altruism, resources move in one direction, but exchange is just what Sarason meant by a "resource exchange network." What is needed for schools to build partnerships on exchange rather than altruism is not new wealth but a willingness to think about giving as well as receiving and creative thinking about what the school already has.

That point is crucial for considering a third type of partnership, *mutualism*, and what would enable an exchange to develop further. In mutualism, parties serve common interests. For instance, a church and a school, thinking of themselves as strengthening a shared community, might convert a lot into a park and play space for students, congregants, and other residents. To envision such possibilities, parties would have to imagine sharing an identity. That is what Emery, Trist, and Warren meant when emphasizing creating a new way of thinking, or culture, that would allow institutions to learn with one another to solve shared problems. Resource exchange may be a means to forming networks, as well as a payoff, but organizing networks to make these exchanges depends on newly imagining interests and relationships.

Southeast Baltimore Partnerships

Rather than "networks," Southeast Baltimore actors commonly spoke of "partnerships," meaning one- or two-way resource exchanges, without changes in how organizations conceived of themselves. Examples include school system transmittal of data to the Task Force, organizing at William Paca that produced an addition, Salem United Methodist Church's contributions to Highlandtown #237, and EBLO's assistance to General Wolfe's Hispanic parents.

On the surface, many "partnerships" were simple, involving only two parties—three, if parents are considered separate from their children's schools. However, in addition, the Task Force was a matchmaker, a catalyst, and sometimes an active participant. And the Task Force itself was a coalition of individuals and organizations. Though invisible, funders were essential partners to many parties. The list can be extended.

The relationships that constituted the Task Force were complex, often ambiguous, and fluid. The Task Force could be considered a sophisticated network, built on imaginative, if sometimes inexplicit, reconceptualizations of institutional interests and engaged in mutualistic collaboration. However, many of the "partnerships" it engaged in or helped develop were simpler. Their domain was restricted to a single problem or purpose. Responsibility was narrow, clear, and fixed. It often was asymmetrical, particularly in altruistic relationships. Partners retained discrete identities and shared little, if any, authority. They kept their boundaries and made few, well-delineated connections. Few members of constituent organizations took part.

The Elusiveness of Networks

The Task Force had little success creating robust, multiparty networks, though the Ad Hoc Group on Education and the Empowerment Zone, described in chapter 10, was a noteworthy accomplishment. The safety assessment, with its mixed results, is illuminating. It involved three main parties: the school, the Task Force, and University of Maryland education faculty and students. In terms of network building, the project aimed to change patterns of thinking at the school in two ways. One was to persuade the principal to think with her staff of themselves as sharing interests in the school as a whole. The other was to encourage her to think of her school and the university as being jointly invested in an effort to learn about and change the school.

Complex factors limited the consultation. Central was the reluctance of the principal, as partner, to broaden the project's intellectual domain to include the school's ecology, to share responsibility and authority for discipline with her staff, and to open school boundaries to consultants' questioning and aid. Instead, she expected the partnership to be altruistic and to focus on transmitting resources, while the Task Force and the university expected it to be mutualistic. In that view, the collaboration would be action research, whereby staff would help the academics learn about school climate and change, while the academics helped staff learn to improve their school. One-way transmittal of university expertise would be useless, because university and school staff could improve the school only when school staff also shared what they knew.

The latter view fits a turbulent environment, where several institutions influence one another in ways that none can fully predict or control. If anything, the safety assessment network was too narrow, not including, for example, parents, who affected children's school behavior. However, the cognitive maps of most school staff, who preferred to see themselves as self-sufficient, did not extend beyond the school—and, for some, not much outside of their classroom. Although many complained about the negative effects of students' homes, many simply insisted that school practices could overcome family influences.

The school system made it nearly impossible for the principal and staff to reimagine their interests and relationships. Its culture rested on the premise that educators could—and should—do it all alone. Its structure encouraged and rewarded strict compliance with myriad regulations. The pace left little time for reflection. Although the school's test scores made it a candidate for reconstitution, the system could not let it take initiatives that might improve conditions. The networking possibilities offered by the consultation were not more resources for current activities (many of which, in any case, were ineffective) but new ways of thinking about what the school should be doing and, then, resources to innovate. However, the principal, perhaps particularly because she was new, felt boxed in and could not move beyond requests for altruism.

In these ways the school system constrained Task Force possibilities for building a Southeast Baltimore education field in which schools actively participated. These conditions discouraged active parent involvement. They set limits to what churches or businesses could do with schools. As the Task Force acquired resources—such as parent organizers, funding for parenting and adult education programs, and access to university faculty—it could engage schools in new partnerships, but most remained altruistic.

The Logic of Participation

Though the logic of participation would have it that anyone interested in something is entitled—and likely—to take part in public talk about it, multitudes do not clamor to deliberate about the schools. Few parents feel that they have the authority to speak, and professional educators, proclaiming that they alone know about education, discourage parents from taking active, questioning roles. These conditions, plus a narrow equation of education with schooling, suppress issues that affect children's education and life chances but seem to have nothing to do with the schoolhouse. In addition, they lead the childless, businesses, churches, public agencies, and nonprofit organizations to conclude that they have nothing to say about education.

The logic of participation goes on that as talk gets closer to action and as stakes increase, participants try to push out rivals. The situation in education seems different. Public participation is scant, and education reform does not move toward well-defined decisions. Though participants have stakes in education generally, there are few immediate issues in which they have specific interests. They are more likely to drop out from boredom or discouragement than be forced out.

Yet beneath this surface a logic of participation operates, which Forester's (1989) distinction among three types of decisions makes visible. On the surface are overt decisions about policies and programs. Just below are decisions about which issues get on the agenda for public debate. Still further down are "decisions" about which aspects of everyday life are even considered issues that might go on an agenda.

The school system has high stakes in current policies and practices. It discourages parent and community participation in formal school and system decision making. But, more generally, in promulgating a culture that defines schooling and education as beyond lay understanding, it keeps the public from even identifying school practices or community conditions as education issues. Thus sparse public involvement reflects the school system's success in restricting participation in defining issues. Much of what concerns community members never reaches the school agenda, much less comes up for overt decision.

Part 4

Action

Chapter 9

Doing Something

Volunteers get satisfaction from doing good. Organizations that deal with large or poorly defined problems—that want volunteers to study before acting—need people who are comfortable with research and reflection; otherwise, desires to do something will displace analysis and planning. Although the *Southeast Community Plan* recommended a "study-action group" on schools, parents and community members were interested more in action than in study. Anyone who took education seriously could at once feel overwhelmed by problems and impelled to do something—anything—to make things at least a little better.

The next two chapters look at projects that the Task Force carried out because participants wanted to do something that satisfied their interests and fit available opportunities. We might describe them as pulled from a "garbage can." Yet to say so does not imply that the projects were not reasonable, nor does it mean that they were not based on tested knowledge—participants took knowledge seriously, and some were professional researchers. Rather, the projects illustrate the logic of action, in that their creation and direction were shaped primarily by participants' interests in finding something that they could do together. We examine three projects of increasing complexity: a small "tutoring-mentoring program," a broad initiative to develop a full-service community school, and an interorganizational network to influence the Empowerment Zone.

A Tutoring-Mentoring Program

In March 1996, School-Family-Community Relations Work Group members, meeting for just the fourth time, wanted to do something for the schools. Three weeks later, at the next meeting, someone proposed a resource fair. People quickly reserved space at a school and invited twenty-five organizations with programs for children to put up displays for teachers and principals. The group prepared resource directories and arranged food. Five weeks later, they held the event, with 100 attending, and had the satisfaction of *doing something.*

However, when the new school year started in the fall, they faced the question of whether they could do something more far reaching. At the end of inconclusive talk in September, they decided that anyone with specific interests should bring a proposal the next month. Three ideas came in. One was a campaign to organize churches, businesses, community organizations, and service agencies to put education on their agendas. A second was an initiative to help schools find ways to involve parents. A third was a "tutoring-mentoring program" for schools.

Steve Kain, who worked with an adult literacy program, introduced the tutoring-mentoring proposal. He had worked in a restaurant that, with other businesses, sponsored a program at a suburban elementary school where employees visited monthly and read stories and talked about their jobs. He proposed to do something similar in Southeast Baltimore. Adults would visit a class to talk about their jobs and familiarize students with the work world. This would stimulate children whose parents' limited economic success provided few compelling models of work. The visitors would read the class something, perhaps related to their jobs. If they wanted to put in more time, they could tutor children. Those with more interest could become mentors. Schools might start longer-term partnerships with some of the workers' firms.

Work group members liked the proposal, but no one volunteered to implement it. Hence, they decided to see what response it got at the upcoming principals' meeting. Meanwhile, Robin August, a fifth-grade teacher at Holabird Elementary School, became interested in the idea, and she persuaded her principal to try a pilot program, which she would coordinate. In January, Mae Kastor, another work group member, offered to help August. Kastor was a social worker who had moved to Southeast Baltimore a few years earlier and wanted to get involved in her new community. She and August would start modestly in the spring and might expand in the fall.

Kastor recruited supermarket staff, an athletic coach, bakers, and journalists to talk with students. At the end of the spring semester, she reflected on the project with the Task Force. In the beginning, children had shyly asked a few questions, mostly focused on speakers' personal lives, with little understanding of the work world. As time went on, students developed a sense of people's jobs and asked more sophisticated questions. Children and adults enjoyed the discussions. Kastor and August would expand in the fall. August would integrate presentations with academic work. Kastor would get business volunteers to spend more time with students, and she hoped to recruit high school students to tutor.

That fall, she arranged a partnership between Holabird and Patterson High School. Starting in the spring, students in Patterson's Sports and Wellness Academy with teaching interests would come to the elementary school as interns, for half a week each. When February arrived, each of Holabird's fifteen teachers had an assistant, and August was training the interns, who helped with various activities. In addition, other high school students tutored on Wednesday afternoons. Older and younger students seemed to benefit from the time together.

However, the high school staff changed over the following summer, and no one continued the earlier arrangement. The tutoring-mentoring program lapsed.

This project was typical of early Task Force initiatives. One or two individuals became interested in something, and they acted in the Task Force's name. Here, people wanted to get community members somehow to help students. Someone mentioned "tutoring-mentoring," a couple of people liked the idea, modified it, and did what they could to carry it out. In putting the project together, they relied on professional judgment, personal experience, and common sense. Research did not seem necessary, and, in any case, they did not have time for research or more planning. They wanted to do something, the idea had an intuitive logic, and so they went ahead.

Creating a Full-Service Community School, Incrementally

The Genesis of an Idea

A lot of energy went into meetings in 1996, with few definite results. By the fall, the School-Family-Community Relations Work Group was the lone surviving group. After some talk about disbanding, parent organizing and the safety assessment started. Finally, the principals' meeting at year's end offered reassurance about a Task Force role, if not specific direction.

In January, as the Task Force was restructuring, Bobby English took stock by drafting an outline of a Southeast Baltimore education plan and formulating ten recommendations based on the group's experience. She proposed that every school have extended school day programs, making schools neighborhood centers. They would offer students after-school academic enrichment and offer parents adult education and family programs. English's proposal, drawing on her Julie Center work with children, addressed the question about a niche where the Task Force could effectively act. It sketched the beginnings of what Joy Dryfoos (1994) called "full-service schools," what others, with different emphases, labeled "community" or "comprehensive" schools.

The general concept was to open up school boundaries to the community. Those who talked of "community schools" called attention to the ways a school could become a community center, where children and adults gathered and conducted their affairs outside of normal school hours. The proponents of "full-service schools" talked about how social and health services, adult education, and other community resources could be brought or linked to the school to provide support for children and families. Among the benefits, children would learn better.

The idea's virtue for the Task Force was its tie between community interventions and educational outcomes. Task Force members were most experienced working with families and community groups, and the concept drew links between what they did best and a school's teaching efforts. The idea was familiar to members who knew about New York's Beacon Schools. The Task Force began thinking about creating a comprehensive school and organized a March 1998 symposium on "Community Schools and Partnerships" to spread the idea and snare the commitment of a principal or two. Martin Blank, from the Institute for Educational Leadership in Washington, D.C., spoke.

Twenty-five, including educators from six schools, other professionals, and community activists, attended, and Blank noted that their activities already comprised the rudiments of comprehensive schools. At the end, two principals voiced interest in making their schools comprehensive: Elizabeth Turner at Tench Tilghman Elementary School and Yvonne Garner at Highlandtown #237. Task Force members met with each to discuss children's social and health needs. The Task Force decided to seek a grant for a two-year planning and development process to create comprehensive, coordinated service programs at the schools. However, though one foundation encouraged a proposal, the Task Force did not find funding.

Finding Life for the Idea

To move ahead, Bobby English counseled incrementalism. If the Task Force could not get planning money, it should imagine what studies would find and develop components of a full-service school in anticipation of eventually creating a comprehensive program. It would do what it could to see that each new piece was integrated with existing activities. In fact, English had been proceeding in this fashion with Tench Tilghman for some time. She had met Elizabeth Turner during the original Task Force school interviews and admired her leadership, and Turner invited her to join the school improvement team. English thought about locating Julie Center services in the school.

In the fall, she sent her lead health promoter to Tench Tilghman to help the parent liaison get parents emergency assistance with housing, food, health, and utilities. She asked a community health nurse who worked at the center to recruit Johns Hopkins student nurses for internships in which they would conduct in-depth home visits. She found funding for adult education and GED preparation. English continued these activities in the 1999–2000 school year. She got nine Notre Dame AmeriCorps volunteers to tutor children. A Task Force grant paid for an enlarged GED program for parents.

While Turner gratefully urged the Task Force to help further, Highlandtown was a different story. Yvonne Garner retired just as the GED grant proposal went in. When it came through in September 1999, a Task Force delegation met the new principal, reviewed the history of the full-service community project, and asked whether she wanted the GED program. As a first-time principal, she would not commit herself to a full-service school. She accepted GED training after much hesitation.

That fall, English found funding for Agnes Rose McNally, who had taught and managed with the Sisters of Notre Dame, to coordinate the nascent Family and Community Resource Center, which would be the hub of Tench Tilghman's services. McNally set out to direct the growing network of resources and to connect them to the work of the school's health staff provided by the City Health Department. A social service intern joined the center to work with families.

In addition to managing the center, McNally took on casework responsibilities. The center would focus on thirty-five families whose children school staff considered at high risk of educational failure. McNally began meeting with children to assess their needs. With nursing students' assistance, she visited homes to meet parents, talk about children, and help parents support their children at school. The center began parent workshops.

Just before McNally arrived, the Abell Foundation had approached English and Ken Strong to invite a proposal for a program to train parents to take active roles in their children's learning. Abell, headed by Robert Embry, former Baltimore Commissioner of Housing and Community Development, former local school board member and state school board chairman, and long-time civic leader, was the third largest foundation in Baltimore and put much of its resources into school reform. Eventually, Abell funded a new Parents Promoting Success in Schools starting at Tench Tilghman and at another school in the beginning of 2000.

McNally found that doing casework with thirty-five needy families, coordinating the Center's activities, and seeking new resources was more than a full-time job. She was awed by the burdens and traps of children's lives. Few had working parents. Most lived in bad housing, and some were homeless. Most did not eat regularly or well. Few had decent clothing, and many parents could not afford laundry. Parents cared about their children, but many lost their aim as they let drugs take over their lives. Child abuse or neglect displaced nurturance. These conditions humbled McNally. As much caring as she gave the children, there was little she or the center could do in short order that would substantially change their lives.

By the next fall, the resource center's thirty-five high-risk families had become fifty-two, and staff were stretching to assist them. Casework, whose clients could not be put off, easily displaced resource development. Responding to children's immediate needs took priority over planning the center's development or getting resources that might relieve the burden.

The next step emerged serendipitously. Early on, McNally concluded that parents' drug problems were a big obstacle to children's success. When looking for funding for the center, some Task Force members had met Rebecca Ruggles, director of program development for Baltimore Medical System (BMS), which ran two Southeast Baltimore health clinics, provided medical services for Medical Assistance families, and was starting school-based health clinics. She became interested in Tench Tilghman. As McNally talked about support groups for children whose parents had drug problems, Ruggles thought about getting funds for BMS to provide that service. Eventually, Ruggles and Tench Tilghman, Resource Center, and Task Force staff fleshed out a proposal for group work, individual counseling, case advocacy, teacher education, and health interventions. BMS found funding to start some of these activities in the fall of 2001.

The Ascendancy of Action

Development of Tench Tilghman as a full-service school followed the logic of action. Task Force members wanted to do something to affect teaching and learning. Only Bobby English was trained as a teacher. Several were professionals who planned, managed, or delivered social services. As activists in a community with few resources, the group believed that cooperation between the needy and the resourceful was desirable and possible. As advocates, they saw the community as more than a collection of problems; it contained assets that could help schools.

English thought about extended school day programs, because the Ad Hoc Group on Education and the Empowerment Zone was talking about their potential to stimulate children's learning, and because they fit needs she encountered at the Julie Center. A number of Task Force members were looking for ways in which family and community interventions could be useful in education. Publications and the March symposium congealed, legitimated, and directed these interests under the label "full-service community schools."

That phrase covered what English had already started with Tench Tilghman, and it pointed toward a comprehensive planning and development process to implement the concept at two interested schools. While the Task Force sought a planning grant, English continued to aid Tench Tilghman through the Julie Center. When planning money did not come through, the Task Force turned to GED training because it was needed and fundable. A Task Force grant for McNally aimed to give coherence to what had come and what would follow. English regarded the Resource Center as a pilot project to test the possibilities for collaboration between community organizations and a school. If it succeeded, she wanted the school system to take it over.

The Julie Center, while a Task Force member, acted as a community agency in getting grants for the full-service school. The Task Force, for its part, as it followed this path to action, inexplicitly crossed from organizing, planning, and relationship building to service delivery. Would responsibilities for services place heavy demands on scarce Task Force resources? Would investing in service delivery shift the group's attention from organizing and loosen its ties to a parent or community constituency? How would it differ from other service providers? Because the Task Force faced a foundation world where funds were limited, would asking for money for services in schools jeopardize getting grants for parent organizing or planning?

Even if social, health, and adult education programs should be linked to schools, why should the Task Force raise funds for schools rather than, as it had offered at the principals' meeting, teach school staff to prepare their own proposals? Some staff knew how to apply for grants, but they lacked the time. However, with funding finite, a Task Force proposal for school services competed with a proposal for Task Force staffing. These questions about the opportunity costs of action offered no simple answers.

Chapter 10

Education and Empowerment Zone

Participation in the Service of Action

Years earlier, in 1993 and 1994, while the last members of the Southeast Planning Council struggled to implement their plan, the Clinton administration was designing its centerpiece initiative to aid distressed urban areas, the Empowerment Zone. As eventually conceived, the program would give $100 million in federal funds to a city while requiring it to raise matching money. Funding would be accompanied by policy innovations, including tax incentives for development (Gittell and Newman 1998; U. S. Department of Housing and Urban Development 1994). Baltimore applied in the first round in 1994, and the federal government designated it one of six urban Empowerment Zones (EZs). This chapter looks at how two Task Force members helped form an interorganizational network that influenced the city's Zone education activities.

Federal policy makers recognized the importance of money for dealing with city problems but also believed that the myriad entities aiming to affect local conditions had to be coordinated to have an impact. Hence, they emphasized that the EZ should catalyze systemic change in how cities addressed problems. Thus while at the least the local organizations managing Zones would be funders, at best they would intervene in policy, changing how public agencies, private firms, nonprofit organizations, and community groups interacted. They would develop relationships among diverse entities with interests in similar problems, so all could begin to think of themselves as a common domain, to define common problems, and to set common directions. Much more than managing funds, these corporations would manage interorganizational fields.

At the same time, EZ management corporations would add to the complexity of local action. While they provided financial benefits, they also brought new catchment areas and eligibility requirements, and they disturbed existing relationships. Any lasting impact, after the money was spent, would depend on the will and ability of the actors in those arenas named for their potential coherence—such as the "housing system," the "community development system," and the "education system"—to build networks capable of collaboration. Otherwise, policy would remain occasional, disjointed, competitive, and ineffective.

The Baltimore Empowerment Zone

Empower Baltimore Management Corporation

Baltimore's EZ application included proposals on community mobilization, community development, public safety, housing, health and family development, youth support, economic development, and education. The Zone would consist of three noncontiguous areas: the west side, including Sandtown-Winchester, which the city and the Enterprise Foundation had been trying to revitalize for years; the east side, centered on the Johns Hopkins Medical Institutions and including part of the area where the Education Task Force would work; and an industrial area at the city's south end. The city proposed to create six Village Centers to organize residents and to administer EZ programs (Office of the Mayor 1994).

The proposal reported that 41 percent of Zone residents lived in poverty. The official unemployment rate was 17 percent; only 44 percent of those over age sixteen were in the labor force (Office of the Mayor 1994, 2–5, 2–6). The document attributed unemployment problems to low education and noted that more than half of those over twenty-five had not completed high school, and only 5 percent had college degrees (Office of the Mayor 1994, 2–9). Further, 40 percent of students dropped out of school, and 21 percent of adults over twenty-five had not completed even the ninth grade (Office of the Mayor 1994, 2–6).

The proposal emphasized business development as the engine of revitalization. Education was tangential. The education section of the document was a hodgepodge of current programs and new proposals, including (1) school-based management, a limited ongoing initiative; (2) establishment of an academy to train teachers in curriculum and conflict mediation; (3) leadership and management training for principals and school improvement teams; (4) preparation of personal education plans for every student; and (5) creation of before-

and after-school and weekend programs in each Village Center. The latter would

> provide a rich mix of educational, recreational, artistic, and multi-cultural activities as well as community service projects to students and other zone residents. Schools will become a more integral part of community life after school hours and provide a place for young people to gather to develop their interests, skills and abilities. (Office of the Mayor 1994, 3:6–8)

After the federal government designated Baltimore an Empowerment Zone in December 1994, the Empower Baltimore Management Corporation (EBMC) was created to run the program. The mayor, Village Centers, and various others selected a board of thirty. In December 1995, the board named Diane Bell, interim president following a first president's brief term, president and chief executive officer (CEO).

Education came under the board's Economic Opportunities, Education, and Community Development Committee, where, as the name indicated, it took second place to economic development. One reason for this subordinate role was that federal EZ policy emphasized economic development. Also, jobs were countable, short-term outcomes. Further, no one on the EBMC staff and few on the board knew about education. The board included Superintendent Walter Amprey (who left after the first year, when public officials yielded places to community representatives); Robert Embry, who had extensive school board experience and strong education interests; and Douglas Becker, president and CEO of Sylvan Learning Systems, a for-profit education firm. Only Embry served on the Economic Opportunities, Education, and Community Development Committee. Its chair, Decatur Miller, a lawyer, had served on the boards of a private school and three universities, but he had no expertise in school program design.

When the committee began to decide on education initiatives, it faced the superintendent's opposition to extended school day programs, which would take nearly $5 million of the $6 to $7 million EZ education budget. Amprey said that the school system could not sustain these programs after EZ funding ended. In response, the committee gave new consideration to curriculum and site-based management. Curriculum proposals included implementing tightly structured instruction in elementary schools and developing an advanced mathematics and science program. School-based management proposals included training principals and decentralizing personnel responsibilities to schools (Rosenfield and English 1996).

Because community participants approved the application that included extended school day programs, a change would require new community involvement. Committee members felt that they lacked the educational expertise to decide. EBMC hired a consultant to elicit community sentiment on priorities.

The School System and the Empowerment Zone

The decision to choose an education initiative after interviewing parents, teachers, and community members, rather than negotiating with the superintendent, was emblematic of the lack of relations between the Zone and the school system. The Baltimore City Public Schools (BCPS) was an isolated institution. EBMC was developing relationships from scratch. It created six Village Centers to connect with communities, but their boundaries bore no resemblance to the school system's administrative areas, or any other political or service areas.

During the year the superintendent was on the EZ Board, BCPS and EBMC had a formal link. When Amprey left, he designated a deputy superintendent as liaison; she in turn assigned her executive assistant, but no one gave the assistant information or authority needed for the role. Even off the board, if Amprey had considered the Zone important, he could have maintained relations. After opposing extended school day programs, he apparently lost interest.

Different organizational cultures made it difficult for the two institutions to understand each other or cooperate. EBMC focused on economic development. Its board included many corporate leaders. It implemented its plans by soliciting proposals from bidders. Staff helped committees work, but only some were experts in their committees' fields, and they did not help applicants develop programs. The school system focused on programs. Its staff had educational expertise. They justified activities in terms of children's benefits, and they resisted the idea of running schools like businesses. EBMC talk about evaluation and accountability and school system talk about students and learning easily crossed without engaging.

Organizational structures made it hard to connect. The school system was a centralized bureaucracy with 10,600 employees, 183 schools, 110,000 students, and a $700 million budget (Lambert and Reynolds 1997). Top administrators expected subordinates to follow detailed directives, and many principals checked with superiors before acting in any way not explicitly mandated. EMBC, also tightly managed, was small, with a staff of twenty and a ten-year budget of $100 million, including less than $7 million for elementary and secondary education. It expected Village Centers to develop programs, including those in education, while school system managers would want to control any EZ education initiative.

THE AD HOC GROUP ON EDUCATION AND THE EMPOWERMENT ZONE

As cities began organizing their Zones, U. S. Department of Education staff grew concerned that they were giving schools little attention. The department was a minor player in the federal program, but USDE had an Empowerment Zone/Enterprise Community (EZ/EC)[1] Task Force to monitor and assist Zone education activity. Its director, William Smith, wanted to boost education's standing in the EZs. His associate Laurence Peters, a special assistant to the Assistant Secretary of Education who directed the Office of Educational Research and Improvement (OERI), had met Sylvia Rosenfield in another connection. Peters talked to her about working with the Baltimore EZ as an experiment in helping a Zone act on education.

Rosenfield talked with me, and we contacted members for an Ad Hoc Group on Education and the Empowerment Zone. We recruited Clarence Stone, a University of Maryland political science professor directing a study of education policy innovation in eleven U. S. cities, and Bobby English, who was not only Task Force chair but also an EBMC board member. Other federal education officials, academics from two universities, and education activists rounded out a group of about a dozen.

No one thought of the group's mission as trying to manage an interorganizational field; people saw themselves as offering advice, albeit to an unspecified audience. Yet the group's influence would depend on its ability to create relationships with significant actors, including EZ and school officials. Success in that respect would help manage the field. The practical question concerned what resources a small group could contribute to governing a turbulent domain. Individuals had expertise, networks, some time, and some authority, but no money. They invited Decatur Miller, chair of EBMC's Economic Opportunities, Education, and Community Development Committee, to their first meeting on April 18, 1996.

Empowerment Zone Views of Education

Rosenfield opened the meeting by describing the Group's purpose as strengthening education in the Empowerment Zone. Miller discussed EZ interests in education. The board, he said, considered elementary and secondary education less important than job training and placement, economic development, and recruitment of employers. In deciding how to spend the $6 to $7 million for elementary and secondary education, Miller said that EBMC was working closely with Amprey, now off the board. Because Amprey opposed extended school day programs, Miller's committee was looking at curriculum and site-based management. Uncertain how to proceed, the board had just hired a consultant.

Ronald Pedone of USDE spoke for federal education officials, saying that they wanted to see Zones combine EZ funding with local resources to make systemic educational change, not just to add projects in a strategic vacuum. Peters, representing USDE's research unit, emphasized the importance of incorporating research into Zone planning for education and offered OERI's assistance. Miller responded that $100 million was not much money and that the board wanted to spend it carefully. They were not education professionals, and they would value help. Pedone added that the EZ/EC Task Force could help Baltimore find money from other sources.

Asked about links between the EZ and the school system, Miller said that contact was sporadic but good. Rosenfield urged EBMC to work with schools and community members. Miller agreed but noted that community groups held diverse positions. He waited for the consultant's report to find any consensus.

What the Ad Hoc Group Had to Offer

The second meeting, which Miller did not attend, left group members to ponder who they were and what links they brought to the education and Empowerment Zone field.

Membership was ambiguous. Federal employees had clear roles: they represented—and were bound by—USDE policies. Working with the group was part of their job. When two members got new assignments a year later, they stopped attending. In contrast, university faculty represented themselves. They brought their institutions' names but lacked administrative authorization or recognition. English, considering herself a Southeast Baltimore representative, claimed roles in the Julie Center, the Education Task Force, and the Empowerment Zone. Members had geographically, politically, and intellectually diverse interests. The group would focus on the overlap: improving public education in the Baltimore Zone. Six of thirty-five EZ schools were in Southeast Baltimore.

The Empowerment Zone's relationship to the group was ambiguous. English, serving on the EZ board and chairing its Housing and Public Safety Committee, later renamed the Quality of Life Committee and given responsibility for education, linked the Zone to the group. However, Miller and top EBMC staff saw the group as one of many acting in their domain and came only when they thought it was useful. The education committee staff member attended regularly.

The group weighed alternatives in connecting with the education and Empowerment Zone field. Two involved the school system. One was to help individual schools. That seemed manageable with the group's limited resources and practical in avoiding the school bureaucracy and EBMC, and it appealed to grassroots sympathies. A second possibility was engaging the system administration. Two options involved the Zone. One was working at the grassroots level with Village Centers. However, it was unclear whether they cared about education. The final option was engaging EBMC. That fit federal interests in influencing a Zone and, in starting outside the school system, could offer leverage for innovation.

The number of alternatives reflected the domain's fragmentation. A case could be made for starting anywhere; practically, working with one entity would require links to the others. The group had educational expertise, but it was uncertain that it had the organizing ability—and political position—to create a network.

The group gravitated toward EBMC. For one thing, there was no getting around it. For another, Miller's brief participation and English's ongoing membership linked the group to EBMC. Moreover, if the group wanted to use the Empowerment Zone to change the school system, then working with EBMC seemed the best option. Finally, group members, with limited time, found it easiest to connect with a small, professionally staffed organization.

Building a Network

The Ad Hoc Group added one more entity to the EZ education domain. Four episodes show how it moved into vacant policy space and built a network to help manage the domain.

Episode 1: Deciding on an Empowerment Zone Education Initiative

During the summer of 1996, the EBMC consultant met with school staff, parents, students, community members, EZ Advisory Council members (a community group that formally approved the original proposal), and Village Center boards to advise the Zone on priorities.

The report documented fragmentation, mistrust, and frustration. Teachers and parents felt excluded from EZ education planning. Teachers criticized parents for taking little part in their children's education. Parents felt that teachers and principals did not want them in schools. Parents and community members did not trust school staff and "experts" to design or run any education initiatives. The Advisory Council wanted to give EZ education funds to Village Centers or to other community entities but not to schools. Many parents, however, considered Village Centers unrepresentative of community interests. Of the alternatives, participants most strongly supported extended school day programs (Strauss 1996). The consultant presented the report to the Economic Opportunities, Education, and Community Development Committee on September 3.

On September 30, the Ad Hoc Group held its fourth meeting, with a focus on the report's implications for the group's work with EBMC. The group invited the superintendent's EZ liaison, an area assistant superintendent, and the EZ's planning and administrative officer. Two days before the meeting, the Zone official said that EZ staff would not discuss the report with school representatives present before it had been formally distributed to the consultant's interviewees. The official would come only if the school system representatives were disinvited. With explanations and apologies, they were asked not to attend.

William Smith came with the USDE staff. He asked Decatur Miller to describe the situation. Miller recounted little progress in developing an initiative. The consultant's findings showed continuing support for extended school day programs, but his committee was unsure that these programs could be sustained after EZ funding. He would value the group's help.

Smith described his experience as a principal who had run extended day programs. He said that they could reinforce students' academic learning and offer social and cultural experiences. They could involve parents and community institutions in teaching. Parents might enroll in programs with their children. In bringing community resources into schools and building alliances among schools, families, and community members, these programs increased schools' impact. There was no question that they contributed to community development. Further, they served EZ goals of employment and economic development by giving children work skills. He urged EBMC not to abandon the extended day idea, which the original proposal supported. He touted it as a way of linking community and schools, and he urged the EZ to leave curriculum reform to educators.

He suggested looking at Title 1 of the Elementary and Secondary Education Act to sustain the programs. A Title 1 expert he had brought in described various federal funds. Smith said that EBMC should find out how the school system currently spent federal funds and consult with the State Department of Education in considering ways to use the money for systemic change. He urged EBMC to push the school system to develop innovative programs, instead of using EZ funds for minor program changes, and to force the system to be a partner. He suggested that EBMC lead in developing relationships by meeting with educators and including them in its board committee. Miller agreed that EBMC had let the school system give up responsibility for education in the EZ. That was in the past, Smith replied; the consultant's report offered a new mandate.

Miller proposed convening EBMC CEO Diane Bell, the planning and administrative officer, his committee's staff person, English, and Robert Embry to discuss directions. They met and reaffirmed extended day programs as the EZ education initiative—not just at Village Centers but at each EZ school. They encouraged the group to help schools develop programs.

In this episode, the group influenced EBMC with information about extended school day programs and Title 1 funding. It gave EBMC authority to endorse these programs—from Smith's experience, research he invoked, his role as EZ/EC Task Force director, and group members' knowledge and positions. The group noted that those with whom the consultant met gave authority to extended day programs. Finally, the group gave EBMC a link to USDE.

When EBMC started drafting a request for proposals (RFP) for schools to apply for funding, it asked the group for help. The group located Toks Fashola, who studied extended school day programs, at Johns Hopkins University. Contributing an RFP, she deepened links between EBMC and the group and connected Hopkins to the group and the Zone.

Cultural changes accompanied these social exchanges. Substantively, EBMC staff and board members moved toward the view that extended school day programs were educational and contributed to job readiness. As important, procedurally, EBMC moved toward the position that it had to collaborate with other organizations if it were to improve education in the Zone.

Episode 2: Preparing Empowerment Zone Schools to Plan

In January 1997, shortly after EBMC began preparing an RFP, the Ad Hoc Group held a workshop to help east side principals and Village Centers develop proposals. Staff came from eleven of eighteen schools, and both centers sent representatives. Speakers and resource people came from USDE, the Maryland State Department of Education (MSDE), the National Science Foundation's Urban Systemic Initiative, a New York Beacon School, the Child First Authority (a local entity setting up after-school programs), Baltimore Reads, the University of Maryland, Johns Hopkins University, and Temple University. They described model programs, funding sources, and evaluation methods.

This was an example of how the Ad Hoc Group could use members' networks to reach people who could give useful information to principals and community members. By facilitating the exchange, the group encouraged school staff to think favorably of extended day programs, laid the groundwork for a network of EZ schools, involved state education officials in the Zone, identified resources that schools could contact, and established the group in a growing network.

Still, as two later workshops made increasingly clear, most principals needed more aid than a conference could offer. Planning required familiarity with program models, the ability to conduct a planning process, and time to review research, plan, and move a proposal ahead. Few principals had all three. Most needed training, coaching, and/or assistance from someone with time to take care of administrative details.

Episode 3: Getting Technical Assistance

Group members told EBMC management what schools needed to develop proposals that would use EZ funds well. Zone staff said that they did not provide technical support to "bidders"; applicants should get help from sources that did not depend on EBMC and could sustain them after it went out of existence. Group members explained that there was no infrastructure to which schools could turn. Unless principals received help, programs would be disappointing.

In March, MSDE Director of Compensatory Services Ronn Friend, responsible for State Title 1 expenditures, convened a conference of Title 1 schools, including all EZ schools. Because he had attended the Ad Hoc Group's January workshop, he invited the group to conduct another one for all EZ schools as part of the conference. At the end of this workshop, he announced that the MSDE would commit Title 1 money for at least one staff person to help EZ schools plan.

In May, as EBMC was publishing its RFP, Friend hired Dale Parker-Brown, a former Baltimore principal, to be a liaison between EZ schools and EBMC. He brought her to the Ad Hoc Group. She had already met with EBMC staff and had started contacting EZ principals. She joined the group and began using its members as resources.

The RFP invited schools to submit proposals for extended school day programs that could include basic academics, educational enrichment, social development, leadership training, career education, community service, art and cultural activities, and sports and recreation. Schools should prepare proposals with parents, students, and Village Centers. To the twenty-eight schools in the Zone and the seven outside it with 35 percent of their enrollment living in the Zone, EBMC offered up to $40,000 a year, dependent on an even match, for up to three years (Empower Baltimore Management Corporation 1997).

For the school system, Parker-Brown met with principals and Village Centers, helped interpret the RFP, and took questions to EBMC. In September, as EZ schools were developing proposals, Robert Schiller Jr., the interim school CEO succeeding Amprey as part of system restructuring, announced that all schools would have after-school programs, focused on remedial academic skills, and the school board gave each school $35,000. It gave EZ schools $40,000 to make the maximum match and thus overcame a big obstacle for them.

Parker-Brown arranged help for principals developing programs, including a third Ad Hoc Group workshop. She created a process for reviewing school proposals and submitting them to EBMC. She helped principals by doing many of the administrative tasks for which they lacked the time. Her aid was crucial in developing and advancing many proposals, and she built relationships among EZ schools and between the school system and the Zone.

Interlude: Education and the Empowerment Zone

School system restructuring formed the backdrop for EZ education initiatives. In April, settlement of litigation established a new school board and the positions of chief executive officer, chief academic officer, and chief financial officer to replace the superintendent. In May, the mayor and governor selected a new board. In July, the board hired Schiller as interim CEO. The new system raced to meet state deadlines for producing plans and hiring permanent executives. Thus the CEO was new, preoccupied, and on the way out during the time that EBMC issued a request for extended school day program proposals.

When the RFP came out in May, principals struggled to develop proposals over the summer. They had to send them to the Baltimore City Public School System (BCPSS) administration for approval before they went to EBMC. In October 1997, one month into the school year, five months after the RFP came out, and eleven months after the EBMC board approved the extended day initiative, the Zone received six proposals, which it sent out for review. Over the next five months, proposals were forwarded to EBMC as principals wrote them and BCPSS approved them. EBMC reviewed the thirty-third proposal in March. (One school did not submit a proposal, and another closed.) After each review, EBMC prepared questions for a school to answer in a contract negotiation meeting. These meetings took place from December to March.

Meanwhile, with $40,000 from the school system in hand, a growing number of principals made commitments to their staff or vendors to conduct programs in anticipation of having $80,000. In April, EBMC signed contracts for four schools where vendors ran programs. Still, with only two months of the school year left, twenty-nine schools had no contracts and no EZ money. School and EBMC staff traded accusations, while matters moved into the hands of the accountants and lawyers, who were proceeding meticulously.

Episode 4: Building a Network to Act

Ad Hoc Group members considered three issues crucial. One was technical assistance. The second was funding: short-term matches for EZ money and long-term continuing support. And the third was the stalemate between BCPSS and EBMC.

Ad Hoc Group meetings were the only place where school and EZ staff regularly discussed the situation. No basic conflict prevented agreement. Rather, each organization simply had more pressing things to do. To the interim CEO, EZ programs were irrelevant to political restructuring mandates, and $4 million over three years was not much compared to a $700 million annual budget. Moreover, EZ money required a match. If BCPSS provided the match, then that would raise expectations that it would come up with full funding indefinitely. Schiller did not want to back into setting any priorities while he and the new board struggled to allocate funds among master plan goals. Hence, for EBMC, which succeeded by using money to leverage other funds and start projects, working with the school system did not lead efficiently to results.

In February 1998, the Group concluded that the two chief executives had to resolve matters. Bobby English, as chair of the Quality of Life Committee and Ad Hoc Group member, convened the CEOs and their staff in April. The Maryland State Deputy Superintendent for School Improvement came at the group's invitation. Laurence Peters represented the federal EZ/EC Task Force. Four Ad Hoc Group members attended.

Group members presented proposals for funding, technical assistance, and collaboration. Quickly the discussion stuck on the current stalemate. Schiller expressed surprise that schools had not yet received EZ funds, and Bell reviewed EBMC's good faith, timely efforts. A Group member observed that, despite problems, the parties wanted to cooperate, and Bell and Schiller agreed. Bell would make it easy to apply for funding in the second year, and Schiller would continue to provide a match for EZ schools. Schiller said that technical assistance was a good idea, but he was unsure whether he could pay for it. He was noncommittal about the Group's proposal to add the BCPSS CEO to the EBMC board, but Bell was willing to issue an invitation. Meanwhile, BCPSS' and EBMC's financial and legal staffs had plans to talk, and the meeting ended with anticipation of a contract agreement and authorization to the Ad Hoc Group to reconvene the group afterward.

Negotiations dragged on for more than a month, and only on June 27 did the school board approve the contract signed by Schiller and Bell. EZ money would reach schools in July, after the end of the fiscal year. Schools could roll over unspent money into the summer and the next year.

The Ad Hoc Group was able to expedite the process by convening this meeting because it had a reputation for knowledge, concern, and neutrality, because English had dual roles, because Parker-Brown had contact with Schiller, and because both parties had interests in an agreement.

Conclusions

Education and the Empowerment Zone as a Turbulent Field

The local school system is only one element in an educational field that includes the community, the economy, the housing market, child welfare policy, and more. When the Empowerment Zone came to Baltimore, it brought new money, but it also added an actor, created new districts, called for new community organizations, and established new requirements for getting money. EBMC had only a marginal interest and no expertise in education. It regarded the school system as just a potential bidder among many, rather than recognizing it as a pivotal institution. In tacit challenge to a system that insisted on top-down control, EBMC, emphasizing community initiative, solicited proposals from schools and Village Centers. Rather than managing the field, it increased the turbulence.

Notably, the mayor was absent from all of this. Although he appointed a majority of the EZ board and shared responsibility with the governor for the school board, although BCPSS was a city department, and although Kurt Schmoke had promoted Baltimore as "the city that reads," he took no part in getting the systems together. It is unclear whether he knew much about EZ education initiatives.

Many actors shared interests in the potential results of collaboration, such as children reading. But most were so busy with their routines that they could not see how their actions affected others and, in turn, made their own success unlikely. If they thought about coordination at all, they calculated that it was safer to keep at conventional, independent missions rather than risk struggling with others to define one without precedent. Thus most had greater stakes in continuing to fail to educate students than in trying to educate them better. That is the epitome of a turbulent field.

Possibilities for Managing the Field

One might characterize the domain as chaotic: no one is in charge. In reality, however, anyone can be in charge. More precisely, different people can be in charge of different things. A turbulent domain has a lot of empty space. New actors can enter and establish their own goals with some hope of realizing them, and a new actor might enter and coordinate others' efforts.

This case suggests ways a small entity can help manage a turbulent field. The group was itself a network, a loose association of individuals, variously representing themselves and organizations, linking their knowledge, authority, and material resources to work on building relationships that would enable others with overlapping interests and resources to collaborate.

Depending on the issues, actors, interests, and costs of acting, a few resources may effect action. The main requirement is that some in the field have reasons to collaborate. These reasons may be self-evident, but more often they remain to be discovered. Hence, the first way a small group may help coordinate is by illuminating or providing reasons for collaborating. It may show a party how it can benefit from working with others. It may show several organizations that they have common interests, that conflicts can be resolved, and that there are ways to work together. The Ad Hoc Group made this effort with EZ and school staff. State money for an EZ liaison was one result.

Still, actors may want to cooperate but may be unsure what to do. Thus a second way a small group can aid is by providing substantive knowledge. For example, EBMC wanted to do something with schools, but it did not know enough about education to decide. The Ad Hoc Group got Smith to persuade Miller and, through him, the board to adopt extended day programs. Later, it conducted workshops to help principals design programs.

However, even with such knowledge, potential partners may fear the costs of trying to work together. Where the costs are mainly time, a third way a small group can aid in coordination is by using its time to arrange meetings, facilitate discussion, and develop common activities. For example, the Ad Hoc Group convened the CEOs.

Sometimes the feared costs are risks of failure. No one can prevent failure, but a small group can help coordinate, fourth, by reducing the perceived probability of the risks. By providing authoritative knowledge about possible actions, it may persuade parties to pick courses likely to be successful and give them confidence that they are not taking unwarranted chances. Even if results disappoint, that confidence can support a willingness to continue collaborating, to learn from experience, and to make changes. The Ad Hoc Group persuaded the EZ to adopt extended day programs by invoking Smith's educational experience and his political role, as well as group members' knowledge and positions.

Still, coordination is necessary but insufficient for effective action. Organizations may work together on a problem but fail to find resources for solving it. For example, principals needed training and coaching to develop sophisticated extended day programs.

Resources

There are limits to what a group with few resources can do. One of the group's constraints was time. It borrowed from members' work. Influencing Zone education was a long process. Some members got tired, some federal employees moved, and some academics went back to scholarly work. A related constraint was money. The group had none. It needed staff. Someone with time to develop relationships would have let members conceptualize issues, strategize to build up the domain, and help actors in the field use knowledge.

A staff member could have helped the group remedy a third constraint, participation, which could bring time, authority, and perhaps money. For about a year, the group had representation from the Zone but not the schools. Parker-Brown worked for BCPSS, but on loan from the state. The group considered adding Village Centers, and Parker-Brown talked with them, but they had no time for meetings. A staff member could have involved others.

The story's conclusion highlights the importance of resources. In May 1998, the Annie E. Casey Foundation, which had not taken part in education and the Empowerment Zone, funded the consultant who had surveyed community opinion on EZ education priorities to help EBMC move ahead with extended day programs. The foundation was a natural place for the Ad Hoc Group to have sought funding, but no one had time to approach it. Now Casey, unaware of the group, tried to fix a problem it discovered. The consultant found the stalemate between the schools and the Zone and focused on getting an agreement. She took over the group's follow-up on the April meeting. Meanwhile, state funding for Parker-Brown ran out, and several group members pulled back. Casey apparently defined the consultant's work in terms of facilitating an agreement on contractual details, and once she had set up work groups to do that, funding stopped. Then no one was left to try to coordinate the education and Empowerment Zone field.

The Empowerment Zone went on to give thirty-three schools $40,000 annual grants for extended school day programs for two years and $25,000 for two more years, with the school system providing equal matches.

Lessons about Action

Through the Ad Hoc Group, the Task Force helped build an interorganizational network that influenced the Empowerment Zone and school system, even while the Task Force as a community organization struggled to connect with the school system. This seeming paradox offers lessons about networks. One is that networks offer alternative paths among actors. The Task Force could reach the school system when linked to the U. S. Department of

Education and the Empowerment Zone, particularly when the latter had money, whereas it met frustration when tied just to parents. Second, networks are possible because much social and political space is empty. Institutions influence a great deal, but many details are up for grabs. That was Long's (1958) point in describing local communities as ecologies of games and Stone's (1993) in emphasizing the necessity of building regimes.

Third, networks are possible because organizations are not monolithic. The Ad Hoc Group linked strategic parts of federal, state, and local educational agencies, universities, and so forth. A crucial related point, fourth, is that institutional links depend on personal relations. The Ad Hoc Group started and built on personal ties. Finally, fundamentally, networks develop when parties share interests in solving a problem. The Ad Hoc Group grew and influenced EBMC, because parties had stakes in deciding how money would be spent. The Task Force had difficulty convincing schools or the system administration to see payoffs in community partnerships.

The Ad Hoc Group was more elaborate and self-consciously strategic than the tutoring-mentoring project or the full-service community school, but its logic of action was similar. A core group assembled a network for a general task and then took specific steps on the basis of members' interests and abilities. They added participants to increase competence, and the newcomers, in turn, reshaped the agenda. This evolution was thoughtfully opportunistic. In each project, success turned on finding parties that increased possibilities for action.

Part 5

Research as a Means to Action

Chapter 11

Acting as a Way of Knowing
Action Research

The Task Force made efforts to tie action to research. This chapter examines ways the Task Force learned from action. We review two early initiatives where people wanted to do something but were unsure what to do and the logic of action outweighed the logic of research. Yet participants treated action as a means to knowledge, and the Task Force drew on experience to develop an education plan. The next chapter recounts later episodes where the Task Force used or engaged in research to decide what to do and the logic of research was ascendant.

Knowledge and Action

Theodore Sizer admonishes educators to "plan backwards." They should specify what students should be able to do, and then reason back through sequences of classroom, school, and, one might add, family or community activities that would enable them to act in these ways. Many planners think in terms of "program hypotheses" (Kettner, Moroney, and Martin 1990): while some interventions have relatively consistent, sure consequences, the complexity and uncertainty of society and nature often make action an experiment. It is possible to draw on a great deal of knowledge and still be unable to predict what will happen. Thus knowledge used to design an intervention can be framed in hypotheses: for example, "if teachers of A or B characteristics do C with students of D characteristic or E with students of F characteristic under G and H conditions, then students of D and F characteristics are likely to accomplish I." Planners should base hypotheses on knowledge tested in practice and fill in gaps with inferences from social theory. Weiss (1998), similarly, urges basing interventions on "program theory" or a "theory of change."

Still, some interventions are more experimental than others. Program hypotheses may be plausible but rest on spotty evidence. They are worth testing, because they make enough sense in addressing urgent problems, but they lack precedent. Implementation is research: acting to see what happens. Knowledge about the world comes from trying to influence it and noting how it reacts. These premises underlie "action research" (Greenwood and Levin 1998; Greenwood, Whyte, and Harkavy 1993; Whyte 1991). It involves assembling any available knowledge, from formal research findings to ordinary people's everyday understandings, to plan action and then systematically noting results. Observation may suggest ways of modifying actions to come closer to goals, or it may show that initial goals were inappropriate and should be reformulated. In any event, observation sets off a further process of developing knowledge, planning, intervening, and reflecting.

In this way an intervention offers three types of learning. First, observant participants, by trying to influence conditions, can learn about a substantive field, such as education or housing. Second, in trying to affect a social system or an institution, such as the schools or housing market, interveners can learn about a system. Third, reflective practitioners (Schön 1983) can learn about themselves as actors. Thus Task Force efforts to improve schools offered participants knowledge about education, the school system, and their own desires and capacities for action.

Action as a Source of Knowledge

The Tutoring-Mentoring Program

The people who developed the tutoring-mentoring program drew on professional training in teaching and social work and supplemented it with personal experience and common sense. The program's main feature when it started—presentations on work—rested on the assumption that if successful adults talked about their jobs, the youths would find out about interesting work opportunities, think more concretely about jobs, develop more specific and hopeful ideas about their vocational futures, feel more motivated to study, and do better academically. This was not all spelled out, and the creators might have felt shaky about positing some of these results, but this was the gist of the underlying program hypothesis.

Tutoring rested on the premises that if adults or adolescents helped elementary school students in reading, then the students would learn to read better, develop self-confidence, be more interested in learning, manage their behavior better, and accomplish more academically. However, though the project could be justified in these terms, it was not explicitly, deliberately planned; its knowledgeable creators were moved mainly by the logic of action.

They intended to evaluate the results but did not do so systematically. Nevertheless, Task Force members drew lessons from periodic reports. The clearest, in the early years when people looked for ways to be useful, referred to the group's capacity to act. The project showed that it could mount programs with schools and, further, arrange partnerships between schools and businesses or other schools. It illustrated Task Force ability to recruit volunteers for schools, and it showed that the Task Force could organize tutoring. Regarding the substance of education, some, considering the project a success, took it as evidence of the efficacy of job presentations and tutoring. Finally, the project offered an encouraging lesson about schools' interest in working with the Task Force.

At the same time, the project's brief life told about the difficulties of establishing even modest programs on volunteer effort. Someone could put in time for a year or two, but continuity depended on institutionalizing the activity. This might mean getting a project into the core of a school's program or securing funding.

One could question the rigor of observations that led to lessons drawn, particularly with regard to educational outcomes. However, there was no question that Task Force members, starting with little confidence in their expertise or authority, took their actions as data from which they developed knowledge about education and their ability to act.

Organizing Parents

A Gathering of Premises

Parent organizing, which started around the same time as tutoring-mentoring, was a complex set of interventions that depended on a much more elaborate theory of change. People supported parent organizing for different reasons and gave it different places in program hypotheses. For some, it was an end in itself, a matter of democracy. Others spelled out relationships between parent organization and educational improvement. A few believed that active parents would break up an ossified school system and create political space for change, which would make schools better. More moderately and specifically, some believed that cooperation between parents and staff would reduce animosity and anxiety and create a climate where educators and parents could reasonably consider innovations. In particular, staff would take parents' knowledge of their children into account in deciding what and how to teach. Parents, staff, and organizers could get community institutions to contribute needed resources.

A few were less interested in involving parents in school decisions than in helping them parent well at home—care for and discipline their children, expect them to do well at school, make sure they were rested, fed, clothed, and otherwise ready for school, and help them with homework. Those who emphasized "parent development" believed that organizers could get parents training and services from which parents would learn or get support to be better parents, with expectable results in children's academic achievement.

In this general theory about organizing and educational change, two links were tenuous. One involved the basic assumption that organizing affected parents. Earlier we noted obstacles to parent organizing, including parents' doubts about their knowledge and authority and educators' resistance to parent activity. Even parent development, which is uncontroversial, is difficult for organizers, because it is hard to contact parents and get them thinking about parenting, much less help them learn to take better care of their children.

In addition, there was considerable uncertainty about the specific steps through which short-term accomplishments of parent organizing—involvement in schools or parenting at home—helped children academically. Part of the difficulty involved fogginess about what good education was, and some reflected explicit uncertainty about what to take as outcome measures. In the end, much came from an intuitive recognition of the elusive complexity of connections between, say, an organizer's activities, meetings of a parent organization, teachers' actions in a classroom, and children's learning. The causal web was no firmer with respect to parental actions at home.

How, then, could Task Force members endorse parent organizing, with uncertainty about how it would accomplish its ends and, indeed, what those ends were? Part of the answer is that people acted on faith, assuming that, somehow, organizing worked its way toward better education. Part is that research and experts seemed to support this view. Prominently, Joyce Epstein had been conducting research, working with Baltimore schools, and writing about parent involvement's impacts for years (Epstein 1995, 2001).

Efforts to get funding for organizing encountered foundations asking what it would accomplish. In response, the Task Force gave up claims to a comprehensive theory of organizing and identified various types of parental involvement and educational improvement as equally worthwhile expectable results. Realistically, organizing could do more to recruit parents to a PTA, get them to volunteer at school, or persuade an agency to offer services to students' families than to raise test scores. Arguably, all of the former were valuable in themselves.

The Task Force went on to distinguish three types of educational "outcomes": attendance, behavior, and academic achievement. Even if conceptually imperfect, this move was a grasp at realism. It was easy to imagine that parental involvement, improving relations between home and school, would make school more welcoming to children and thus increase attendance. Similarly, students who felt that parents and teachers both wanted them at school learning would more likely act appropriately. Attending more consistently and acting more constructively, they would more likely learn reading or math. That too was plausible, though the Task Force emphasized the suggestive quality of test scores, the time necessary for changes in attendance and behavior to work their way toward grades and tests, and myriad intervening events that flood over small, if real, effects of organizing on academic accomplishments.

Thus though parent organizing started with a medley of justifications, those most closely associated with it approached agreement on a few program hypotheses that linked organizers' activities to expectable results. Instead of planning systematically at the outset, they planned retroactively, justifying what they seemed able to accomplish in terms of research and associated claims and modifying their aims to fit changing views of what was worthwhile. Although this planning was more "forwards" than "backwards," the logic of action, as Weick notes, makes this approach likely: "Organizations formulate strategy *after* they implement it, not before. Having implemented something—anything—people can then look back over it and conclude that what they have implemented is a strategy" (1979, 188, emphasis in original).

Knowledge Drawn from Action

Crucially, Task Force members believed that the organizers were acting on and testing knowledge, and they drew conclusions from the results.

Task Force Capacity to Act

Parent organizing offered two contrasting but related lessons about Task Force capacity to work with parents in schools. The first was that organizing was hard. The second was that organizers could get along with schools when they got resources that advanced principals' agendas or made them look good. In part, these conclusions were linked developmentally: the beginning of an organizing relationship was tough going, but, as things got sorted out, organizers could find ways for parents and staff to work together. In part, the conclusions reflected the shift in emphasis from organizing toward resource development. People might take one lesson or the other as paramount, depending on when they saw the organizing and what they expected of it.

Organizing was continuously difficult. Principals, teachers, and parents were busy, anxious about one another, and often indifferent to one another. Rarely did parents or staff act as a unified group. Agreements between parents and schools usually involved a few individuals, and busy-ness, mobility, and second thoughts often undid commitments and made it necessary to start over.

In this constellation, the principal was key: the Task Force could work in a school only with his or her permission. Getting and keeping it depended on being sensitive to the pressures of the principal's position, as well as personal idiosyncrasies. That effort, however, when parents and principal disagreed, easily subjected organizers to role conflict. Starting with interests in serving parents but needing to get along with principals, they could get pulled back and forth.

In the long run, it was less important for organizers to help parents win specific conflicts than to build their capacity to analyze issues and act on those they thought important. However, the logic of participation strongly pulled organizers, and the difficulty of action made any possible action precious. Role and time pressures combined against analyzing issues. Hence, supervision was important in helping organizers make decisions about particulars in the context of an organizing model that stayed focused on developing parents' capacity to act. The Task Force learned this lesson partly from an inability to provide the supervision that organizers required.

One way organizers could get action at a school was by involving parents in principals' projects. Another was to get resources, such as volunteers or services, for school or student needs. The latter successes gave succoring satisfaction to organizers and Task Force members who felt discouraged by organizing difficulties. In addition, resources' tangibility made them easier for many members to understand than organizing processes.

Yet partly for this reason, the variety of resources, programs, and partnerships led some to question whether this activity added up to a coherent initiative that benefitted students. If the organizers were to act strategically, then what should they concentrate on? To answer this question, organizers needed educational expertise, to help parents and staff develop sophisticated views of problems and remedies. Otherwise organizers would simply see disagreements as political conflicts and identify issues as discrete problems to be "solved" with a "resource." This lesson emerged from the results of sending organizers off without this support.

The School System

More than anything else the Task Force did, organizing taught it about the school system. Organizers sometimes attributed principals' resistance to personal quirks, but the fact that they could call on the bureaucracy to expel organizers showed that they were integrally part of the system. The administration's unrelenting demands on principals frustrated most and, in any case, left few with the time or patience for parent organizing. On top of this, several Southeast Baltimore schools were threatened with state takeover if test scores did not improve. Those principals had to detail remedial strategies and host state monitors who regularly checked for progress.

The threat of reconstitution was only the sharpest weapon in a widespread public attack on the schools. As a new school board carried out restructuring by creating new structures, drafting and moving to implement a master plan, and hiring new top managers, principals confronted new relationships and added demands. Reconstitution-eligible schools adopted model curricula. BCPSS added a local test to three state tests. System managers drew in the wagons, defended their intentions and efforts, formulaically invoked bureaucratic routines, and tried to keep everyone in line. They expected principals to do the same.

Principals had little room for slippage. Parent organizing was risky. Hence, the Task Force modified its organizing approach. Even so, the paranoid strand in the system culture made many principals highly anxious about organizing and parents and unable to see common interests.

Education

Parent organizing offered nebulous lessons with respect to the substance of education. Simply, it was difficult to know how an organizer's actions, or the resources an organizer got, affected children's learning. Funders' pressures to specify organizing outcomes were at once illuminating and humbling regarding education's complexity. Task Force leaders, increasingly sensitive to evaluation difficulties, most confidently believed that organizers' improvements in the quality of school life and family-school relations contributed to increased student attendance.

Developing a Plan for Southeast Baltimore Education

Even though the USDE proposal promised to develop a plan, few in the early years saw much purpose in one. They had little idea what the inchoate organization could do. When at last it got involved in the safety assessment, parent organizing, and the Empowerment Zone, people were relieved to be acting, but a bigger picture eluded them. As projects increased, some thought a plan unnecessary because, after all, the Task Force had figured out what to do.

In January 1998, with a year of university funding left, I urged preparing a plan. It would codify the Task Force's learning and report on its work; it could clarify goals, set priorities, and guide action. Now people readily moved to outline a plan, draft a mission statement, and flesh out recommendations. They regarded the previous three years' work as research and planning. Textbooks advocate planning as preparation for implementation; they treated implementation as a means of planning. Not knowing what to do, they took small steps and noted the results.

Recommendations

At the April Task Force meeting, Bobby English presented fourteen draft goals representing her conclusions from three years' activity. The list did not so much delineate an educational vision as endorse projects and ideas encountered over the years. Some concerned school structure: forming a Southeast Baltimore school district, reconfiguring schools into pre-K–8, holding school size to 500, and reducing student-teacher ratios. Some referred to school programs, such as serving special education students and establishing extended day programs. Others described family or community involvement: governing schools by home-school associations, establishing student-parent-teacher contracts, and developing community partnerships. Three mentioned safety, including creating an alternative high school for disruptive students and establishing conflict resolution programs. One goal supported teacher professional development.

Members discussed the proposals in terms of whether they were reasonable solutions for problems, whether they could be implemented, whether the Task Force could say something specific enough to advance public debate and guide its own course, and whether it could do something to implement them. They added other recommendations.

Following the meeting, English drafted a mission statement, which made explicit what the Task Force had been doing all along. It began, "The Task Force acts in the areas where community support makes a difference," and it identified five activities: conducting research and planning, increasing parental involvement, forming partnerships, getting resources, and advocating for school needs. Task Force members quickly endorsed the statement in June.

Over the next months, members talked among themselves and with educators, activists, school system staff, and school board members. Revised recommendations in October reflected three changes. First, the Task Force backed away from proposals about system structure. A school board member told them that the system would not create a Southeast Baltimore district. Rather than advocating for small school size per se, the Task Force subsumed this in a more actionable proposal to create K–8 schools. Second, they added activities that would connect families and community institutions with schools, with an emphasis on parental involvement and church or business partnerships, for tutoring and mentoring, promoting attendance, and developing full-service community schools. Third, noting the costs of all of this, they added proposals to increase funding.

The Task Force sent the recommendations to principals, teachers, and parents at the sixteen Southeast Baltimore schools, asking for reactions and suggestions. Two hundred responded, putting priority on increasing funding and improving reading and math instruction, with creating neighborhood K–8 schools close by. They gave weight too to supporting parent organizations, promoting attendance, teaching social skills, creating alternative schools, tutoring and mentoring, and preparing children for careers.

The Task Force prepared a draft plan and invited school staff, parents, and other community members to comment on it at a November community meeting. A racially and economically mixed group of 100 reviewed the document and endorsed its recommendations, adding details and suggesting implementation strategies.

The *Southeast Community Plan on Education*, published in February 1999, reflected growing coherence about accomplishments and purposes. The plan demarcated a clear role in school improvement. While educators worked on curriculum and pedagogy, the Task Force would work in the community—organizing resources to support families in preparing children to learn and schools in teaching them, as well as advocating for programs and practices about which community members had expertise. The plan emphasized what a community group could do by itself or in partnership with schools (Southeast Education Task Force 1999).

Recommendations were organized in the four areas adopted in 1995: (1) building school-family-community relationships; (2) developing school-community programs; (3) organizing for safe, positive learning environments; and (4) advocating for more resources. The plan started where the Task Force could do most, building relations between families and community members and the schools. It emphasized strengthening parental involvement in schools, establishing partnerships, recruiting tutors and mentors, and informing the public about educational issues.

Turning to school programs, it emphasized those that linked curriculum to community issues, opened the school to the community, or used community resources. On curriculum, it recommended promoting art and music and developing links between school and careers. Addressing family and community issues, it advocated for early screening and sufficient staffing for students with learning difficulties and creating full-service community schools. The plan offered schools community help running after-school programs and promoting attendance. It advocated research on K–8 schools as a means of tying schools to community members.

The next recommendations looked at ways community members could help make schools safer. Physically, the plan recommended making buildings safe and healthy and organizing community efforts to make the environs safe and clean. Socially, it urged effective schoolwide discipline programs and social skills training for students. Finally, for students who could not get along with others and risked failing, the plan argued for alternative settings.

Concluding recommendations addressed the bottom line: resources. The plan advocated for increased public funding and also recommended community fund-raising.

Few were new or remarkable proposals. Rather, what was noteworthy was the way a community group developed a vision of good education and a partnership between community and school in giving life to it. The recommendations covered broad ground and identified community interventions that could make a difference.

Sources of Knowledge

Some recommendations directly reflected research. Planning faculty and students had reviewed studies of K–8 schools and analyzed local attendance zones, and the plan recommended continuing in order to develop a workable Southeast Baltimore model. The recommendation on attendance followed research that shifted emphasis from punishing parents for absenteeism to giving families supports that made attendance possible.

Some recommendations reflected experts' views. Epstein's research shaped recommendations on linking families and community members to schools. Sylvia Rosenfield's consultation stressed the importance of coherent schoolwide discipline programs and led to recommending social skills curricula. Martin Blank's community school symposium clarified how family and community supports mattered to education. Extended school day program experts assembled by the Ad Hoc Group showed how after-school programs could help children develop.

Other recommendations grew from personal observations. Bobby English's work at Tench Tilghman convinced her of the importance of special education and early screening for learning difficulties. People involved in programs often advocated for them. Parent organizing, tutoring, church-school partnerships, and the full-service community school were examples.

Task Force discussions alerted people to problems and remedies. Unsafe and unhealthy building conditions led to one recommendation, as dirty school environs did another. An advocate for school-to-career programs convinced people of their importance. These talks pointed to increasing funding.

Thus Task Force members saw the plan as a codification of their learning, and it symbolized their authority to participate in public debate.

Program Hypotheses and Theories of Change

The *Southeast Community Plan on Education* did not base recommendations on a systematic analysis of educational issues. One reason was acknowledged uncertainty about the nature of problems and the assumption that careful analysis would precede specific actions. Another was Bobby English's distaste for talking about problems and her penchant for emphasizing the positive and possibilities for action. A third was the inclusive Task Force culture: almost any proposal was accepted; recommendations proceeded from disparate premises toward diverse goals. What they shared was an opportunistic interest in action.

The goals referred, variously, to educational outcomes, programmatic activities, and resources. The great majority recommended instituting or enlarging programs, on the premises that they removed obstacles to learning (e.g., making buildings safe and healthy) or supported teaching (e.g., promulgating discipline programs) and would thus contribute to academic achievement. Whatever the focus, each described likely benefits. One noted research linking parent involvement and educational outcomes. Another mentioned studies showing "that when a significant portion of the day is devoted to the arts, the academic abilities of students improve" (Southeast Education Task Force 1999, 25). Still another noted that after-school programs offered academic and social instruction at a time when many youths would be unsupervised and prone to crime, substance abuse, or pregnancy, which could end their education.

One could read the plan as a broad attack on various educational problems based on tacit hypotheses about problems and remedies. In this respect, recommendations were strikingly consistent. The plan said that much was right in the schools. Implicitly, problems in children's education were attributable not so much to shortcomings in curriculum or teaching as to the great or special needs of children from low-income communities and troubled families. At the least, the plan was silent on curriculum and pedagogy; drafters believed that they lacked relevant knowledge, and, in any case, some schools were trying new models. At the same time, the plan said a great deal about family and community interventions, because they were areas of Task Force expertise.

The plan assumed that teachers knew what to do and could do more and better under three conditions. The first was if schools had more resources, from money to improved facilities to volunteers and institutional partners. The second was if special treatment were given students who could not adjust to normal learning expectations. Thus students should be tutored, mentored, screened for learning disabilities, taught social skills, managed according to schoolwide discipline plans, and, if these measures failed, removed to alternative settings.

The third, important condition was if schools were tied to students' communities, so teachers would teach more effectively because of sensitivity to children's backgrounds, and students would feel motivated to learn because of school's connection to their lives. Thus many arguments for K–8s had less to do with education than the expectation that these would be neighborhood schools, keeping middle-grade children near home and giving parents continuing opportunities for involvement. Full-service community schools made the social connection, after-school programs and school-to-career curriculum the intellectual connection, and safe school environs the physical connection.

In these ways, the *Southeast Community Plan on Education* represented the community approach to educational improvement. The plan focused on the structure of relations between schools and the community rather than on the technical substance of schooling. In addition to building school-community ties, strategies aimed to improve community conditions that influenced teachers' and children's motivation and ability to work together.

One might dwell on gaps in program hypotheses or inconsistencies in theories of change, but these assumptions held recommendations together. The community group was concerned less with developing a conceptually tight analysis of problems and prescription of strategies than with finding practical opportunities for doing something.

Observations

This chapter looks at relations between the logics of research and action in community organizations. The organizations have compelling reasons to plan action based on research: they must use limited resources efficiently. Yet participants push for action. They do not necessarily oppose research, but they have little time for it. Especially if they have limited formal education, they are unfamiliar with research studies and methods. Few are accustomed to consulting formal research, much less conducting it. Hence, because resources are scarce, participants' pressure easily bypasses research and planning. This is community organizations' predicament.

Researchers who want community organizations to use more research have encouraged university-community partnerships, with the aim of changing organizations' culture or, at least, temporarily, their way of proceeding. The Task Force sometimes used the university for planning studies. More often, however, members wanted another kind of assistance—help in turning action into action research. This may be the most fruitful university-community collaboration.

Even so, it is not a simple matter for a community organization to reflect. Members participate part time. Few, if any, know about everything the organization does. Rarely do members have the time to think about more than one or two projects. Neither members nor staff meet enough to share all they know about the organization's activities. A core group knows a great deal, and they occasionally take time to discuss an initiative in detail. Within that group, individuals specialize in particular projects and are best equipped to reflect on them. They may discuss their observations and conclusions and learn from doing so. Those who take part in these periodic discussions develop specific knowledge and general understandings of the organization's activities, and they draw their own conclusions. Deliberate engagement in action research may make such inquiry more formal, data collection more systematic, and meeting more routine. Still, changing participation and pressures to act work against institutionalizing reflective practice.

In the Task Force, the university's presence encouraged people to think more systematically about what they were doing. I raised questions about projects' purposes, strategic soundness, and feasibility, and I asked what could be learned from what happened. These inquiries supplemented didactic symposia, workshops, discussions with experts, and reading. Members learned from interviews and meetings with teachers and principals, parents, students, activists, and school officials. And throughout, tacitly, participants learned by reflecting on action. Cumulatively, these experiences transformed a group who felt they knew too little to do anything into one that confidently initiated projects and drafted a plan.

Chapter 12

Knowing as a Means to Acting
Research for Action

The Task Force used research to make some decisions. We look at an effort to decide whether to support K–8 schools and another to determine what school facilities Southeast Baltimore needed. In aiming to change schooling, both focused on what Task Force members understood most confidently: its structure rather than its technical substance. The essence of creating K–8s was altering schools' grade structure, though much of what proponents liked was their potential to improve the structure of relations between schools and communities. Facility issues were concerned with physical structures, which also had implications for school-community relations. Besides playing on Task Force intellectual strengths, structure was a good strategic choice for pulling together people from around Southeast Baltimore. The sixteen schools had common structures, whereas the substance of education in each was distinct.

These cases shed light on conditions affecting whether community action follows a logic of research. In addition, they look at information in relations between a community organization and a school system to see whether the system gave the organization information needed for planning and whether, in turn, the organization could use knowledge to influence the system. Answers have implications for forming interorganizational networks.

K–8 Schools

Beginnings

In May 1994, a Baltimore City Public Schools K–8 Schools Study Group issued a position statement that reported: "The number of K–8 schools in our system has been increasing over the past several years. It has become clear that support for K–8 schools has increased in communities throughout the city and in the school system itself" (Baltimore City Public Schools 1994b). In fact, only seven of the city's 184 schools were then K–8s, but the parent and teacher initiatives that produced them and would create nine more in the next three years raised questions about how the system would educate young adolescents. The document asserted that students were succeeding in K–8s, noted that the middle school model could be implemented in K–8s, and offered assistance to principals who wanted to develop K–8 schools.

The Abell Foundation, whose president, Robert Embry, wanted to evaluate reform ideas, pulled together data on middle-grade students in the city's K–8 and middle schools. A review showed higher sixth grade attendance at K–8s than at the middle schools where students would have gone. Comparisons of MSPAP and CTBS scores showed that eighth graders generally did better at K–8s than at middle schools. However, eligibility for lunch subsidy suggested that K–8 students had higher family incomes than did middle school students. It was hard to unscramble grade configuration from socioeconomic status from the activity of middle-class parents in creating many of the K–8 schools. Even so, the story's headline gave breath to further interest in K–8s.

In Southeast Baltimore in the early 1990s, parents were concerned about children's safety going from small elementary schools to big, anonymous middle schools outside of the neighborhood. Some of the worry was racial. For children in historically white areas, going to middle school meant leaving predominantly white schools for significantly or majority black schools. For example, in 1990, students went from 96 percent white Highlandtown Elementary #237 to 29 percent black Southeast Middle, from 97 percent white Hampstead Hill Elementary to 34 percent black Canton Middle, and from 92 percent white Highlandtown #215 to 69 percent black Highlandtown Middle. The black presence at Highlandtown Middle stood out sharply against surrounding white neighborhoods. All four Southeast Baltimore middle schools were becoming blacker. If K–8s were neighborhood schools, whatever their educational merits, they would be racially more homogeneous.

Thus educational considerations, social and psychological arguments about community-school connections, and racial anxieties mixed in interests in K–8s. Bobby English, endorsing K–8s in her January 1997 draft plan recommendations, argued that they would avoid a painful transition to middle school, lower the dropout rate, and make schools safer. Ed Rutkowski convened a work group to look at ways of turning Southeast Baltimore schools into K–8s.

University planning faculty became involved in two research efforts. Rutkowski asked Alex Chen, who was helping him on a USDE-supported housing project, to map where students lived to see whether it was feasible to redraw school zones to create K–8s with existing building capacities. Chen began plotting student residences and experimenting with zone boundaries.

At the same time, I doubted the academic effects of grade reconfiguration alone. Most community arguments turned on the social benefits of students' attending small neighborhood schools for nine years, with the assumption that these arrangements would bring educational gains. I wanted to see academic data on middle-grade students in K–8s and middle schools. If evidence did not clearly favor K–8s, then it might be reasonable to try to improve middle schools. After all, converting elementary and middle schools into K–8s would be costly, to redesign facilities and to support and develop staff to implement a coherent K–8 concept. The money could be invested in middle schools. Even if K–8s were a good idea, there was no guarantee that the school system would implement it any better than it had the middle school idea earlier. I contacted education experts, and Kristen Forsyth, a graduate assistant, searched for published studies.

A Review of Research

The research was scant, and the findings were inconclusive. The research summary that Forsyth and I prepared for the Task Force began with difficulties of comparing K–8 and middle schools:

> Many K–8 schools (74%) are private schools, and some of those are religiously affiliated; many of the public K–8 schools are in rural areas. . . . On average, K–8 schools are smaller than middle schools, and the number of students in a grade is smaller in K–8 schools. . . . [Hence,] it is difficult to be certain whether any differences are simply the results of K–8 groupings. (Southeast Education Task Force 1997)

Available research found that grades and test scores were higher in K–8 schools than in middle schools. The difference was not associated with family income or school size. Since comparisons solely among public or private schools found little academic difference associated with grade configuration, the variation seemed due to distinctive characteristics of private and religious schools, such as their culture and families. Truancy, violence, and substance abuse were lower in K–8s. Their students felt more prepared for and interested in classroom work than middle school students. These differences, too, might result from K–8s' private or religious sponsorship, students enrolled, or smaller size.

The report noted that some desirable school characteristics, such as small size, were likely in most K–8 schools but that many, such as curriculum and teaching methods, were matters of choice. More important than grade configuration were the educational program, teacher-student relations, and school climate. Many issues in designing K–8s had not been systematically studied. The document ended with Eccles, Lord, and Midgely's conclusion from their research review:

> [T]he K–8 system has many advantages for early adolescents, but [t]o recommend a return to the K–8 system would shift focus away from the classroom environment and back on grade ranges and time of transition. . . . We recommend that serious efforts be made to improve, and expand, the nature of student-teacher relationships in schools that serve early adolescents regardless of the grades included in the schools. (1991, 539)

When Forsyth and I presented the report to the Task Force in late spring, people were appreciative, but Rutkowski asserted that Southeast Baltimore conditions were distinct, and that K–8s there would have noteworthy results that future research could document. Alex Chen was beginning to produce useful maps, and Rutkowski's K–8 committee would examine them at a July meeting.

Moving Ahead: Hurrying Up and Waiting

By plotting students of various ages on each block in Southeast Baltimore, eyeballing the results, and experimentally moving zone boundaries a few blocks at a time, keeping existing school capacities as a constraint, Chen managed to create potentially workable K–8 zones. Rutkowski considered the results most promising for zones associated with three of the four middle schools (Canton, Highlandtown, and Southeast), because all or most of their students came from the eleven Southeast Baltimore elementary schools. The committee talked about how K–8 schools' neighborhood connections and long-term relations between teachers and students would stabilize schools. Members strategized to build support for K–8s in the three middle school clusters.

Rutkowski conferred with Sandra Wighton, assistant superintendent for the Southeast area, which included the three clusters. Wighton liked K–8 schools. She believed that Highlandtown and Canton and their feeder elementaries were most feasible, but she worried that some principals would not support the idea. To make sure it was practical, she would ask BCPSS' planning department for its best estimates of building capacities, with attention to what K–8s required.

Rutkowski opened the K–8 committee's August meeting with an announcement of this study. He would get current enrollment data from the planning department and see if K–8s were still feasible. Rebecca McAndrew, interim BCPSS board executive, talked about the process of converting an elementary school into a K–8 school. Bobby English suggested waiting for the student and capacity data before embarking on a campaign. Meanwhile, the group would prepare a position statement.

The committee emphasized three largely social arguments for K–8s. The first concerned the benefits of neighborhood schools. Walking to school would be safer, parents could be more involved, and students would be less anonymous. Second, the reconfiguration of specific schools under consideration would reduce significant overcrowding at three schools. Finally, K–8 schools would improve schools' climate. The sixth-grade transition would be gone. Teachers would know students better and thus teach them better, older students could help the younger ones, and a longer time at the school would increase students' attachment to it. The committee recognized that redesigning buildings was costly. They concluded with questions for further study.

In January, Rutkowski reported that the planning department had not sent enrollment data, and Wighton's requested facilities evaluation was not taking place. He now thought that Canton Middle and its feeders were the best place to start K–8s. In February, he said that he had talked with some Canton zone principals and had heard encouraging responses. However, there was still no progress on student data or a facilities study. He made similar reports for several months. In May, he said that Wighton had told him that there would be no facilities study before the next school year. Nevertheless, he was trying to work out details among Canton principals.

Over the summer, Wighton moved on, to head the system's new Office of High School Improvement. She was succeeded by Patricia Abernethy, who, as later discussions would reveal, doubted that K–8s had academic advantages. The Task Force lost steam on K–8s.

Perhaps one reason the facilities study had been put on hold was that the school board was hiring 3D/International, consulting engineers, to assess all city schools. The firm and its subcontractors started in August, finished inspections the following February, and issued a report in late March 1998. However, this study, focused on buildings' physical conditions, shed no light on the feasibility of K–8 schooling, which concerned how buildings could be used.

The assessment's staggering price tag of $606 million to bring facilities up to standards caught everyone's attention and gave further weight to the new school board's interest in taking an overall look at the system. The next year it launched a comprehensive rezoning initiative. The city had been losing population, neighborhoods had risen and fallen, and buildings poorly fit enrollments. Schools would be closed, new ones would be built, and zones would be redrawn. This initiative touched on questions that the Task Force cared about.

Planning Southeast Baltimore School Facilities

In September 1999, Ken Strong received an invitation from the BCPSS Rezoning Task Force Curriculum Subcommittee to a meeting to review a draft report on standards for types and sizes of spaces that schools required, desirable class sizes, and school capacities. Dottie Fried attended, and the Task Force began to think about school facilities again.

While the 3D/International engineers wanted to know whether school buildings were physically sound, the Curriculum Subcommittee's educators and parents wanted to know whether the buildings had enough space of the right kinds for teaching and learning. The subcommittee proposed standards for different school levels, with attention to programs and buildings at schools that did well in the MSPAP. Although their initial "Facility Utilization Plan" did not include K–8s, a later version, noting school board interest in K–8s, identified standards for pre-K–8 schools and called attention to issues regarding whether a building was suitable for K–8 conversion.

Comprehensive rezoning offered Task Force members an audience and decision points for reformulating and promoting their interests. Everyone on the Task Force knew of schools with deficient, and even harmful, conditions. Those that lacked air conditioning, for example, were oppressive in late spring and summer and dangerous to asthmatic students. Three elementary schools were severely overcrowded. All were designed without classroom walls, but they were not the only Southeast Baltimore schools where the absence of walls created constant noise and distraction. Some schools lacked playground space, libraries, or both, and one did not have a cafeteria.

Task Force members recognized that teachers were more important than buildings in educating students, but they noted that certain building conditions, such as overcrowding and a lack of air conditioning, hindered teachers' and students' best efforts. Moreover, members could understand building conditions, and they were an issue on which schools and community could join forces.

I asked the BCPSS office of facilities planning and school construction for a copy of the 3D/International report and the system's facilities plan, with capital improvement priorities. I emphasized that the Task Force wanted to work with schools to get better facilities and wanted to proceed knowledgeably. After wary questioning about Task Force intentions and the passage of time, the system provided copies of the documents, which made it possible to identify structural deficiencies and repair costs.

With these documents and the draft space standards in hand, in January the Task Force began its own research, contacting Southeast Baltimore schools to see whether the engineers' report accurately described conditions and whether schools had the spaces identified as necessary for good programs. Volunteers reached eight of sixteen principals. Most were pleased to show deficient conditions to potential allies, though some referred the Task Force to the area office or central office, and one rebuffed the caller as an agitator. During early spring, an ad hoc facilities group analyzed the documents and principals' responses, drafted a summary, invited principals and area executive officers (AEOs) to discuss findings, and planned a report to the school board.

In May, the facilities group met to prepare for a June school board meeting. Bobby English noted that an AEO had urged the Task Force to take the case for facilities to the board. Laura Weeldreyer, now director of the BCPSS New Schools Initiative, a quasi-charter school program, noted that principals hesitated to lobby with the central administration. Elizabeth Turner, Tench Tilghman's principal, wanted to focus on immediate building needs. The group created committees on short-range needs and long-range plans. The first, under English's leadership, would prepare a statement for the board.

Short-Term Facility Repairs

The Task Force issued a report on the "Critical Need for Capital Improvements in Southeast Schools." Task Force members, it explained, were compelled to bring unacceptable conditions to public attention. Bold print proclaimed a series of "critical immediate need[s]" that

> directly impact learning: Overcrowding: Overcrowded situations negatively impact learning. . . . We claim the following needs to be of critical and immediate concern to the health needs of children: Heating, Ventilation, and Air Conditioning Systems: Unhealthy environments due to lack of air conditioning, poor air flow, and irregularities in central heating and air negatively impact both student learning and student health. . . . We claim the following needs to be of critical and immediate concern to the well-being of children: [one open classroom school needed walls, two schools needed playground space, and one school needed exterior light repairs for night use]. (Southeast Education Task Force 2000, 2–5, passim)

The report did not simply catalogue problems but suggested solutions. Thus the Task Force was not just one more complainant but a collaborative problem solver.

After English presented the report to the board, Turner illustrated it memorably. She explained how the failure of Tench Tilghman's air conditioning the previous week had raised the building's temperature to ninety-five degrees, unbearable for students starting the MSPAP that day. By coincidence, her AEO stopped by to see how testing was going, and he discovered the problem in sweaty detail. After many futile efforts to get the school's ancient air conditioning fixed, now he responded, and repairmen came. The next day, the school was a little cooler. School board members could understand this. They asked Colene Daniel, their member responsible for facilities, to meet with the Task Force and schools.

Daniel met in June with Task Force representatives; the parent organizers; Turner; teachers, parents, and community members from General Wolfe; Wolfe's AEO, Gary Thrift; and Pete Dixit, the system staff member responsible for maintenance. Daniel arranged for adjustment of Tench Tilghman's air conditioning and for repair of its outdoor lights. Most of the meeting, as well as one in July, was concerned with trying to get General Wolfe more space, described earlier. Though that effort failed, English, Dottie Fried, and Wolfe faculty and parents seemed to conclude that school officials had done what they could with limited state funds.

Long-Term Facilities Planning

While English focused on short-term repairs, Ed Rutkowski chaired a Long-Range Capital Improvements Committee, which would prepare a Southeast school facility plan. This was a context in which he could reintroduce K–8s. During the summer, his committee looked at different sections of Southeast Baltimore. They considered how boundaries could be redrawn to reduce overcrowding and to make K–8 schools feasible. They found an area north of Patterson Park with many children and no schools, where they concluded that a new school should be built.

The committee knew best the area around Patterson Park. They knew less about west of Broadway, where many lived in public housing, and east of Haven Street, which combined public housing tenants and immigrant families. They planned public forums in each section to let educators and residents respond to initial ideas and to suggest others. The first would be in Canton, south of Patterson Park, on September 18. Pastor Neil Carrick of the Chesapeake Good Shepherd Union Church, who wanted to start a new school, would host it.

Six days before the meeting, BCPSS issued recommendations from its facility utilization study. It proposed closing twelve city schools. It would build two pre-K–8s and a middle school, and it would reconfigure twenty-four schools into pre-K–8s, magnet middle and high schools, a zoned high school, early childhood centers, and 7–12 schools. No Southeast Baltimore school would be closed. In fact, the system expected rising enrollment in Southeast Baltimore and would build a new school. It would be a pre-K–8, intended to reduce enrollment at Tench Tilghman, Paca, Highlandtown #215, and Highlandtown Middle, which would be replaced by a new school of some kind. Other schools would continue as at present, with four exceptions. Highlandtown #237 was being renovated to accommodate a larger enrollment. Lombard Middle's zone would be redrawn to include more students. General Wolfe, because it was small, might be closed after the new school was built, and Southeast Middle School might be assigned new students or closed if enrollment fell significantly. Rutkowski's committee viewed these recommendations positively.

The first forum convened on the evening of September 18 to full pews at Good Shepherd Church. Among the 100 attendees were Carmen Russo, who had just become the system's CEO; Betty Morgan, the chief academic officer; Gary Thrift and Patricia Abernethy, AEOs for thirteen of the sixteen Southeast schools; and Laura Weeldreyer, whose New Schools Initiative had received proposals from Carrick and three other Southeast Baltimore groups. Two school board members, two city council members, five state legislators, two of the mayor's staff, three principals, five pastors, two foundation staff members, two community organization directors, and a couple of citywide education activists joined the meeting.

Bobby English explained that the Task Force believed in partnership between the community and schools. The forum would not dwell on problems but would move to solutions. Ed Rutkowski presented the draft plan. The Task Force proposed a new K–8 northeast of Patterson Park, with Highlandtown #237 converted into a K–8 during its renovation. The Task Force wanted to replace Highlandtown Middle with a smaller K–8 on the same site or elsewhere. He described an international school proposed under the New Schools Initiative. South and west of the park, the Task Force wanted to create three K–8s in the Canton zone and to develop a community plan for General Wolfe. Plans for the far west and east remained to be filled in.

The audience formed small groups to discuss specifics. Regarding K–8s, parents talked up the safety benefits for children going to school near home. A middle school teacher gave a positive review to a K–8 in a nearby neighborhood that, like Southeast Baltimore, was racially and economically mixed. Administrators called attention to details and possible trade-offs: for example, small K–8s offered intimacy but had fewer resources for middle-grade students than large middle schools. Parents and teachers from overcrowded schools north and east of the park emphasized the need for a new school and rezoning to make schools manageable.

Some black parents worried that the international school would just be a new way of getting the best resources for whites; the school's advocates emphasized that they would balance immigrants and other residents. Parents from west of Broadway, many in public housing, opposed the system's rezoning proposal for Lombard Middle: the boundaries would keep the school nearly all black. They favored increasing enrollment, but they wanted students from Commodore Rodgers and General Wolfe, which had whites and Hispanics. Parents and teachers at the overcrowded schools who wanted rezoning insisted that new boundaries maintain the neighborhoods' racial mix.

At last CEO Russo spoke. She had been on the job only ten weeks, she said, but she knew about facilities and Southeast Baltimore. She had opened international schools. The issues were familiar. She called the forum a model for other communities and then asked for help in lobbying the state for money for city schools. The Task Force looked ahead to the other forums.

Interlude: Rethinking K–8 Schools

Parents at the forum had little question about K–8s but had not thought about specifics. Advocates seemed interested more in children's safety and, perhaps, the racial homogeneity of small K–8 schools than in specific educational benefits. Yet any educational or social advantages of K–8 schooling depended on the details. I decided once more to canvass experts.

Research was still scarce. Academics and practitioners could recite plausible arguments on each side, but no one had much evidence. I asked BCPSS Chief Academic Officer Elizabeth Morgan for the research on which the system based its support for K–8 schools.

Whatever the merits of K–8s, implementation also was a question. Good arguments supported K–8 schooling, and research might confirm them. Even so, there had been good arguments for middle schools. The history of Baltimore middle schools, which educators and parents alike found disappointing, did not show the arguments to be faulty but rather revealed a failure to implement the model as designed. These problems raised questions about whether K–8 schools, either, could be set up as planned. Whatever had made it hard to establish effective middle schools also could scuttle K–8s. Implementation of either required that the system select a strong principal, support that leader in recruiting and developing a faculty committed to the school's educational philosophy and skilled in implementing it, permit the faculty to structure student activities consistent with the philosophy, and provide the school with continuing support, from professional development for teachers to resources for students.

I raised these issues with one of the system's strongest K–8 advocates. He did not know of a lot of research. Middle-class K–8s did better than middle schools on the MSPAP. As some of these neighborhoods declined economically, the schools still seemed to do better, though the record was ambiguous. Middle-grade attendance was higher at K–8s than at middle schools. Parent involvement was higher. He did not think that the middle schools could be fixed. He was confident that the system would appropriately support K–8s. I asked for any research that he had.

A few days later, I received identical packets from Morgan and him. In fact, the familiar documents were the 1997 Task Force materials on K–8 schools, which I had faxed to Laura Weeldreyer in April 2000, when she was starting up with the BCPSS Middle School Task Force. Those ambiguous research summaries were all the system referred to, besides administrators' impressions of local middle-grade trends.

Graduate student Elin Zurbrigg helped prepare a "K–8 Fact Sheet," incorporating new evidence. Some studies favorably compared K–8s to middle schools; the summary identified elements of good K–8 schools that seemed to make them effective. Some, such as years of continuous contact among teachers, students, and families, were distinctive to K–8s. Others, such as small size, student advisories, and team planning, were possible in any configuration. When we reported to the Task Force in October, we suggested that if people wanted K–8 schools, then they should focus on the details that made them good. Discussion generally accepted this view.

Continuing Facilities Planning

In November, the Task Force convened a second forum, at New Harvest Ministries Church, north of Patterson Park. Because the Canton forum was the first, people came from many neighborhoods, and participants were racially diverse. In contrast, this meeting, focused on north and east of the park, drew mainly from the nearby African-American population. Attendance was smaller, about fifty. The school system was represented by board member Camay Murphy. Yale Stenzler, executive director of the Maryland Public School Construction Program and staff to the Inter-Agency Committee on School Construction, attended for the state.

After Ed Rutkowski presented the plan in progress, discussion focused on K–8s. Bobby English passed out the "K–8 Fact Sheet." The K–8 schools, she said, were family oriented, and teachers knew children. As a result, absenteeism was lower, and fewer students dropped out. These schools had little transition "jolt" between the fifth and sixth grades. Students could maintain self-esteem. As a result, they behaved better, and test scores improved. Moreover, parent involvement continued into middle grades. Some of this was not unique to K–8 schools, she noted, and K–8s worked best when they incorporated the elements of all good schools.

A mother commented that schools were too crowded to become K–8s. That was why the area needed a new school, English explained. Stenzler observed that few K–8 buildings in the city were designed for K–8 curriculum. That kind of detail mattered for K–8 to work. Irona Pope, the City Springs parent liaison, talked about K–8 school zones. Zone boundaries often were racial ones, and racial boundaries were boundaries in school quality. She wanted details about which students would be included in a K–8 school. A mother worried whether putting older and younger children together would create problems for the young ones. As for parent involvement, her children went to a school where staff were hostile to parents. Could parents choose the school administration? Another mother complained that her child's principal was crooked. And the mother who had spoken just before her jumped back in: K–8 or any other school, "Show me it's a good school." She had considered Catholic school for her children, because the public school was so bad.

And, a grandmother said, if you improved a school, you just attracted more students, and you got overcrowding all over again. And what would be done with students who disrupted schools and made learning impossible? A parent liaison who had seen many changes of school administration and policy challenged the proposal to turn Southeast schools into K–8s. Just building two new schools would not solve all of the problems. There were the problems of curriculum, administrators, and budget. Parent involvement would still be a problem. Before going along with any of this, she wanted details. She would not vote for K–8s, because the Task Force did not have community or parent input into these proposals. English said that the meeting was part of a process to find out what community members wanted; the Task Force had no agenda to push.

After this discussion, Camay Murphy spoke for the school system, repeating much that Russo had said earlier. The school board was interested in Southeast Baltimore and wanted to build new schools to relieve overcrowding, but State money was needed. The board had sent Stenzler a proposal for a new Southeast Baltimore school and was awaiting a response. Stenzler acknowledged the proposal and emphasized that enrollment projections would have to support it.

Two weeks later, Rutkowski brought draft "Recommendations of the Long-Range Capital Improvements Planning Committee" to the Task Force. The document described areas around Patterson Park in detail and presented clear proposals for them. The areas on the far west and east remained sketchy. With anticipation of meetings in those areas, Task Force members were satisfied with the draft. Over the next two months, English organized meetings in the west and east. Though they filled in details, they did not substantially alter the plan.

On February 16, Bobby English, Ed Rutkowski, and I presented the plan to CEO Carmen Russo and Southeast AEO Patricia Abernethy. Russo noted that the system's plan included a new Southeast Baltimore school, which it proposed making a K–8 with a math-science-technology emphasis, and was trying to get Stenzler's approval to move ahead. Stenzler was waiting for the system to specify a site. English turned to K–8 schools. She acknowledged that research was inconclusive but underlined the virtues associated with good K–8s, such as small size, community ties, and consistent relations between teachers and students. Abernethy responded that research did not favor K–8s over middle schools. Still, Russo said, she took community preferences seriously. Even so, she noted that redesigning elementary school buildings for middle-grade use was costly. After a wide-ranging discussion, Russo concluded with a request for help in securing a site for the new school, and Rutkowski and English pledged to find one.

The school system identified a site and informed Stenzler. Stenzler responded with more fundamental concerns—whether enrollment projections justified a new K–8 school at all. New State Rated Capacity (SRC) figures were higher than previous numbers from the State Inter-Agency Committee on School Construction.

Russo, convinced the SRC figures had little relation to actual conditions in overcrowded schools, particularly those with few classroom walls, invited Stenzler to join her in visiting three Southeast Baltimore schools to see how space really was used. School board member Kenneth Jones and Jeffery Grotsky, AEO for some Southeast schools, joined a tour of Tench Tilghman, William Paca, and Highlandtown #215 Elementary Schools in April. Afterward, Stenzler concluded that the usual method of determining capacity could not be used for schools like these, and he proposed working with BCPSS to develop a comprehensive plan for six existing schools and the possible new school. If a new school seemed justified, his office would help choose a site.

Rutkowski and English tried to advance the cause of the new school on two fronts. In June, they invited Stenzler to meet with them and members of the state legislative delegation, whose presence added political weight to the community's educational preferences. Rutkowski and English bolstered their case technically by assembling data on population changes and enrollment trends. They discussed the influx of Eastern European, African, and Latin American immigrants, attracted by a new resettlement center. They noted home ownership initiatives.

Over the next year, discussion went back and forth between BCPSS and Stenzler's office. The state wanted to be sure that projected long-term enrollments justified a new building, and Task Force members worked with the school system to make the case. If a new school were justified, then Stenzler favored rehabilitating an existing building, at half the cost of new construction. Some unused Catholic schools were suggested, but none had a suitable location. The question of the site for a new facility resurfaced, as several possibilities met objections. The Task Force interested the school system in building on part of Ellwood Park and organized support from the area's state legislators and city councilmen, who persuaded Mayor Martin O'Malley to endorse the location and the BCPSS proposal to the state. Again, the state was uneasy about enrollment projections. Finally, in May 2002, the state approved construction of a K–8 in Southeast Baltimore. However, soon after, the city found that the park had been built with federal money, and, therefore, land taken for a school would have to be replaced by the city elsewhere. While weighing these costs, the school system has been looking for alternative sites that would offer sufficient land for a pre-K–8 school in a location that would permit construction affordable with an austere budget and that would draw students from overcrowded Southeast schools.

CONCLUSIONS: RESEARCH, ACTION, DEVELOPMENT, AND NETWORKS

Task Force Use of Research

Planning

Research can assist with three tasks in "planning backwards." First, it can help set goals by studying community values and preferences and identifying realistic conditions that fit them. Second, it can help choose strategies by examining past experiences. For example, if teaching children to read is a goal, research can assess curricular strategies. Finally, in a similar way, research can help assemble tactics for strategies—identifying what teachers, students, parents, and administrators must do, with what support, to implement a curriculum.

In setting goals, Task Force members used research differently in the two cases here. With K–8s, the Task Force did not use research. K–8 proponents invoked various goals, more social than educational, in support of the schools that they wanted. The main effect of the research summaries was to add language to some of the arguments for K–8 schools without changing the goals in terms of which people advocated for them.

In the facilities case, Task Force members used research in setting goals. They started by adopting the engineering consultants' facility condition standards and the rezoning subcommittee's space standards as goals. They accepted the standards because experts set them, and because they seemed reasonable. At the same time, they interviewed principals to ascertain whether their experience led them to different standards. This research led to modifying some of the original goals, and the new set influenced strategic recommendations. Two factors contributed to using research to set goals in this case but not the other. One is that Task Force members believed that they could understand space requirements and building standards, in contrast to school organization and teaching, and hence they considered research useful. The other is that K–8 schools had such strong symbolic importance to many Task Force members as their primary remedy for what ailed schools that they resisted examining premises.

The Task Force made consistently different use of research for selecting strategies. The K–8 advocates put weight on social goals for schools—they should be small, should keep the same children together for a long time, and should be close to home—and K–8 schools inherently satisfied those requirements. Common sense suggested that students would be safe, parents would be involved, teachers and students would get to know one another—and students would do well. In any case, those who liked K–8 schools valued the social goals so much that research on the fit between K–8s and educational goals could not challenge this preference. At the least, sketchy data left room for assuming academic results for a program chosen first for satisfying social goals.

With facilities, in contrast, Task Force members knew about some problems but had no definite agenda. They conducted research to answer three questions: How many students would Southeast Baltimore schools need to accommodate? What was the current school capacity? And what actions would create needed capacity? To estimate future enrollment, they looked at current enrollment, Alex Chen's maps, and state enrollment projections. In addition, they considered trends affecting enrollment, such as home ownership initiatives and immigration. For context, they relied on their own knowledge of neighborhoods.

Task Force researchers began with state figures for school capacities. However, they found some recent revisions unrealistically high. Further, they considered space needs not included in state calculations—uses identified in the curriculum subcommittee's standards, as well as room for parent and community activities. Finally, they interviewed principals and toured schools to refine their calculations. This research led them to estimates of the match between enrollment and usable space.

In researching strategies for increasing space, the Task Force talked with principals and school officials about structural possibilities and costs of altering or adding space at existing schools. Finding limited opportunities and recognizing a large area that had a growing number of children and no school, they considered new construction. They talked with school officials to test their interest in renovations and a new school. They conducted public forums to get responses to emerging ideas and to generate other proposals. Facility recommendations reflected research on engineering possibilities, costs, school board priorities, and community preferences.

In both cases, the most specific tactical details were locational—where to draw zones to make K–8 reconfiguration feasible, and where to locate a new school—and Task Force members made careful use of the research. They studied Chen's maps. They tried, unsuccessfully, to obtain updated maps from the school system. Particularly with the new site, they used their knowledge of population changes, street traffic and safety, and property availability and ownership.

Influencing the School System

Did Task Force research influence the school system? In the fall of 2001, the CEO proposed creating seventeen new K–8s, on the ground that research supported them: eighth grade test scores were generally higher at K–8s than at middle schools. None of the seventeen was in Southeast Baltimore. Task Force research did not obviously affect this proposal.

Research had clearer influence in facilities planning, including the BCPSS proposal to make the new Southeast Baltimore school a K–8, for four reasons. First, the Task Force worked within the system's comprehensive rezoning plan. Second, especially with short-term repairs, it identified practical remedies for recognizable problems. Third, Task Force members knew about the local details that could make or break a system initiative. They could tell officials how to fit zones to community boundaries or which sites were available and would work physically and socially. Fourth, the Task Force organized elected officials who could get school officials' attention to consider proposals.

Research and Community Organizations

Task Force history suggests that a community organization is likely to conduct or use research when four conditions are present. First, organizations must have leaders who are interested in research, who care about the action implications of knowledge. Many Task Force members had college educations, and some had research experience. They might not have time for conducting studies, but they could understand and would use research on issues that concerned them.

Second, organizations must have the capacity to conduct research. Though volunteers can collect information about local conditions, they have limited time and cannot engage in ongoing or systematic reconnaissance. Moreover, few residents, particularly in low-income communities, have the training for collecting and interpreting published research. Organizations need staff for research. The Task Force benefitted from university participation, which made possible reflective practice, action research, and formal research.

Third, beyond these preconditions an issue must be researchable. Participants must believe that additional information would be useful in deciding what to do, and that it is possible to get that information. They must feel confident that they have relevant expertise. The K–8 and facilities issues satisfied these conditions for Task Force members.

Finally, an organization is more likely to engage in research when others on whom it depends will base their action on knowledge. They constitute an external client or constituency for research. The school board commissioned a facility assessment and launched a comprehensive rezoning initiative to obtain information about schools and students before making decisions about closing, building, or reorganizing schools. The Task Force could best influence the system by collecting information that framed Southeast Baltimore positions in terms of those studies.

Building Networks on the Exchange of Knowledge

The cases show how turbulent environments require organizations to collaborate in defining and addressing problems that none can manage alone. System officials and the Task Force both believed that schools' current location and organization did not fit students' needs. They had different, complementary knowledge of the education field. System administrators knew most about the central office, less about schools and classrooms, and least about families and communities. The Task Force knew most about community life, less about school and classroom activity, and least about the school board and management. Together they could make sophisticated proposals for Southeast Baltimore schools.

However, while the Task Force was trying to involve the school system in a network for Southeast education, school officials did not see the Task Force as a partner. Board and staff considered it one of many interest groups with which they had to contend. The administration responded warily, slowly, and incompletely to Task Force requests for policy, budget, student, and building information that would enable the community group to join schools in developing realistic proposals. Lengthy staff interrogation about Task Force intentions suggested that the reason was not lack of time as much as resistance to sharing information with the public. Nevertheless, board and staff asked the Task Force for information that they wanted.

The Task Force and school system could have worked more closely in planning Southeast Baltimore facilities. They could have built on these efforts to consult and collaborate regularly. However, this development was unlikely, because the system lacked resources for staff to make and sustain connections, and because school culture disparaged community experience and knowledge.

Part 6

Money

Chapter 13

Money Matters
The Costs of Participation, Research, and Action

Much of what the Task Force did would have been impossible without money. Community members must lead an organization, but they lack the skills, time, and resources to maintain one and to take extended action on their own. They must persuade others to give them money for these purposes. We look here at money in the life of the Task Force: what it needed money for, what money was available for, and how the availability of money affected its work.

GETTING STARTED: RESEARCHING THE FIELD

The Southeast Education Task Force was an unusual idea. Few community organizations were active in education, and fewer still took education as their sole domain. The public character of American education means that a professional bureaucracy has a virtual monopoly on schooling and that little education funding is available to nongovernmental organizations.

The Task Force did not start, however, as an idea in search of funding. It began opportunistically: the U. S. Department of Education was giving universities grants for partnerships with community organizations, and the University of Maryland included the Southeast Planning Council's "study-action group for schools" in a five-project proposal. Federal funders provided $200,000 over four years for creating an organization, conducting research to produce a plan, and implementing the plan.

The Task Force consisted of community volunteers, with Bobby English taking leadership. She put in the most time—sometimes two days a week. She offered the Julie Community Center, which she directed, as the Task Force office and meeting place. Besides acting as what could be considered the board chair, English carried out many staff activities, contributing Julie Center supplies and materials to the work. Later on, others, such as Ken Strong at SECO and Ed Rutkowski at the Patterson Park Community Development Corporation, would do similarly. However, the federal grant funded the main initial staffing. A graduate student worked twenty hours a week, and I averaged nearly two days a week. From time to time, the Urban Studies and Planning Program contributed a second graduate student, as a match for the grant, for ten or twenty hours a week.

The grant assumed that because many parents already were active in education, little organizing was necessary, and research and planning would dominate the first year. Activists would lead, and the university would assist by researching questions and formulating issues. In fact, much of the core group's activity the first year was research, and it was labor intensive. Members engaged in self-education, meeting frequently to identify and understand issues, to think about priorities, and to design a process for taking action. English managed the 160 school interviews, which produced a wealth of narrative material. Analysis of published school and student data was exceptionally straightforward.

However, there were few education activists, and the university contingent tried to cultivate participants, in addition to meeting potential allies or resources. Its time also went into normal staffing responsibilities—arranging meetings, preparing documents, recording minutes, developing databases, circulating materials, and debriefing. Establishing an organization, nurturing commitments to it and to an agenda, and identifying resources competed with research for attention and time.

The fruits of the first year's efforts, in finding volunteers for work groups, which also needed staffing, compounded tensions between organizing and research. Much of the time for research went into analyzing data that the system started to provide. After organizational maintenance, little time was left for organizing or extending the Task Force network. The Task Force needed additional staff for two purposes: to recruit participants, particularly parents, and to extend research to in-depth study of neighborhood schools and substantive examination of educational programs and policy issues. We look first at efforts to increase participation.

Organizing Participants

The CPHA grants for parent organizing in mid-1996 enabled the Task Force to extend its network toward parents and toward schools. SECO's addition of an organizer, first through the grant turned over by CPHA and later with a grant of its own, increased network building. By the following fall, however, two considerations led the Task Force to consider getting its own funding for organizing. First, it wanted to increase parent organizing and direct it more closely than the CPHA arrangement allowed. Second, the university grant would end in little over a year, and the Task Force would need staff who could do more than organizing.

Although four funders, including the national Edward Hazen Foundation, had supported the CPHA and SECO organizers, the Baltimore foundation scene was sparse. Historically, Baltimore, unlike, for example, New York and Chicago, had few corporate headquarters; it housed regional offices. Thus the 1996 directory of the Association of Baltimore Area Grantmakers (Association of Baltimore Area Grantmakers 1996) listed only fifty-eight funders, a mix of foundations and local corporations. Many were small. Of the thirty-four listing total assets, the national Annie E. Casey Foundation and the local Harry and Jeanette Weinberg Foundation stood out at over $1 billion, and three others registered between $100 million and $200 million. Twenty-four were under $25 million, and half of those were under $5 million. Although several listed education as an interest, only about a half dozen had given nonprofit organizations money for education activities.

Fortuitously, a large local foundation was developing philanthropic interests in the city's east side. The France-Merrick Foundation was formed from two foundations whose founders had close Johns Hopkins University ties. In the mid- to late-1990s, the foundation began looking for a comprehensive way to support community development as an alternative to categorical program funding. Its Hopkins relationship and the institutional strength of the Johns Hopkins Medical Institutions in East Baltimore moved it to consider investing in East and Southeast Baltimore communities.

In 1997, France-Merrick assigned a program officer, Jack Bovaird, to think about funding strategies in the Hopkins area. He became ubiquitous, showing up at meetings, asking questions, developing contacts, and trying to figure out how the Foundation could improve neighborhoods. I talked with him about the Task Force and took him to schools. France-Merrick seemed like a possible funder for staff needs. Bovaird was interested in schools as part of community development, but the foundation held a vivid memory of a disappointing education project that it had funded in a Southeast Baltimore school, among several sites. Arguably, that failure reflected the reformers' cookie-cutter approach rather than a problem with the school, but the foundation board was cautious about getting involved with public schools again. It pondered how to use its resources effectively in relation to the great, expensive challenges of school reform. Bovaird wanted to be persuaded that the Task Force could make a difference.

One of his early, continuing contacts was Ed Rutkowski, who, with Marcus Pollock, had written *The Urban Transition Zone: A Place Worth a Fight* (1998). Their thoughtful analysis of economic and racial transition in their neighborhood and recommendations for stabilizing it appealed to funders, city officials, and others looking for a handle on dissolution in the city. Bovaird not only enthusiastically read Rutkowski's report but came to share office space with him. Because Rutkowski was a Task Force member, his analysis, which described the necessity of restoring schools, added authority to Task Force efforts to work with seven schools in what he called the "Patterson Park Urban Transition Zone."

In February 1998, after several meetings with Bovaird, the Task Force sent him a letter, asking about foundation interest in activities for which it sought funding. The document described what the Task Force considered necessary for organizing, research, and action: two parent organizers, a church partnership developer, a business partnership developer, a coordinator for the organization, a part-time planner from the university, and a graduate assistant, for a two-year total of $460,000. Bovaird asked for a detailed proposal.

The resulting document was even more ambitious—and expensive. In March, the Task Force submitted a proposal in partnership with SECO (which would be fiscal agent) and the Patterson Park CDC for $642,000 over two years. The text presented the activities as a second stage of school improvement efforts, following the Task Force's first three years. It reported that $780,000 had been spent during the first stage, including the federal grant, university contributions, parent organizer grants, Sisters of Notre Dame AmeriCorps tutors whom Bobby English placed at two schools, salary of the Empowerment Zone school coordinator that the State Department of Education paid for after the Ad Hoc Group's work, and volunteer time.

After discussion at the foundation, Bovaird asked for additional commitments and information. He wanted the Task Force to coordinate with the Patterson Park CDC. He wanted the schools to agree that they would take part in proposed activities. He wanted more detail about activities' outcomes. Finally, he wanted to know how the Task Force would sustain activities that needed to be continued after the two-year grant; the foundation did not accept new requests from grantees for two years after a grant ended.

A revised proposal in May responded to these questions. Still requesting $642,000, it now identified matching funds of $476,000, including CPHA and SECO parent organizing grants and contributions of time, facilities, equipment, and the like from schools, church partners, business partners, the university, and individuals. Bovaird asked for a more modest, more realistic proposal. In June, the Task Force halved the request and focused on two parent organizers, a church and business partnership developer, and the researcher and planner, plus a four-hour weekly supervisor and coordinator. The new two-year budget was $333,000.

Time moved along. This was the Task Force's first fund-raising effort. France-Merrick seemed interested, but the Task Force had nothing else to fall back on. Bovaird seemed sympathetic and was encouraging, but he had reasonable questions about whether parent organizers and a partnership developer could affect children's learning. His board was still uncertain about how to get involved with schools and doubted that organizing was a useful strategy. Around this time the Task Force sent a small proposal to the Hazen Foundation for part of a parent organizer's salary, but that alone would not support the Task Force as an organization.

In July, Robert Schaefer, France-Merrick's executive director, reflecting conversations with his board, raised six issues. Two were concerns about outcomes and sustainability. A third was an interest in seeing other foundations in the project. Fourth, France-Merrick wanted assurance that the seven principals were strong leaders, that parent organizers could work productively with them. Finally, the foundation had two questions about Task Force structure.

One involved internal structure: how would the Task Force, an informal coalition, coordinate things? Who would manage and supervise staff? These were realistic questions. The Task Force framed its responses in terms of a second question, about external structure: why did this proposal not simply come from SECO? Hazen had raised that question about the proposal sent there and said that it would not accept the proposal unless it were transferred to SECO, which the Task Force agreed to do. The Task Force told France-Merrick that it would make this change if the foundation insisted, but it preferred a grant to the Task Force because these were Task Force projects. As for oversight, Task Force members, though informally organized, could guide an education project more closely than SECO, where education was a peripheral interest, and SECO would manage the parent organizers as part of its organizing staff.

When the board grant review committee met in mid-September, it still had questions. It wanted to know more about what results it could expect, who would run the project on a daily basis, and how it would be funded afterward. It would make a decision on October 1. In response, the Task Force identified organizational results (parent organizations and school partnerships), educational results (improvements in attendance, safety, academic achievement, and overcrowding), and community results (neighborhood stability). With regard to day-to-day management, the two organizers and partnership developer would work at SECO with its current parent organizer. One would be lead organizer and supervisor for all. Bobby English would consult to them as needed. Policy and strategic direction would be given by a steering committee composed of Task Force and SECO board members and schools' designees. After the grant ended, parent organizations, aided by church and business partners, would support themselves.

Bovaird called after the board met to say that it wanted more information and had postponed a decision until the end of the year. The request was too big. I said that our priorities were two parent organizers, a partnership developer, and a researcher-planner from the university. And the board still doubted that they could influence the schools. Was there someone in the school system who knew Southeast Baltimore and could reassure the board about the project? I would find a school official to talk with the board.

Three weeks later, Bovaird said that the board had met with Sandra Wighton, the former Southeast area assistant superintendent, and that she had spoken supportively. Bovaird would urge Schaefer to talk with the system's CEO. Now Strong wrote to Schaefer, detailing new developments and revisiting old arguments. First, the Hazen Foundation had given SECO $30,000 for a parent organizer to work with organizers in the France-Merrick proposal, as well as SECO's current parent organizer. Second, a community assembly had endorsed the *Southeast Community Plan on Education;* Strong enclosed a *Baltimore Sun* article. Third, he reminded the foundation of past Task Force accomplishments in parent organizing, most conspicuously getting the William Paca addition. Finally, he reiterated the importance of school improvement to SECO's board.

On January 11, Bovaird called to report that the board had given $80,000 a year for two years. The Task Force should select the projects to fund. English and Strong decided to use the combined grants to hire two parent organizers and to keep me as consultant for two years. At the last hour, the Task Force had been sustained; indeed, it would expand. Endorsement by two significant foundations was affirming. In addition, funders had pushed the Task Force to think about crucial organizational questions. However, though it devised governance and managerial arrangements, scarce time and attention, which additional funding might have remedied, limited their implementation.

Moving into Action

While the Task Force sought France-Merrick and Hazen funding, it began developing a proposal for a full-service school. The Task Force approached a large local foundation to fund planning and development of full-service community schools at Tench Tilghman and Highlandtown #237. The foundation made many education grants; however, after encouraging a proposal, it turned down the project. It had big continuing commitments and strong competition for new funding. In addition, a staff member suggested, the board was reluctant to invest in a planning and development process two steps removed from influence on student achievement. Subsequent contacts with national groups supporting full-service community schools and national foundations indicated, consistently, that funders were much more likely to pay for specific programs than a planning process to determine what programs were needed, or to organize service providers to develop those programs.

Hence, Bobby English urged incremental development of programs toward a full-service school at Tench Tilghman after Highlandtown #237 changed principals. Service program proposals were easy for foundations to understand, and these Task Force funding efforts proceeded straightforwardly. In July 1999, the Task Force sent a proposal for GED programs at Tench Tilghman and Highlandtown #237 to the Lockhart-Vaughan Foundation. The Julie Center would be fiscal agent, would hire staff, and would take responsibility for the programs. The relationship between the Task Force, the Julie Center, and the schools might be unusual, but a grant for a GED program was clear cut. In the fall, Lockhart-Vaughan approved three years' funding.

English used Julie Center resources to add services at Tench Tilghman, as described earlier. Starting in 1998, she sent over a health promoter, located nurse training there, got Notre Dame AmeriCorps volunteers for the school, and initiated adult education. She secured a grant for Agnes Rose McNally to coordinate a new Family and Community Resource Center. Around this time, an Abell Foundation program officer encouraged English to develop a program to engage parents in their children's education. Abell funded her proposal for Parents Promoting Success at Tench Tilghman and City Springs starting in January 2000.

That spring, the Task Force began looking for continuing funding for the full-service community school and other projects and approached the Erickson Foundation. Its board was openly skeptical about school system management and liked "outside" strategies for innovation. The full-service community school appealed to interests in involving communities with schools, and Erickson made a grant to support the Resource Center's coordinator.

Engaging in Research

The Task Force carried out significant research in later years without much earmarked research money. Volunteers conducted research, including two interview surveys, a tutoring need assessment, school facility site visits, and the learning from action that produced, among other things, the *Southeast Community Plan on Education*. Ed Rutkowski, at the Patterson Park Neighborhoods Initiative and, later, the Patterson Park CDC, consistently engaged in neighborhood study, including research on K–8 feasibility, analysis of facility conditions, and preparation of a long-range Southeast Baltimore school facilities plan and implementation strategies.

Most of the rest of Task Force research was supported by the changing university-community partnership. The original USDE grant funded faculty and student assistance for four years. When that ended in 1999, similar relations continued under various arrangements. The Task Force paid me for two years as a consultant, the only time that a grant to the Task Force paid for research and planning. During this time, the Planning Program gave me a graduate assistant, whom I committed to the Task Force. When the grant ran out, coincidentally, I received a one-year professorship that supported continuing the work and provided a graduate assistant. The next year, I stayed on as a volunteer, and the university funded the graduate student.

Faculty and students conducted a number of formal research projects, including analysis of student data, an examination of attendance-promotion programs, research reviews on K–8 schooling, mapping to assess K–8 possibilities, a feasibility study for a community fund for schools, and an analysis of the school capital budgeting process.

The feasibility study for community funding was the only research project specifically funded, by the Abell Foundation. Other efforts to support research and planning fell short. When the school system considered building a new school and demolishing and replacing another, the Task Force wanted someone to work with parents and school staff to help them participate in planning and developing new facilities and programs. This person would conduct research on school needs and model facilities and programs to help Southeast stakeholders put their preferences into workable plans for system action. This was an extraordinary opportunity to affect Southeast Baltimore education. One foundation, while seriously interested in community revitalization on the east side, was skeptical about investing in schools. Another, despite public praise for the Task Force, preferred citywide, systemic initiatives over neighborhood projects.

Community Action in Education and Funders

Community organizations interested in education do not find ready funding matches. Few local foundations have sufficient confidence in the school system to put money into education. Although a community organization proposing to aid and change schools from the outside presents the virtue of independence from the system, still it is concerned with education, a seeming morass where tremendous effort is necessary to accomplish even the tiniest result. Some large national foundations, in contrast, are investing in education, but in their interest in getting leverage for their money they are unlikely to support community organizations. They concentrate resources in a few locations, invest heavily in school systems in which they have confidence, and focus on what goes on inside classrooms. A neighborhood organization, if not invisible, is, at least, unimportant in this strategy. As for government funding, virtually all public money for education goes to school systems.

Thus simply locating interested funders takes a lot of time. Even if a community organization finds one interested in its agenda, many local foundations' small size means that a grant may fund a project for only a year or, alternatively, part of it for a couple of years. Organizations must piece together multiple grants to support initiatives of any size. Most projects entail four types of activity—organizing participation, conducting research and planning, implementing action, and managing and maintaining the organization. However, most funders want to invest only in action; they regard organizing, research, planning, and managing as inefficient, unimportant, or, at least, someone else's fiscal burden.

Funders rationalize their biases in terms of an emphasis on outcomes. Although this focus is reasonable, most conceptualize outcomes in two ways that work against organizing, research, planning, and particularly against education projects. First, they want outcomes that can be measured quantitatively. In this perspective, development of a parent organization, research on promising programs, or formulation of a community plan is hard to see. Second, funders think of outcomes in terms of the end of the "production line"—in education, student learning—rather than anything along the way—such as parent involvement in the PTA, church partnerships with schools, or community participation in planning a new school. In education, these biases converge in a one-dimensional emphasis on raising test scores. Community organizations should know why they want to involve parents or create partnerships, but the dual difficulties of measuring these activities and linking them to academic results preclude them from many funders' consideration.

Even when funders take a sophisticated view of educational processes, even when they support community action in education, community organizations have difficulty sustaining projects long enough to have a significant impact. Funders want to get as much action as possible from their assets. Hence, many prefer to keep moving on to new projects rather than continue supporting old ones, regardless of their success. Some like to stay with grantees in whom they have confidence but want to support new "innovative" projects rather than extend past programs. Some funders do not accept new proposals from grantees for a period after a grant has ended. In short, few foundations have anything like the "brand loyalty" by which consumers continue to buy the automobile that has performed well for them. Funders rarely purchase the same automobile twice. They expect automobiles continually to find new purchasers. They keep looking for new models to buy and then commend to others. Funders like to consider their grants seed money, which will start up significant programs that will then succeed without further support. Some foundations eschew long-term funding because it might seem to make them responsible for running programs or sustaining organizations. Routinely, grant applications ask how a project will be continued at the end of funding. Whatever applicants write, they often try their luck with other funders, or they simply let projects lapse.

Many funders, from small local foundations to large federal agencies, lack staff time and expertise to visit or even talk with applicants to discuss their plans, to examine their organization, and to consider thoughtfully how, if at all, the funder could best assist the organization (perhaps besides giving money). Funders rely on cues, such as a past relationship with an applicant (those who performed well in the past probably will reflect well on the funder in the future); an applicant's reputation (a well-regarded, even if an unfamiliar, organization should do well and look good); the conventionality of a proposal (a "normal" project may not be innovative but will be a credible investment); and narrow conformity to funding specifications. Unconventional activities, such as community action in education, face a handicap.

Some funders, especially large national foundations, are not interested in addressing local problems in a specific place as much as creating national models that might enable locals in many places to solve their problems. This expectation assumes that such models can be developed at a low enough level of abstraction to be useful. In any case, this orientation tends to rule out community organizations, for two reasons. First, few of them, struggling to stay in existence, sustain programs, and maintain communities, have interest in problems outside of their immediate neighborhoods. Second, even if they did, they lack the time to examine related conditions elsewhere and to design interventions that, while dealing with local problems, would test general theories about intervention and problems in far-flung cities.

A number of funders, more likely national than local, are interested in "systemic change": rather than continue to treat symptomatic problems, they want to alter structural conditions that cause them. This expectation also works against community organizations. First, they are too small to wield much leverage. Second, they lack the resources to be concerned with changing institutions—for example, to develop a realistic strategy for changing a school system. In addition, funders tend to think of "systems" in terms of formal institutions. Thus "systemic change" in education typically means changing the local school system. That is important, but a broader view of the system in terms of all of the actors and institutions that influence children's education would include parents and community members, as well as labor markets, housing markets, race relations, and political culture. No funder can hope to change much of this system at once. However, talk of "systemic change" is frequently too narrow, excluding influences outside of formal institutions, and too abstract, overlooking the specific events in children's lives that affect their learning, to recognize roles for community organizations in changing systems.

FUNDERS AND THE LOGIC OF ACTION

Community action, which builds on participation and research, depends on significant, consistent, long-term funding. However, funders' priorities, culture, and size all reinforce a logic of action that displaces both participation and research.

Most funders can make only small grants. Few give multiyear grants or, in any case, continue funding projects beyond a single grant. Hence, community organizations must put considerable effort into raising money, taking time and intelligence from organizing, research—and action. Pressure to produce results for each of several grants pushes organizations into executing conspicuous, short-term projects rather than organizing, conducting research, and planning for more knowledgeable, comprehensive initiatives.

Although some funders expect action to rest on community involvement, and many want action based on research, few pay for either. Many funders encourage organizations to form partnerships, to develop local resources, and in these ways to become self sufficient, but few support organizing or maintaining complex networks. Funders want community organizations to take action based on solid knowledge, but few give them research grants that could investigate problems, search for promising practices, or evaluate actions taken.

These conditions push community organizations to propose action based on participants' immediate ideas rather than on research, and to assert without much knowledge that action will have specific, visible, and significant results. Minimal time for consulting with potential partners or constituents limits not only the knowledge underlying action but also personal and institutional investments in it, its legitimacy, and its efficacy. Because funders rarely pay for evaluation, few community organizations or funders know whether money is well spent.

In part, these problems reflect limited resources, but availability is a question of interest and will, in addition to fiscal capacity. In part, too, they reflect most funders' hands-off stance toward potential grantees, whereby they simply receive and judge proposals rather than help develop good programs. In part as well, these conditions reflect an anachronistic organization of funders. While encouraging grantees to form partnerships, most grantors operate solo rather than form networks to build collective intelligence and funding ability (see Baum 2000). Thus they push community organizations to pull together programs without participation or planning.

Part 7

Tensions between Attachment and Knowledge

Chapter 14

Realities and Fantasies in University-Community Partnerships

The next three chapters analyze challenges in forming interinstitutional networks. We begin with university-community partnerships, move to community-school partnerships, and finish by looking at tensions between attachment and knowledge in interorganizational practice.

The Southeast Education Task Force letterhead reads: "A project of the Southeast Planning Council and the University of Maryland, College Park Urban Studies and Planning Program." The announcement for the USDE Urban Community Service Program described its purpose as "provid[ing] grants to urban academic institutions to work with private and civic organizations" (*Federal Register* 1994, 15810). The U. S. Department of Housing and Urban Development's Office of University Partnerships lists Maryland's work with the Task Force among "University-Community Partnerships in America" (U. S. Department of Housing and Urban Development 1999).

Links between universities and communities can be mutually beneficial. Universities can conduct research and practice in communities. Communities can get help improving conditions. Both can benefit financially (Benson and Harkavy 1994; Feld 1998; Maurrasse 2001; Nyden, Figert, Shibley, and Burrows 1997; U. S. Department of Housing and Urban Development 1995, 1996, 1999). Such accomplishments buoy a growing, but often uncritical, enthusiasm for "partnerships" as solutions for many, wide-ranging problems. Advocates may exaggerate partnerships' potential, minimize their requirements, and ignore evidence that development often is disjointed and tenuous. They may imagine that simply creating a "partnership" magically produces "resources" that will solve problems, obviating realistic analysis of conditions or strategies for changing them.

The case of the University of Maryland and the Southeast Education Task Force helps understand what university-community partnerships may be and do. This partnership is near the small end of a continuum in terms of funding, the number of individual or institutional participants, and activities, in contrast with some well-funded, long-term, multiinstitutional partnerships. Even so, it resembles many partnerships, and its predicaments pertain to university-community partnerships of all sizes.

PARTNERSHIPS AND FANTASIES

The partnership is the first human relationship, in infantile attachment to the mother, a partner who seems to offer infinite nurturance. Soon enough, the infant becomes aware of another partnership, the mother's relationship with the father, which, among other things, produces new life in the form of siblings. For infants, fantasy and barely distinguishable reality endow parental partners with seemingly infinite power to create and sustain life. Though these early experiences with partners recede from conscious memory, the assumptions about parents continue to influence beliefs about and involvement in partnerships throughout life.

Organizational partnerships are a world away from the relations of infancy. They are institutional, formal, and often deliberately planned. Moreover, they make good sense in turbulent environments, where organizations cannot control enough to accomplish their purposes alone. If groups and organizations combine resources, not only can they draw on a larger pool, but they may cross-pollinate in ways that create new resources.

Yet studies of institutional relationships, including business partnerships, joint ventures, corporate mergers, managerial teams, and interdepartmental initiatives, reveal an interplay of realism and fantasy that echoes life's early moments. Organizations often form partnerships with exaggerated expectations of what they can accomplish, and then, if the going gets rough, they imagine that what they are doing, despite contrary appearances, will somehow succeed.[1] Partnerships are especially likely to grow on and nurture fantasy when reality resists strongly held intentions.

Common talk of cross-pollination offers a clue to unrealistic expectations. The language is metaphorical, yet its usage expresses a widely shared belief—or wish, reminiscent of early life fantasies: if only two bodies came together in the right way, they could give birth to abundant new resources. This is a satisfying thought, but differences between flowers and bees and universities, community organizations, and business firms signal confusion between fantasy and reality.

In fact, the desire for cross-pollination resembles a fantasy that groups sometimes indulge when they conclude that rational planning cannot solve a problem. Bion (1961) found that frustrated groups unconsciously redefine their purpose and the means of success in order to feel effective. One stratagem is to assume that the task of the group, rather than to solve a problem instrumentally, is to allow two individuals or units to pair up and watch them, as if by immaculate conception, give birth to a leader or program of action that will miraculously bring a solution. Without effort, with only hopeful expectation, the group will succeed.

For example, members of a committee may imagine that if only the chair and co-chair meet often enough, regardless of what they know or do, somehow their being together will lead to success. Groups convene meetings without realistic preparation because of a fantasy that the mere presence of a couple of central members will automatically accomplish the work. Perhaps just "getting the key players together" will solve problems. These wishes arise in many groups, organizations, communities, and networks (Baum 1987, 1997; Diamond 1993; Gould, Ebers, and Clinchy n.d.; Hirschhorn 1988, 1991; Janis 1982; Kets de Vries and Associates 1991; Kets de Vries and Miller 1984; Schwartz 1990; Stein 1994).

Thus the conditions that can realistically justify institutional partnerships—when problems exceed one party's capacity alone—can encourage fantasies about a partnership. Imaginary ideas that survive from life's earliest relationships encourage partners to idealize one another's abilities instead of strategizing to increase them.

UNIVERSITY-COMMUNITY PARTNERSHIPS

University-community partnerships have burgeoned. Some are initiated by universities, others by community groups. In one case, a state legislator required a university to work with her district as a condition for getting its budget allocation (Reardon 1998). Many universities would never have gotten involved with community groups if someone had not paid them to do so. Funding comes from various sources, including the government, foundations, corporations, nonprofit organizations, universities, and community associations.

Activities include research, planning, organizing, and service delivery. They involve single, time-limited projects and long-term relations and multifaceted programs. The work covers many fields (Benson and Harkavy 1994; Cohen 1995, 1997; Dewar and Isaac 1998; Feld 1998; Harkavy and Pickett 1991; LeGates and Robinson 1998; Maurrasse 2001; Mayfield, Hellwig, and Banks 1998; McCall, Groark, Strauss, and Johnson 1998; Nyden et al. 1997; Reardon 1995, 1998, 1999, 2000; Rubin 1998; U. S. Department of Education 1997; U. S. Department of Housing and Urban Development 1995, 1996, 1999; Wiewel and Lieber 1998).

Partnerships rest on overlapping interests in improving community conditions. Success depends on planning that is clear, specific, and realistic. For instance, the *target* of partnership activity may be a more or less discrete problem or a broad institutional structure. The boundary between the two is fuzzy: a problem may be a symptom of institutional functions, and institutional change may be necessary to reduce the problem. In any case, the target must be explicit. A partnership's *goals* may be to alleviate distress associated with a problem or to change a system that produces it. Either way, the goal should fit the target and should be realistic.

A partnership may bring different *strategies* to these goals. One is to implement a more or less free-standing, time-limited program. Such a partnership can dissolve after the project has been set up. Alternatively, a partnership may establish an enduring relationship, which may create various programs but also builds connections, or social capital. What matters is that strategies realistically fit goals. Finally, partnerships must have *resources* to implement the strategies.

Partnerships may begin with agreements that are clear and specific but unrealistic. Proposed strategies may not fit intended goals, or resources may not support strategies. For example, a GED program may be insufficient to get parents employment, and, in any case, meager funds will not pay for an effective GED program. However, even when planning is realistic, rigid adherence to initial aims may hinder learning or fail to accommodate changes in membership or thinking. Perhaps after people consider adult education, they will redefine problems. As they work together, maybe as participants change, they may want to take on child care and transportation and, in so doing, drop and add partners.

Two interests can lead to unrealistic specificity. One is a strong desire for major social change. People may conclude that they cannot settle for anything less. The other is a blunt insistence on "accountability." Parties may interpret accountability in terms of predefined results and benchmarks rather than reciprocity in a partially defined but developing and trusting relationship. Both interests easily converge in simplistic agreements about who the partners are, how they will relate, and what they will accomplish. In such innocent beginnings, fantasy can displace realistic analysis and strategizing. Later on, obdurate reality may require further fantasizing to continue.

Funders, expecting significant social change from their investment, often encourage unrealistic aims. Two federal agencies that have supported many partnerships provide examples. The U. S. Department of Education's Urban Community Service Program

> provides grants to urban academic institutions to work with private and civic organizations to devise and *implement solutions to pressing*

> *and severe problems* in their urban communities (*Federal Register* 1994, 15810, emphasis added)

The U. S. Department of Housing and Urban Development describes its Community Outreach Partnership Centers Program as a "demonstration to determine the feasibility of facilitating partnerships between institutions of higher education and communities." The partnerships' aim is "to *solve urban problems* through research, outreach, and the exchange of information." "Applications must be multifaceted and *address three or more urban problems.*" Research "must have a *clear near-term potential for solving specific, significant urban problems*" (*Federal Register* 1997, 13507, emphasis added). Proposals are evaluated for their promise to "*solve or address an urgent need or problem,*" with "measurable objectives to be accomplished during the period of performance" (U. S. Department of Housing and Urban Development 1997, A 30, emphasis added).

These typical statements can be questioned in two regards. One concerns the realism of anticipated outcomes. Funders encourage the belief that universities can provide near-term solutions for significant, pressing, severe, and urgent urban problems. Such expectations encourage disingenuousness, fantasy, or both. They motivate applicants to assert that they can solve major urban problems quickly with few resources, and they encourage faculty, community members, and funders to believe these claims.

The second weakness in common funder statements is that they are unambiguous. They assume that it is clear what "institutions of higher learning" and "communities" are and how they act. However, those who work with communities begin with questions. It is normal to ask who "the community" is and who represents it. Official leaders may speak for only a few. Some people who are the center of extensive networks, and might speak for many, may be suspicious of formal planning or organizing, or may just consider it unimportant. Some groups, typically the neediest, have little knowledge about or skill in developing programs. Competing organizations, each with credible claims to represent a community, may oppose one another on what to plan, how to plan, or whether to plan. Moreover, when community or organizational leaders or members change, newcomers may redefine their group or its directions. A university that aims to form a partnership with a community must not only decide who "the community" is but also must find concurrence on that view by "community members."

Universities present similar questions. Who is "the university"? Who represents it? A university is a formal organization but is notoriously individualistic. Can anyone represent it? Faculty and administrators variously represent the institution intellectually, socially, fiscally, and politically to students, research subjects, elected officials, and members of the public. Those who would form a partnership between the university and a community must persuade members of an identified community that they represent the university and must get others in the university to authorize them to act, to acquiesce in their acting, or at least to ignore them.

These questions frame a third set. What kinds of arrangements might a university-community "partnership" include, allow, or require? Who can be parties to such a partnership? Can single individuals in each entity agree to a partnership; if so, must they be their entities' leaders? Or must a partnership be authorized by a majority or at least substantial numbers in each unit? Would different authorizing procedures by each partner be workable? How much must the entities agree on, and what conditions must they agree to to constitute a partnership? In what ways is a third-party funder a partner, and how should the funder participate? Who else should be a partner? Parties must answer these questions pragmatically.

"The University" Acts

It is misleading to speak of "the University of Maryland" as a partner in the Southeast Education Task Force. Five Urban Studies and Planning faculty members submitted a proposal to the U. S. Department of Education. The proposal comprised five projects, including four in Southeast Baltimore—economic development, housing, and recreation, in addition to education. The document, submitted in the name of the campus, described the efforts as being consistent with the University's urban mission, and campus officials endorsed it with their signatures.

The campus administration valued research about and service to cities, but the University has many missions. The administration consistently rewards research—particularly its funding and publication. The administration appreciates, though it does not necessarily reward, service to community groups, especially when it leads to public recognition or budget appropriations. The USDE proposal might bring in money. It included research that could end up in publications. It involved community service that might carry favorable publicity. Beyond this, the administration gave it no special priority.

When USDE funded the proposal in October 1994, "the University" consisted of five faculty members and ten graduate students in one program. I directed the education project, aided at different times by one or two graduate students, eventually eleven by 2002. Although others, including a contingent of education faculty and students, contributed significantly, practically, in Southeast Baltimore education, "the university" came down to one professor and a graduate student or two.

Some funders support university-community partnerships as a means of changing university culture and incentives, so that faculty engage in service to urban communities, the way land grant colleges once aided agriculture. However, under these conditions, where little of the university is engaged in a partnership, those aims are unrealistic.

Clearly, a professor, some occasional colleagues, and a few graduate students could not turn around sixteen urban schools. However, the community partner's expectations were more modest, and, in any case, the partners recruited additional collaborators. Still, false assumptions periodically inflated hopes.

Creating "The Community"

When the university received the grant that made it possible to help the Southeast Planning Council create a "study-action group for schools," Bobby English was the only member of its Coordinating Committee with interest in and time for education. She was not connected to parent activists, and, in any case, there were few of them. The initial "community" was as small as "the university." In the fall of 1994, the two of us constituted the university-community partnership.

Acting in the name of the university, I would help her create the "community" that she would represent. During most of the first year, the core group and associated volunteers interviewed educators, parents, and students. Twenty-five people attended a mini-kickoff, and seventy attended a maxi-kickoff and endorsed an agenda. An education "community" was slowly coming to life.

Yet the next year saw difficulties in sustaining work groups and involving parents. Parent organizing became a way of creating a "community." However, though several dozen parents took part in school activities as a result, they did not come to Task Force meetings. The organizers represented them in the Task Force. By the start of 1997, after the principals' meeting, the Task Force coalesced in a core group of fifteen, with others meeting in ad hoc work groups. The main group grew to about twenty. A few of the original group remained in 2002, but many members had dropped out. The categories of members were similar: community activists, school staff, service agency and nonprofit organization staff, pastors, parents, and Task Force project staff. Most participants have been middle class, often college educated, and many have been professionals. Most are white. Few are parents. They do not resemble Southeast Baltimore's predominantly working-class residents or its majority African-American student population. However, many spend time with parents, children, or educators in their jobs or civic activities.

More than 1,000 people have participated in Task Force activities, including interviews, work groups, symposia, community meetings, and workshops. These people live, work, send children to school, teach, or attend school in Southeast Baltimore, or they just care about the area or education. They represent Southeast Baltimore demographically better than the core group, and they include school and school system staff. Because the core group want to speak for broad interests, they have listened to these others. Still, the occasional, informal character of much of this contact limits what the core group can know and say authoritatively about this "community."

These conditions, though far from ideal, are within the normal range of community activity. However, the result is that though the Task Force kept the same name and a handful of original members, in fact, the organization and its "community" were constantly recreated. Those who joined later did not know those who had preceded them and knew little or nothing of Task Force origins or activities. They felt no obligation to its history, and they brought new images of and attachments to "the community." These facts had implications for "partnership."

Forming a "Partnership"

The Federal Government, the University, the Community, a Foundation, and the University Again

The Department of Education paid for a professor and a graduate student to work with community activists in creating what became the Southeast Education Task Force. Arguably, this constituted a partnership, but partners' identities and relations were both ambiguous.

At the least, USDE, the Urban Studies and Planning Program, and the Education Task Force were linked, but the relationship was asymmetrical. The only formal contract involved the federal funder and the university program. Two Southeast Planning Council members, one of whom became Task Force chair, worked with a professor on the proposal. The Department of Education sent the Planning Program money in return for its commitment to implement the proposal. However, no community member was a party to the agreement with the federal government. The university got the money and was solely accountable for the project.[2]

In fact, once USDE approved funds and I began meeting with the Task Force core group, everyone considered a lot up for grabs. Those who had not worked on the proposal did not feel bound by it, and those who had wanted to rethink what was realistic. Appeals to the federal contract carried no weight. Thus "the university" had money but no power beyond what a faculty member could negotiate with "community" members. The "partnership," rather than being established in a written proposal, would be worked out in action. In performance reports to USDE, I explained that community members had new ideas about what to do and when to do it. The response to the first report asked why the project was not aiming at systemic school reform; later communications did not question changing directions and pace.

"The community" and "the university's" "partnership" with it have been protean. Institutionally, the Task Force was the creation of a partnership between the Planning Program and the Southeast Planning Council, represented by its Coordinating Committee. The latter effectively dissolved in mid-1997, leaving the Planning Council alive only on the letterhead. I began speaking of a partnership between "the university" and "community members." These shifts, about which no one at USDE or the university knew, were too subtle to matter to either.

When the federal grant ended in December 1998, Task Force leaders used a grant to keep me as a consultant. A foundation took the federal government's place as third-party funder of my work, but the foundation did not explicitly pay for a university-community partnership. The Planning Program gave me a graduate assistant, whom I put to work with the Task Force, but the university was no longer formally party to Task Force activity. Yet I continued to act in the university's name, and Task Force members, who knew nothing of these changes, identified me as their university partner. Around the time the foundation grant ran out, the university gave me a year's support to continue with the Task Force, along with funding for a graduate assistant. Formally, the university was once more a party to the relationship. Indeed, the "partnership" was for the first time a two-party relationship. Still, the university's involvement extended only to supporting an individual faculty member on a discrete project. After that, my work with the Task Force has been unfunded, but I have had a university-supported graduate assistant. Observers might see me as simply volunteering, but I can still draw on university resources, and the Task Force continues to see a "university-community partnership."

Few Task Forces members have known of these variations, and for most practical purposes, the "partnership" has stayed the same. The greatest change has been informal: as my experience with the Task Force grew and as relations with members deepened, I gained authority for "the university" as "partner." Institutional partnerships depend on personal relations, and my bonds with Bobby English held the university and community together.

The Vicissitudes of Partnership: Change and Constancy

A "partnership" has continued since October 1994. Although superficially it has remained constant, much has varied. "The university's" participation has been most constant. It started and stayed small. It began as essentially personal and did not become institutional. Bobby English has anchored "the community's" participation, though it has changed in amount, composition, and interests. The partnership began with a third-party funder but moved to a two-party relationship. Under federal funding, elements of the partnership were formal and contractual. Later on, more was tacit, informal, and personal.

Some of these changes are idiosyncratic, not intrinsic to university-community relations. However, community fluctuations in participation are normal. Moreover, though community organizations may enter into contracts with university partners, much that goes on, even under those conditions, is informally decided. In addition, funding can be expected to shift, with accompanying role and relationship implications. Over time, relationships often become less formal and more personal. The advantages of personal connections are obvious. So too is the vulnerability of partnerships that depend too much on individual attachments.

It would be misleading to equate this "partnership" to other relationships to which the label is commonly applied in business. They are similar in being designed to share resources, but they differ in formality and fixity. Whereas business partnerships link incorporated organizations, university-community partnerships connect persons more than institutions. Some universities are more significantly and formally involved with communities than Maryland, in this instance, but the case is not atypical. Sometimes universities and community representatives sign formal contracts, but communities are not solid entities, only aggregations of individuals. Although community organizations can commit resources or paid staff, community participation is an accumulation of individual actions. A university may have an understanding with a community organization, but in an important sense it is a partner to a number of separate persons.

Some other terms applied to the Task Force capture these aspects of university-community partnerships. It has been called a "coalition" of individuals and organizations interested in improving Southeast Baltimore schools. The university is one of those organizations, or, at least, I am one of those individuals, as are several dozen others who regularly attend meetings or take part in projects. Sometimes the Task Force is considered an "umbrella," a name and a structure under which those interested in schools can find like-minded collaborators. I have brought a few of the university's people and some of its resources under the umbrella, to be available to community members, school staff, and others there at the time. One also could liken the Task Force to a "floating crap game." Players enter and leave with fluctuations in their interest, opportunity, and wherewithal. I have been "in," often bringing others' stakes, playing in the university's name with others who feel that their own chances of winning are reasonably good.

Fantasies and Realities of University-Community Partnerships

This partnership's initial funder expected it to "implement solutions to pressing and severe problems" in four years.[3] If this phrase meant making Southeast Baltimore public schools as good as, say, those in upper-middle-class suburbs, then a partnership of community activists and a few professors and graduate students was strikingly unequal to the task.

A changing small group of people working part time cannot alter social institutions. Yet funders treated such efforts as plausible. Federal policy makers, even though they had lived in real communities and attended real universities, thought of "university-community partnerships" as likely relationships between solid, unitary, intentional institutions. Funders assumed that universities and communities could make formal, binding agreements. They expected universities to provide matching funds that would increase resources for problem solving and commit universities to new missions. They imagined that universities had storehouses of resources from which faculty could take away loads to designated community partners. Yet Cohen, March, and Olsen (1988; Olsen 1976) have seen universities as "organized anarchies." That characterization should surprise no one who has taught or studied in one.

Moreover, much of the social scientific literature, journalistic reports, and anecdotal accounts of lower-income, minority communities, the target of many partnerships, was less than encouraging. Even if Moynihan's "tangle of pathology" (Rainwater and Yancey 1967) was not a phrase still in good currency, the image was pervasive. Wilson (1987, 1996) described "the new urban poor," and others chronicled the ways their lives often were organized around drugs or violence (Anderson 1999; Simon and Burns 1997). A countervailing voice called attention to these communities' strengths and abilities to accomplish positive collective purposes (Boyte 1984, 1989; Fisher 1984; Kretzmann and McKnight 1993; Medoff and Sklar 1994). Nevertheless, as heartening as these examples were, they were exceptional, and published accounts often played down difficulties. No matter what a community's income or education, a few individuals' good intentions did not easily translate into organized collective action. Wishing otherwise about universities or communities did not make it so.

Unrealistic assumptions encouraged optimism about not only the formation and continuity of university-community partnerships but also what they could accomplish. School reform illustrates the point. Any significant improvement in children's education must involve the schools, yet the schools resist joining forces with any community group, regardless of university participation. University-community-school partnerships, while necessary, are elusive, as many educators assume that they can solve problems on their own.

Even if such partnerships formed, much would be necessary to enable them to "implement solutions to pressing and severe problems." For starters, a period of four or five years is too little to develop these partnerships and to get them moving. Moreover, the marginally additional funding offered by university-community partnerships would provide little incentive or means for changing structures, policies, or programs. In addition, school improvement depends on not just money but also new ways of thinking about educational problems and purposes, institutional missions, programmatic strategies, and teachers' and students' everyday work (Bascia and Hargreaves 2000). Universities and communities can help school systems in these ways, but university-community partnerships as conceived do not lead toward success.

Improving children's learning depends on much beyond the schools. This fact, on the one hand, offers community organizations reasons for working with families and local institutions. Yet it also points to limitations of even a university-community-school partnership. Much that affects schools' power to educate children lies beyond these three parties' influence. Local actors, including the government, have little purchase. Control over funding for city schools lies with suburban jurisdictions and beyond. National and regional economies have a great deal to do with adults' financial opportunities, men's marriageability, families' strength, and children's motivation to learn. Not even university-community-school partnerships could "implement solutions to pressing and severe problems" in this complex domain. The example here is education, but the same could be said of university-community partnerships in many other fields.

These partnerships, as now typically constituted, present two risks. One is that well-intentioned faculty, students, and community members expend great effort trying to get leverage with basic institutions, only to fall far short. Those who fail to accomplish what they intended and promised feel inept and blame themselves. Alternatively, university and community participants, recognizing that their partnership's formal aims are unrealistic, struggle to save themselves by finding something that they can do with the resources at hand, but their results are merely decorative and trivial. In either event, the participants, those who have watched them, and their funders become cynical about communities' or universities' ability to address problems that matter.

Perhaps funders should stop paying for university-community partnerships. The Southeast Education Task Force, after all, was unequal to most of what constrained Southeast Baltimore education. And yet community members did not have a choice between this partnership and more efficacious organizations. The Task Force was the only game in town. Even if this university-community partnership did not meet the funder's fantasies, it gave a group of parents and community members an opportunity and resources to organize and work for at least small educational improvements that would not have occurred otherwise.

Funders might issue more realistic requests for partnership proposals, recognizing the value of modest accomplishments and encouraging faculty and community activists to speak honestly about conditions and possibilities for ameliorating them. Alternatively, funders could take their ambitions seriously and consider ways of making common cause with one another and with the major institutional actors whose investment would be necessary for success.

Chapter 15

Why Community-School Partnerships Are Unlikely

The Southeast Education Task Force believed in parent and community involvement in education because it was democratic and because, as research showed, it benefitted children. Yet the Task Force had little success in developing substantial community-school partnerships. We look here at the nature of communities and schools as potential partners. Metaphorically, we can think of communities and schools as different species and ask whether they can mate. Anatomic fit is essential. Genetic compatibility is important. Desire matters. We look first at communities and then at school systems and schools. Many of the observations about both are familiar; we emphasize here their implications for the possibility of partnering.

Communities As Partners

Voluntary Communities, Communities of Limited Liability

A community is a group of people who interact in significant ways, identify with one another, and share behavioral norms, beliefs, or other culture. Traditional rural towns or urban ethnic neighborhoods, with their closeness, coherence, and inclusiveness, are familiar models of community. Familiar, too, however, are changes in communities over the past century. Physical mobility and institutional differentiation have separated people and places of home, work, religion, education, and commerce, particularly for those who have the means to get around.

Community membership has become increasingly voluntary, and individuals, albeit the middle class more than the poor, have choices about whether to belong to a community and which community—or, more likely, communities—to join. People frequently choose communities on the basis of interests, from intellectual or occupational concerns to those associated with a lifestyle or a stage in the life cycle. Whereas in the old ethnic neighborhood people interacted with the same community members in working, doing business, socializing, raising children, and worshiping, they now are likely to be part of separate communities for different purposes. Some of these communities are networks that extend far beyond the neighborhood of residence (Wellman 1999).

Each community pulls on its members but without reinforcement from other communities, and people selectively apportion commitments and loyalties. Hence, communities vary in intensity and meaning, as experienced in the nature and significance of social interaction, the content and salience of a common identity, and the breadth and force of cultural norms (Baum 1997; Fowler 1991; Mandelbaum 2000; McMillan and Chavis 1986). When interests become a basis of community, it is easier to think of individual interests than to search for common interests, and people feel relatively free to enter and leave. Thus many communities are communities of limited liability (Janowitz 1952).

The Contingency of Community Organization

Because communities are informal networks, they do not act in any deliberate collective way. Tacitly and often unconsciously, individually and cumulatively, members promote certain community ideals or interests (Baum 1997), but communities lack a structure for reasoned thinking and calculated action. They create organizations to act in these ways. More precisely, some people establish or participate in organizations that they say represent the communities of which they are members.

Normally, a small minority of people participate in a community organization, often without widespread knowledge or authorization of their activities (Cnaan 1991). One reason is the voluntary character of communities: when personal interest becomes a basis for joining, and when exit is an alternative to participation, it is easier for people to consider themselves members and yet refrain from collective action. Other reasons, already noted, are the time, skills, knowledge, and confidence that activism requires.[1]

Community organization is rarely simple. Many communities have several organizations—such as a "community organization," a church, a business association, and a political club—each of which does or could claim to represent the community, and people may divide their allegiances. Even so, many people may not feel that they are represented by any organization. Further, organizations change. One that has widespread endorsement may lose legitimacy as new leaders replace old ones and as policies and practices change. Even if an organization stays the same formally, community members' preferences may change, or new members may take the place of departing ones. The relationship between a community organization and a community is fluid.

Still, many communities have no organization. Many others have simple, informal organizations. Even many formal organizations are small. They probably have officers and a letterhead; they may have bylaws, formal membership, and dues; they are less likely to have offices or staff. Few communities have both the interest and the resources.

The Tenuousness of the School Community

Schools often are characterized as "community institutions." With public schools that have geographic zones, the community most likely to be concerned about a school is the people who live in that territory, particularly if they have children or do business there and identify with the area. The relationship between a family and a school is specific and consequential, giving community members reasons to organize and act. However, generally limited community attachments reduce this likelihood, as do other types of mobility specific to schools.

Children move from one school level to the next, changing the formal membership of schools' communities. Although parents might continue to identify with their children's former schools in anticipation of younger siblings' entry or become involved with schools that their children will attend later, most families feel attached only to the school their children are attending at the time. The relationship with the school is so specific that, once the child has gone on, the family no longer feels part of the school community. Moreover, families, particularly those with low-incomes, move, and in many urban schools one-half of the students enter or leave during a year (Hartman 2002).[2] Not only do many families have brief connections to schools, but those who stay have difficulty identifying with a specific, constant group of community members.

The most stable members of an urban school community are likely to be the diminishing number of middle-class families, if they send their children to public schools.[3] Their formal education enables them to understand their children's schooling, and their education and social status give them confidence to talk with teachers and administrators. They are most likely to know what goes on at school and to evaluate it in terms of broad education issues. Nevertheless, consistently involved parents are the exception.

When parents or other community members take active roles in schools, they focus on what they understand best, even if they care more about other things. Thus they may complain about inadequate buildings rather than students' inability to read, because they find it easier to talk about peeling paint, unsafe drinking water, and lack of play space than about curriculum and pedagogy.

For these reasons, few members of a school's community have both the motivation to engage the school and the assurance and ability to go ahead. Parents can most easily be tacit, parallel partners to the schools, raising their children well at home and perhaps helping with schoolwork. Fewer can keep in touch with teachers or volunteer at school. Fewer still are ready to take part in community action on education or school decision making. Whatever they do is likely to be informal and ambiguously connected to other members of the school community.

Schools and School Systems as Partners

In contrast to communities and even many community organizations, school systems are formal systems: their mission, technology, structure, and environment consistently influence how units and individuals act. Their size, formality, and institutional authority give them great control over the possibility of partnering with communities.

The Environment Shapes the Mission

The Public Character of Education

Even when few community members act to become partners with school staff, communities, individually and collectively, influence schools' missions. Local communities hold certain expectations. In addition, they have voices as parts of larger communities, interests, or publics, such as "the African-American community," "suburban families," "low-income children," "blue-collar families," and "business interests."

Some, especially the better educated and more affluent, speak for themselves. Others are spoken for or about, with varying accuracy and fidelity. Sometimes communities or their representatives speak directly through meetings or publications. Sometimes others record them on television or in the movies, whose pictures have the impact of thousands upon millions of words. Sometimes actions and perceptions of actions, beliefs about actions, and impressions of actions speak louder than words. In short, national "debate" about education is in part a deliberate expression of clearly and widely held views and in part a cacophony of numerous fragmentary, partly thought out, more and less definitely expressed thoughts.

These ideas in the educational environment variously shape schools' missions. They do so legitimately because of education's quintessentially public character. School attendance is mandated by law. Nearly all education is publicly produced. Elementary and secondary education are almost completely publicly financed. Nine out of ten children attend public schools.[4]

For these reasons, many important decisions affecting education are made politically—based on perceptions of interests rather than on an examination of knowledge about teaching and learning. Taxpayers insist on something of value for their coerced contributions, and parents refuse to experiment with their children. Decision makers, attuned to voters' concerns, try to proceed as if there were single purposes for schooling and proven best ways to educate children. Thus elected officials and school boards decide what teachers will teach, how they will teach, what students will read, and how much time students and teachers will spend together.

When in doubt, a public that hardly trusts schools or teachers makes rules restricting the authority of school systems, schools, principals, and/or teachers.[5] National commissions regularly critique public education and recommend reforms; state and local governments follow by introducing new standards, curricula, or incentives; and teachers must drop old practices to adopt new ones (e.g., National Commission on Excellence in Education 1983). However, because reforms rarely take into account what goes on between teachers and students in classrooms, new requirements add to teachers' work without improving students' learning (Bascia and Hargreaves 2000; Sarason 1990).

Limits on teacher autonomy may satisfy public cries for accountability but, paradoxically, may make it hard for parents to form partnerships with their children's schools. Uniform standards and requirements, by prescribing what teachers must do, tie educators' hands in offering parents options for their children and thus preclude open discussion of students' needs.

Numerous, Ambiguous, Conflicting, and Sometimes Unrealistic Expectations of Schools

Not only do numerous members of the public try to control what schools do, but also they do not agree about what students should learn or what teachers should teach. Everyone expects schools to introduce children to knowledge they will need as adults, but that expectation is ambiguous. Some want children to learn traditional basic skills, while others insist that schools teach higher-order thinking. Some want schools to concentrate on cognitive learning, while others want to nurture children's personalities. Some are content to have children learn to reason well about whatever they encounter, while others believe that there is basic cultural knowledge that all young people should have (Bennett 1999; Bennett, Finn, and Cribb 1999; Hirsch [1996; Hirsch, Kett, and Trefil 1988]), and still others believe that children should become conversant with diverse cultures (Banks and Banks 2000; Gollnick and Chinn 1997). Some want schools to stick to "facts," while others believe that there are basic values that all children should be taught, and others yet want children to appreciate a multiplicity of cultural values (Hunter 1991).

In addition, the public wants schools to prepare young people for work. Schools traditionally responded to and reinforced class differences by tracking students into "vocational" and "academic" curricula, with the former leading to physical trades and the latter to college and intellectual work. Those who find "vocational" programs outmoded have reinvented them as "school-to-work" or "school-to-career," but these do not always teach "new basic skills" such as reasoning, problem solving, collaborating, and communicating, and college is increasingly necessary to obtain good jobs (Murnane and Levy 1996). Advocates for children who have difficulty with conventional teaching want "special education" to prepare them. Others argue for advanced courses as vocational education for the "gifted and talented."

At the same time, schools are expected to prepare students for citizenship. Yet this value, too, is contested. Groups with different histories or cultures make different assumptions about whether government can be trusted, whether an active public role is safe, and what men and women may do outside of the home. Middle-class adults trust the public domain more than those who are poorer, have the knowledge, skills, and connections to move comfortably in it, and succeed in ways that affirm a faith in citizenship (Gans 1988). Some parents expect schools to familiarize their children with American history and government. Others want schools to help children analyze the ways society influences race, culture, religion, gender, and class. Still others ask schools to teach skills in community and political activism. And some parents want schools to avoid these matters altogether.

When a cacophony of voices confronts teachers with numerous, conflicting expectations that defy intellectual, political, or practical reconciliation, it is hard for them to concentrate on anything, much less to find time to do what seems to matter. Paradoxically, these pressures encourage educators to focus on circumscribed goals so that they can succeed at something, but those aims are certain not to satisfy the public, which will redouble efforts to "hold schools accountable" for other narrowly defined results that, similarly, ignore broader, more complex educational expectations. School staff are likely to see contacts with parents and community members as just tightening the binds in which they find themselves and to regard possible partnerships warily.

The Service "Technology" of Education Challenges Accountability

No matter what communities expect of schools, the activity that accomplishes the desired results—education's "technology"—eludes easy observation, measurement, evaluation, or control. Its outcomes involve mental capacities, but these are invisible, or at least intangible. It is possible to measure students' performance at specific tasks, such as answering multiple choice questions, but people disagree about which tasks students should perform, and, anyhow, the link between success at specific tasks and general mental capacity is speculative. Further—centrally—educators' interactions with students are far from uniform, their actions have widely varying effects, and many other individuals and institutions also influence children. While some teaching practices have fairly consistent effects, there is vast uncertainty about how children learn, and teaching that leads to learning depends on unique relationships between teachers and students.

Another way to say this is that education is a service, not a good, such as an automobile or a chair. One can see and touch a vehicle. Most people can compare cars not just by appearance but also by performance. Moreover, it is reasonable to assume that all cars of a given model are identical. They are uniform, because they are produced on assembly lines, where people and machines perform unvarying operations on raw materials to create finished products. With chairs, one can distinguish the work of individual artisans from mass-produced furniture. Though both are subject to physical laws, artisans attend to customer tastes and may exploit the characteristics of distinct pieces of wood. Craft work, where products and processes vary, is closer to education than is mass production; nevertheless, there is broader consensus about good chairs than a good education, and far more is known about shaping wood than shaping children.

Teachers are expected to reproduce society one child at a time. They encounter students who vary in abilities, interests, personalities, and circumstances. They must draw on a broad repertoire of skills to develop distinct relations with each. They do so with the knowledge that much remains uncertain. At an extreme, a child's biological or social conditions may hinder the efforts of the best teacher. In any case, teachers do not know what works until they take up with each student, and they rarely see their former students as adults, to assess how they affected them.

The particularities and uncertainties in this "technology" offer anxious taxpayers little to depend on if they lack confidence in teachers' judgment. Laypersons know and care little about the intricacies of pedagogy; they are interested in the apparent results—most commonly, test scores. When many children do poorly, teachers' talk about students' troubled homes or neighborhoods sounds like excuse making. Members of the public and their representatives have difficulty avoiding skepticism and anger about educators' ability to manage an indeterminate "production process" toward intangible ends. In this atmosphere, school staff find it safer to avoid community contact and to resist active partnership with outsiders.

The Professional Culture Constrains Educators' Responsiveness

Though most teachers recognize the uncertainty of their work, their professional culture encourages them to exaggerate its predictability (Katz 1975; Tyack and Hansot 1982). In marking a line between educators and laypersons, the culture portrays teachers as scientists of child development, curriculum, and pedagogy who know best what should happen in the classroom. When assailed by critics or self-doubt, teachers can fall back on the culture.

However, even when educators openly struggle with the messiness of their work, when they realize that they do not know all they need to know, then normal images of teaching make it hard for them to understand what community members think, want, or could offer. People become teachers because they want to teach children, and schools of education aim to prepare them to teach children. This simple observation covers three assumptions. First, the dominant image of teaching, which attracts aspirants to the field and guides teacher preparation, is dyadic: an individual teacher encounters an individual student—and, by extension, a class of individual students. Second, teaching is a hierarchical relation in which the teacher knows and the student does not; hence, the teacher should have authority over the student. Third, the student is mainly a cognitive being; social conditions affect his or her thinking but are marginal to teachers' concerns.

These premises limit educators' ability to respond to community expectations. They may understand individual development, but their inclination and training make it unlikely that they will understand community, because it is a collectivity. Teachers or administrators may think of a community in terms of individual persons or organizations but may have difficulty seeing what is distinctive about it as a whole. At worst, if they find the community hard to understand, they may disregard or even fear it. If staff do work with a community, they are likely to define issues in terms of classroom activities, to see themselves as experts encountering others who know less, and to take a superior position in a hierarchical relationship. This attitude makes it difficult to recognize community members' definitions of issues, which can include conditions outside of the school, and to work with them as equals in learning about problems and solutions.

This orientation also makes it hard for principals to manage schools. Most were originally teachers, interested in working with individual students. Few have much training in either the analytic or interpersonal work of management. Most are inclined to relate to teachers or other administrators as individuals rather than as members of groups and organizations. Operating in this way, principals find it hard to satisfy the central office, with the side effect of having little time or patience to meet with parents.

The "Responsive" Structure Discourages Responsiveness

School systems' dual structure is intended simultaneously to deal with environmental demands and to allow teachers to exercise discretion consistent with educational "technology" and professional culture. The central administration manages institutional functions by responding to opportunities, requests, or requirements from funders, regulators, policy makers, and interest groups. For each, it establishes an office or a program—which may, for example, satisfy a federal agency's funding requirements, comply with special education regulations, manage union contracts, or supervise school improvement plans.

Classrooms, where the system's technical work takes place, are only loosely coupled to this administration, so as to buffer teachers from public pressures and to give them autonomy for using professional judgment in educating students. Pedagogical activities are largely concealed from public view, though, in any case, few laypersons could assess them just by observation. The administration issues test scores, grades, and diplomas to vouch for teachers' efficacy and to certify students as learners (Meyer 1977; Meyer and Rowan 1983; Meyer, Scott, and Strang 1994).

When teachers teach well and administrators manage well, the structure works. However, it can break down in two ways. The central administration can grow cancerously, stimulated by public expectations but losing connections to them; it can become sclerotic, not even superficially responsive to the public; or both. Alternatively, classrooms can become anarchically isolated, at most under the control of only the teachers who occupy them, not just unregulated, but also unsupported, by the administration and unaffected by the public. Still, even under these conditions, administrators may continue to convince the public that the system is working if they can certify students as succeeding. However, poor published test scores vitiate the administration's claims and raise questions about the technical efficacy of classroom practices. Each of these structural problems limits a school system's interest in community partnerships.

Bureaucratization of the Central Administration

The bureaucratization of school systems accompanied the consolidation of schools into districts and the professionalization of education and school administration at the start of the twentieth century (Katz 1975; Tyack 1974; Tyack and Hansot 1982). The move rested on beliefs that there were single best ways to deliver services to diverse individuals, and that scientifically trained experts knew those methods and thus should direct their implementation. The bureaucracy's purpose was to manage teaching and to regulate contact between schools and communities. These premises gave educators little reason to listen to community members, much less to collaborate with them.

In addition, once established, these systems, like all bureaucracies, created conditions that further discouraged administrators and teachers from attending to parents. Here we look at how bureaucratic structures commonly affect those who work in them psychologically, often unconsciously (Baum 1987, 1991). Bureaucracy distributes responsibility for tasks more or less evenly but concentrates authority near the top. Hence, most workers find themselves having less authority than they need to carry out their responsibilities. They depend on authority from others above them to do what they are expected to do. However, because work often is complicated, contingent on many people's efforts, an individual's responsibility may be ambiguous: it is unclear who should do what to ensure overall success. In addition, formal authority is only part of workers' actual authority: expertise, relationships, and strategy also matter. Thus authority too may be ambiguous: it is unclear who can make what happen in specific circumstances.

This predicament of combined inequality and ambiguity of responsibility and authority presents workers with risks not only that they cannot do what superiors expect, but also that those higher up take credit for success and force blame for failures downward. It becomes easy to imagine that responsibilities grow ambiguously larger while authority shrinks ambiguously smaller, adding anxieties about being scapegoated to realistic concerns about getting work done. One way people deal with these anxieties is by trying to avoid responsibility.

At the same time, bureaucratic structure adds anxiety by leading workers to make negative assumptions about how those above will treat them. Administrators are considered to know enough about others' tasks to direct and evaluate their performance. In large, hierarchical organizations, such as school systems, supervisors exercise considerable authority over many individuals with whom they have little contact. Looking upward, subordinates may see these bosses as anonymous, self-sufficient people who share little information about their own work, seem able to satisfy their own needs without help from below, and make consequential judgments about those below with little explanation.

Staff want to understand the motives of those who control so much, but because subordinates know so little about administrators, they must use their imagination to fill in the details. Often people fill in information by unconsciously drawing analogies from early experiences with parents, who also were autonomous and powerful (Baum 1987; Hodgson, Levinson, and Zaleznik 1974; Sennett 1980). As if they were once again children, workers imagine that administrators will inevitably find their work inadequate in unforeseeable ways. They anticipate being shamed for not performing acceptably. This anxiety gets in the way of realistically understanding administrators and the organization. It increases fears of being scapegoated for problems created by others, and it hinders acting assertively to take authority and carry out responsibilities (Lewis 1974; Lynd 1958; Piers 1971). If people exercise authority, they are more apt to prevent action than to facilitate it.

These common bureaucratic experiences block desire to partner with community groups. First, because they make taking responsibility risky, they discourage teachers, principals, and central staff from paying attention to community members. Community requests could lead to new responsibilities, and others might blame and shame them for mistakes. Second, because these risks loom larger than possible accomplishments or rewards, even those with authority are unlikely to exercise it to promote initiatives. Instead they will try to prevent subordinates from acting.

Third, these conditions foster a paranoid culture in which many others look like potential enemies. Facing numerous and often unrealistic demands, educators can easily assume that someone will blame them for failing to do something. Because they know that they do not succeed at everything, they anticipate being shamed. And they encounter many who make it quite clear that they do not trust their competence. Under pressure, the bureaucracy issues regulations that register doubt about teachers' ability to make judgments about educating students. School staff feel that it is prudent to avoid parents or community members, because contact seems likely to lead to blame and shame.

Isolation of Schoolteachers

Thus when the central administration promulgates positions and regulations to manage environmental pressures, it can immobilize staff by leaving them unable or afraid to exercise professional judgment and get work done. In addition, the bureaucracy can isolate teachers by concentrating on external demands and neglecting their needs. The scientific premises that molded contemporary school systems already separate teachers from one another.

One premise is that teaching depends on a relationship between an individual teacher and individual students. Another is that teachers can most effectively instruct students when they are grouped by age. The organizational and architectural result is the "egg carton school": teachers and students in differentiated grades occupy discrete classrooms, isolated from one another, accessible only from a central hallway. A principal walking the halls can observe the rooms, but teachers have difficulty making contact with one another. The building structure, combined with a schedule that keeps teachers in their rooms for all or most of the day, gives teachers little chance to see others teaching, to teach with them, or just to talk about teaching and students. Bureaucratic incentives, which assess teachers for their solo performance, indicate that this is only proper.

The organization of space, time, and rewards makes it hard for teachers to reflect with one another about what works. Further, this arrangement hinders teachers from identifying with the school as something more than their classroom. The principal occasionally comes by, sometimes to help, sometimes to judge. Bureaucracy's psychological dynamics lead teachers to feel isolated and beleaguered and to resist principals' visits and inquiries, and principals may retreat, with the result that while they are expected to manage, they know little about what teachers do. Few principals think of their school as a collectivity of specific staff and students who have aspirations and accomplishments that they might join together. Not many principals or teachers assume that they can rely on others for support when they need help (Bain, Long, and Ross 1992).

Thus teachers or principals approached by community groups commonly respond as individuals. They have little time to test other staff members' interests, they assume that colleagues are busy, and they calculate that with staff working on their own rather than cooperatively, they would have to beg for help rather than appeal to common interests. Hence, they can find even friendly community activities overwhelming and try to avoid them.

Constant Turnover Hinders Connection

Staff in urban school systems continually change. Nationally, 14 percent of teachers leave their school each year. Beginning teachers are especially likely to go: 20 percent of those with one to three years' experience move on annually. In schools with 50 percent or more minority enrollment, 16 percent of teachers leave each year (National Center for Education Statistics 2001, table 73). Three-fifths of urban eighth graders lose at least one teacher during a school year (Olson and Jerald 1998, 17). Principals move often; in big, urban systems, more than half of schools may change principals at least once in four years.[6] Large, urban system superintendents stay an average of four and a half years (Council of Urban Boards of Education 2001).

This mobility jeopardizes existing community partnerships and adds to difficulties of establishing new ones. Constant movement makes it hard for teachers and administrators to know one another and to work together. It hinders their identifying with or developing loyalty to a school system, because the people around them keep changing. New principals often begin anxiously and introduce new priorities and ways of working. New superintendents bring new personnel, make organizational changes, and institute new policies. Teachers and administrators end up trying to succeed at continually changing tasks. Because so many people are new, people are always trying to learn what is going on and whom they can trust, and few feel secure taking initiatives, least of all with outside community groups.

Challenges of Contact and Partnership

Community-school partnerships depend on personal relations between parents or other community members and school staff. People must have time to get to know others, to determine what they can do, to arrange time and resources, and to assess results. To begin with, high community and school mobility makes it hard even to make the contact that might lead to "mating."

Mismatching Morphology

When community members and school system staff size up one another, many complain about mismatching morphology. Community activists charge that schools are too bureaucratic to engage, while school administrators argue that communities are too amorphous.

School systems are hierarchical, with public contact assigned to specialized staff. Although community members may be interested in policies, budgets, personnel, standards, research, or facilities, administrators typically refer citizens to a public information or a public involvement officer. The public information office may not have the information that a community member wants, and a public involvement officer has limited time for many requests. Community members who call other offices to get information or convey views may leave repeated messages without a response, may get through after much time and effort, or may reach someone who lacks the information, time, interest, or willingness to help. Schools are small and less bureaucratic, but many principals try to restrict public contact to themselves or to a parent liaison, and both are busy. Engaging the school system requires exceptional knowledge, time, and patience.

Few community members have all three. Activists who do usually are occupied with several projects. They may come together to contact the school system and to collect information, but some will leave for other concerns, and a diminishing group will analyze the information, meet with school staff to discuss issues, or develop plans for community action. Newcomers may join and may introduce new directions. In any case, few in the larger community know that the group exists, much less what it does in their name. Hence, a community presents to schools a small, changing representation with uncertain ties to any broad constituency.

Superficially, this mismatch between community and school structure makes connection problematic. However, community networks' amoebic structure has the virtue of being able to change shape to fit external objects. Parents and community activists have no protocol describing where, when, or how they should meet with teachers or administrators. They can call anyone, drop in anywhere, attend any more or less public meeting, and buttonhole anyone in a hallway. They are free to say what is on their minds. And many carry their own authority, able to make decisions on the spot. This protean shape aids engagement with schools.

Differently Permeable Boundaries

Partnership requires not just contact but open boundaries—to transmit information and then authority, effort, and other resources. Communities and school systems have different norms regarding external relations and different ability to regulate engagement.

Because communities have little formal organization, they have no power to control members' outside contacts. Formal organizations can most credibly authorize individuals to speak for the community, but many persons can claim to represent it. Conversely, communities are open to outsiders, who may meet and try to make agreements with nearly anyone. Formal organizations are the most reliable partners. However, there may not be a single organization that incontestably represents all or most, separate organizations may be active in different issue or geographic areas, or there may be no organization actively serving many community members. Thus community boundaries are easily crossed in both directions, and many community members may engage schools or the school system in partnership.

School systems differ in three ways. First, their members are employees, and administrators can regulate their contacts. Second, system managers generally discourage outside contact on the grounds that it is unnecessary, it consumes scarce time, and it could lead to problems. Third, school systems divide authority to meet with outsiders from authority to make agreements with them. A public involvement officer meets with community groups, but activists who want a decision must influence a different official, who spends little time with the public, and the board, which limits debate at meetings. At a school, the principal has the authority to meet parents and to make some decisions. However, many principals, already responding to numerous demands and sensitive to norms against letting the community in, limit parent contact and resist using their authority. Thus school systems tightly regulate boundaries.

These conditions do not hinder parents' helping with homework or volunteering, but active community partnerships will be on the system's periphery, at the edge of the central administration or at schools. Idiosyncratic individuals may reach out to community groups or institutions, but their activity will be marginalized within the system and will have little impact on it.

Asymmetrical Desire and Self-Defeating Ambition

One might lament the ways the school system's structure and culture interfere with community partnerships. However, in society, unlike biology, desire influences anatomy. Where there is a will, there is a way. The system's anatomy serves its purposes. Most educators, thinking in terms of professional expertise and authority, if they consider partnerships at all, want community support for their missions. Parents should raise children well, appreciate what teachers are trying to do, help children with homework, and volunteer for nonprofessional tasks. Businesses should contribute money, expertise, or other resources. The PTA should obtain resources for the school. Few educators think about what a school can do for a community.

Parents, in contrast, thinking in terms of democracy, parental rights, and the effects of parental involvement on children's learning, want various partnerships, from discussion of school programs to joint monitoring of children's progress to participation in making decisions. They expect some partnerships to involve them individually and others to include organized parents. Some think of partnerships as ways of improving not just children's education but communities. In approaching the schools, community members are not always highly knowledgeable, skilled, or organized, but frequently they are the only party interested in connecting.

One might lambaste the school system or, alternatively, rue these failures as regrettable but more or less inevitable results of differences between schools and communities. However, either course misses a crucial point: the difficulty of forming partnerships is a product of the *interaction* between the community and the school system. On one side, members of the public make numerous, ambiguous, conflicting, and sometimes unrealistic demands regarding children's education. On the other side, professional educators insist that they can do everything necessary to educate children. They then seize an untenable position, and members of society are glad to find a simplistic view of things that lets them blame teachers and schools for much that is beyond their control. Inevitably educators fail, they encounter critics at many turns, and the bureaucracy has them where they cannot easily learn or innovate. Under these conditions, a professional culture becomes a paranoid culture.

Then partnership is the furthest thing from educators' minds, and they seem like culprits. And yet partnership, beginning with realistic public discussion of how to divide societal responsibility for educating children, also is the remedy. Schools do not have to do it all, and they can share the burden with manifold community partners, from neighborhood parents to regional employers to national policy makers. We return to this theme in the final chapter.

Chapter 16

Building Networks in Turbulent Fields
Tension between Attachment and Knowledge

School reform, as any action in a turbulent field, depends on creating a network that collectively has the capacity to control the environment and the intelligence to bring about results. The Southeast Education Task Force is an effort to design such attachments and knowledge. The past two chapters have described the difficulties of these efforts. Community organizations are insubstantial and fragile. They do not attract the attention of universities or school systems; they have little evident to offer and no power to compel participation. School systems are self-absorbed and defensive. They avoid contacts and shun community organizations. And yet the Task Force managed to develop connections that contributed to educational improvement.

This chapter examines the difficulties and possibilities of what can be called "organizing practice": efforts to organize people in attachments and ideas in knowledge so that efficacious collective action is possible in a turbulent environment. The analysis focuses on how the tenuousness of attachments puts knowledge in jeopardy.

The Turbulent Urban Education Field

Turbulent Environments

The essence of turbulent environments is that entities sharing a field are so large and numerous that action by one sets several others reverberating, with the result that no one can control the field or succeed at much by itself.

Because entities cross traditional geographic, political, institutional, and disciplinary boundaries, problems that arise belong to no one alone—and may belong to no one at all.

Solving problems depends on creating networks whose members can design and agree on new roles, relationships, procedures, and directions (Gray 1989; Schön and Rein 1994). Unlike the formal institutions that send participants, networks are loosely bounded and structured, with fluid, negotiable membership, responsibility, authority, and accountability. Because problems do not match organizational boundaries, the crucial links in these networks are individuals who have distinct skill, knowledge, and personal security, as well as time and other resources, that enable them to connect organizations, communities, and institutions (Sarason and Lorentz 1998).

Actually, "organizations," "communities," and "institutions" misleadingly imply coherence and unity. For example, these entities may have powerful informal structures that bear little resemblance to formal descriptions. More than that, they frequently are not single bodies. Many are themselves networks, of "divisions," "subcommunities," "departments," "groups," and the like. Relations among these components may be stable, but they need not be. Moreover, the units may act autonomously, often connecting more with "outsiders" than those "inside."

These conditions have two implications for solving problems. One is that work may require creating, or at least strengthening, the entities that themselves become participants in an "interorganizational" network. Community organization is a prototypical example, where an organizer must fashion a "community" that can act. The same may be said with regard to school systems. The second implication is that the components of a network spanning a turbulent field often are subunits (including individual members) of entities that are formal members.

The Education Field

In the case of the Southeast Education Task Force, the education field can be described as having six main components: the community (which includes people who live, send their children to school, work, or do business in Southeast Baltimore, as well as organizations that are located or operate there); the Task Force; the University of Maryland; funders; sixteen schools; and the Baltimore City Public School system, represented most concretely by its central administration but encompassing the sixteen schools. These components, in turn, include other actors. The distinction between the schools and the school system, though partly arbitrary, recognizes that schools have some autonomy to act independently of the central administration.

Urban education fields include a school system and schools, by definition. From the perspective of most local school systems, the community is not an actor, at least not one with whom they intentionally interact. Community organizations concerned with education are rare. Similarly, few universities take a role in the urban education field more active than preparing teachers or administrators to join the school system or providing some professional development for staff. Hence, it is unusual to find a university and community organization working together on education. Thus the education field portrayed here may be unrepresentative of American cities, but it shows the challenges and possibilities of developing denser urban education fields.

Truncated Membership

One might object that this field, whatever can be said about difficulties organizing it, is not turbulent in the sense of being the object of uncontrollable dynamics set off by huge organizations. The school system is the sole large institution in this picture. However, it is important to keep in mind that no local school system can dominate the education field if a measure of that control is the ability to educate children. One reason, forwarded by many school staff, is that students' communities contain influences beyond schools' control (Levin and Riffel 2000).

If we take "the community" to be more than just social relations among neighbors, we can see that it is a mammoth entity in its own right. Its members are people who seek employment, want to rent or purchase homes, have and are treated as holding certain racial or ethnic identities, have variable capacities to take care of themselves, and so forth. Thus any community has connections to labor markets, housing markets, social welfare policies, racial institutions, and the like. Each of these is part of the field affecting local communities and, thus, with a community, part of the education field. These institutions clearly influence school systems—in terms of where students live, what parents expect of children, how parents care for children and prepare them for school, and how school staff treat students.

Yet these institutions normally are not seen as part of the education field. To take a simple example, the exodus of manufacturing from cities has eroded families that depended on it for employment and hindered the formation of families by adults who could have worked the jobs. This economic change reduced families' abilities to support children and lowered expectations from children's education. If school systems could influence the labor market, then schools could do much more to educate children. However, the political difficulty of doing this—because some key actors are not local, because incentives for collaboration are elusive, and because American political culture favors a "private" labor market over one that is publicly managed—is a chief reason labor institutions are not in cognitive maps of local school systems. Another is that professional educators choose to see themselves as the primary influence on children's learning.

Thus the apparent simplicity or sparse population of the urban education field reflects widely shared assumptions about which organizations or institutions are "educational" in the sense of bearing responsibility for good schooling—even though there is little disagreement that many institutions, including the labor market, affect educational outcomes. Conventional views of the field exclude a number of institutions that influence the school system because of the perception that it cannot influence them in return.

In fact, even within the narrow definition of the local education field there are a few more actors in the Task Force case. Churches and nonprofit organizations are active in the community. Elsewhere in the city are community-based and nonprofit organizations interested in education and staff members of some public and quasipublic agencies. The state and federal departments of education, academics, and education program developers and experts also are present.

Still, others one might expect to see are absent. The mayor and city council are not active in schooling. Few local foundations make education grants. Partly as a result, there are not many community-based or other nonprofit organizations in education. There are few advocacy groups and few organizations to which any community or grassroots group can turn for assistance. Few businesses play much of a role beyond occasional, and usually small, contributions to partner schools.

In short, what appears to be the city's education field is a truncated version of the actual field. Those who would influence the field locally, such as a community organization, find few of the significant actors at hand.

Few, Spotty Relationships

Aside from links between central school administrators and school staff, prior to creation of the Southeast Education Task Force few actors in the local education field had ties. There were few neighborhood organizations concerned with education and no links between schools and parent groups other than PTAs and PTOs. A few churches, businesses, universities, and other institutions had relations with schools, ranging from donating resources to operating after-school study halls to managing curriculum projects.

Part of the explanation is the conditions that limit community organization. However, even when, as in this case, a community organization forms, the actors in the field have few points of contact. Most funders, for example, react to proposals rather than going out and contacting people who could implement their agenda. Foundation staff have limited time; in addition, they have limited expertise and are uncertain about whom or what to encourage. Most universities have little interest in communities other than, perhaps, their immediate neighbors. Usually their aim in community relations is to maintain peace while town and gown do their separate business. Universities rarely look for ways of joining with community groups and helping them.

A central reason for little contact among actors in the urban education field is the school culture. As a professional culture, it regards outsiders as unnecessary except for supporting school agendas. When the culture turns paranoid, it regards outsiders as dangerous. As school staff feel under the gun to produce higher test scores, they raise drawbridges over moats and defend the system's entries. They learn to turn their backs on the public by ignoring them, not returning phone calls, responding noncommittally or hostilely at meetings, and talking in esoteric language. Consequently, outsiders have difficulty finding anyone with whom to connect.

Instabilities in the Field

On top of this, entities in the field are unstable. School system staff come and go, changing policies, priorities, parts of the system structure, and individuals with whom others might work. Families move, children switch schools, and adults' interests in education change. Though a community organization may continue to be concerned about schools, its members and their interests and capacities alter.

Funding relationships are inherently unstable, because money is limited. Insofar as funders prefer to see grants as seed money, even successful connections are transitory.

Local churches, particularly where congregations are old, small, and dwindling, where national denominational offices place and rotate ministers, or where a minuscule budget requires a minister to work a full-time job elsewhere, experience steady turnover of pastors and lay leaders. Ministers face many demands, and activities outside of the congregation, such as in the education field, take second place to church work.

The university in this case was exceptionally consistent, but it also was the smallest actor.

These conditions make connections elusive and tenuous.

Effects on Organizing Practice

Three realities define practice in an environment like this. The first is that creating attachments must take priority over all else; otherwise there is no one to act. Second, attachments must be continually recreated, to consolidate entities and to connect to them. People must be brought together, given reasons to work together, nurtured in working and staying together, and replaced when they move on. Third, these tasks must be carried out personally. Although people may identify with communities or organizations as abstractions, they form attachments to voluntary organizations and networks by connecting to persons they meet directly.

The truncation of the education field—such that it is defined in terms of a few local institutions centered on the school system, to the exclusion of many others that influence children's learning—has two distinct effects on organizing practice. On the one hand, it diverts attention from actors who matter greatly in education, and it restricts initiatives to a small part of the field. As a result, for example, a community organization may ignore how the labor and housing markets limit children's opportunities and develop initiatives that affect little. On the other hand, the truncation focuses a small organization's practice on manageable aims—connecting to and trying to influence the school system and schools. Deceptively, by holding out the possibility of influence, the truncation persuades a community organization to act.

Even the truncated field extends so far as to require intensive organizing activity. In the case of the Task Force, the small group who started out had to find common ground among themselves, recruit others to a new organization, consolidate the organization, nurture its members, and replace those who left; then they had to persuade school staff to join or support the organization in anticipation of benefitting from its work; at the same time, they had to urge the superintendent to endorse the organization's efforts to principals, cajole research staff to deliver data, and encourage other staff to provide useful information; soon after, they had to convince pastors to involve congregants or at least themselves in developing partnerships with principals; soon after that, they had to persuade funders to invest in the organization. And so on. The elusiveness of contact, compounded by the Task Force's newness, required unceasing effort to develop personal relations that would give others reasons to take part or lend support. Ubiquitous instability forced the organization to start over many times.

The most direct impact for an organization like the Task Force is on volunteers' and staff members' time. They must give priority to developing relationships. If they start a project, they must keep it going by sustaining contacts, persuading a new principal to adopt it, and getting someone to replace a volunteer staffing it who got tired, changed jobs, or moved. They have little time for analyzing or evaluating the project, much less for developing more general knowledge.

Loyalty

Further subtle and pervasive effects on organizing practice derive from the emotional bonds that attach individuals to one another within an organization and between organizations. When staff or volunteers become organizing practitioners and approach others to join their enterprise, the latter expect things of them.

The first is attention. They want appreciation for their virtues, such as their talents, generosity in giving time, and importance to the accomplishment of a task or mission. They want to see how their participation, which has opportunity costs, will bring them benefits, such as general pleasure in doing good, satisfaction with accomplishing a specific good, enjoyment in meeting like-minded others, and personal or professional gains from future contacts with some.

Moreover, people want an organizing practitioner to absorb risks. Their most specific concern is failure. They do not want to fail, they do not want to have to clean up after a failure, and they do not want to be blamed for failure. Some more diffuse risks also weigh heavily. People don't want to reveal their needs and personal, professional, or institutional "secrets" to others, only to see others exploit this knowledge by embarrassing them or negotiating unfairly. And they want to avoid the negative consequences of sticking their necks out in their home setting, for example, in trying something new that few others know about or support.

People want a practitioner to guarantee the security of their boundaries. They do not want their personal or institutional space intruded on or spoiled, and they want to be able to go home again. In calculating the odds on participation, they measure the practitioner in terms of his loyalty (Forester 1999). Does he understand what someone means and cares about? Though partly a question about the practitioner's intelligence, this is mainly a question of whether he listens, whether he asks about what he does not comprehend and stays at it until all feel confident that they understand one another. At bottom is emotional loyalty. One might speak of political loyalty—the practitioner's readiness to support someone's position and stick with him over time—but while that matters, it is only part of a desire for the practitioner to be true on a deeper, personal level. Will he support me and my view of things; is he strong enough to do so?

Different people calibrate the terms of this question differently. One variable is psychological, a matter of personality: some people require total, unambiguous loyalty, whereas others accept less. The latter may recognize and even value a reality of diverse affiliations. Another variable is social: people differ in their involvement in or commitment to specific attachments. Those for whom an organization or a network is central have high stakes in its operations and expect much from responsible practitioners, whereas others for whom a connection is peripheral need and expect less. But all still ask the loyalty question.

For a practitioner, loyalty demands a great deal of time. He must be present to others. He must listen. And he must speak, responding to what he has heard and asking questions and speaking further, until he and others understand one another to their satisfaction, and until the others feel appreciated. And he must speak consistently with those he encounters, because many of them know one another, indeed, knew each other before he appeared and know and care about some others far more than they will care about him. Whether members of a community or a far-flung network, they will compare notes about his performance.

When those whom the practitioner would connect hold conflicting views or interests, these conditions present complicated demands. If conflict is great and stakes are high, it is easy, and likely, for one party to imagine that the practitioner is loyal to others, against him. The practitioner must be an honest broker, loyal to the principle of respect for everyone's concerns, if not necessarily to the primacy of all positions.

These requirements of attachment compete with those of knowledge for scarce time. In addition, a tension between attachment and knowledge arises from the emotional effects of loyalty on volunteers or staff who make the connections in forming organizations or networks. Although for a few loyalty is just a calculation (going along in return for money or power), for most it is partly or wholly an internal commitment. The key is that loyalty affirms not only the other but also the practitioner. Someone's judgment that a practitioner is loyal is an announcement of his competence, value, and even worthiness of affection. (It also may be a means to future business.)

People who act as organizing practitioners come from various home bases. Some may rest securely in relatively large or at least nurturing organizations, and this practice may be a component or extension of their normal role. They can go back to a warm home after the work. Often, however, certainly in many community initiatives, and particularly when practitioners are volunteers, those who take organizing roles do so outside of their formal positions. They may have peripheral institutional roles that bring them into contact with outsiders, and it may be that marginality that enables them to be loyal to others. In them, connections among people and organizations truly are personal, and they hold organizations, partnerships, or networks together.

In this position, organizing practitioners need support and nurturance. They may take some of both from their work's successes, but successes are only infrequent interruptions of long spells of meeting, talking, and writing. Relations with partners provide opportunities for reward and replenishment. Indeed, relationships outside of a home organization offer social and emotional possibilities that are incompatible with formal lines of responsibility, authority, and accountability.

Here is the crux of the tension between attachment and knowledge. Loyalty, which is central to attachment, not only connects others to a practitioner but binds the practitioner to others. However, while connection is the essence of attachment, knowledge depends on sufficient separation to reflect, analyze, and even criticize. Loyalty conflicts with the detachment necessary for developing and offering knowledge useful for action. Attachment and knowledge represent fundamentally different acts, psychological conditions, and social relations. Focus on attachment, which is intensified under turbulent conditions, when connection is constantly in question, hinders attention to knowledge.

When a practitioner works with a partner who is powerful, whom he respects and likes, and who offers appreciation, companionship, or affection, he can easily identify with the other's views and forget about alternatives. He loses the ability to question. A manifestation of this process is the personalization of issues. For example, a coordinator of an education network, instead of systematically considering a range of proposals that the network could present to a school system, simply weighs the views of the persons around him. Conducting research to define problems or to search for solutions could cast doubt on people's positions. If he proposed new policies or strategies, others, feeling challenged, might question not just his analysis but also his loyalty. New positions could upset relations among participants and jeopardize consensus on action. It is easier—if the aim of collaboration is to agree on and carry out action, particularly because time is limited—to accept and work from given positions than to start anew.

Although a staff member or volunteer can decide for practical reasons that an organization will take only a position that incorporates leading actors' preferences, more often this constriction of possibilities occurs unconsciously, in an effort to demonstrate loyalty. Some people narrow their horizons simply because they are uncomfortable asserting their views against others, but the structure of practice evokes a general response. When relationships are personal, people think in terms of politeness more than political calculation. However, both politeness and politics create "garbage cans," where attachment takes priority over knowledge.

Action depends on reciprocity between attachment and knowledge. People must know enough about themselves and others to form useful connections, and their relations become the basis for defining, developing, and using knowledge. This knowledge, in turn, helps reformulate and re-form connections, and so forth. These interactions are encapsulated in Schön's (1983) felicitous phrase "reflective practice."

The challenge is that attachment and knowledge are in tension, one requiring connection and the other detachment. In this way, they resemble the Heisenbergian paradox that it is impossible to know simultaneously a particle's position and its velocity. Attachment involves connecting to a position. Knowledge involves taking a measure of someone or something by observing him, her, or it in motion. While attachment provides an essential basis for knowledge, total attachment precludes knowledge—and, paradoxically, because all are merged, eliminates attachment. While knowledge gives guidance to attachment, total concentration on knowledge prevents attachment—and, paradoxically, makes knowledge impossible. Practitioners experience the impulses toward attachment and knowledge as contrasting emotional states. Attachment demands loyalty, whereas knowledge requires reflection and analysis. Deliberate action depends on pragmatically, imperfectly balancing the two.

Knowledge

The structural question is how to limit the attention and energy invested in forming and maintaining attachments to allow attention and energy to go, also, into developing and using knowledge. The psychological question is how a practitioner can modulate distance from others to be both loyal and analytic. The social question is how a practitioner can organize others so they feel securely enough attached to be able to examine and even criticize their positions and consider an open array of actions. These were Trist's (1985) concerns when he asked what would enable a network to become a "learning network." Warren, Rose, and Bergunder (1971) wondered, similarly, what was necessary for network members to develop an "institutionalized thought structure," where, thinking in common ways, they could act together to solve problems.

There are no formulaic answers. Realistically, attachment demands a lot of time. Yet practitioners have discretion. Many, concerned about demonstrating and benefitting from loyalty, assume that they must continually build or deepen relationships, even when it is possible, and necessary, to develop knowledge. One reason they may avoid research and planning is that they feel overwhelmed by conflicting positions and complicated problems. However, they also may hesitate just because reflecting on matters entails drawing back from attachments, lowers the satisfying intensity of relationships, and seems to raise questions of loyalty.

Those who bring people together to open up issues need to reassure themselves and others that this work is not disloyal but is the essence of loyalty. Asking questions about preferences, positions, or past actions does not necessarily challenge people's competence, virtue, or good faith but asserts all three in the work of inquiry. A practitioner must show others that questioning can serve their interests by clarifying what they are and how to forward them.

That is the crux of Tuckman's (1965) theory of group development, which revolves around tensions between attachment and knowledge. Groups oscillate among "stages" as they try to establish workable compromises. Thus a practitioner must help people *form* (attach themselves to one another) with sufficient security to go on to *storm* (raise questions and look for knowledge about their interests and relationships). If they can agree on *norms* (for their attachments and the knowledge that they will seek and use), then they can move ahead to *perform* (develop and use knowledge in action). The practitioner's burden is to help all manage anxiety about disloyalty, so that they do not avoid or prematurely curtail the storming prerequisite to tempering attachment with knowledge.

Making Space for Knowledge: Possibilities for Organizing Practice

Lessons from the Southeast Education Task Force

Members must be securely attached to explore knowledge. In the Southeast Education Task Force, a personal relationship, between Bobby English and me, provided requisite structure. She put priority on personal attachments but also respected knowledge. I gave primacy to knowledge and appreciated attachment. In the beginning, we pulled in different directions, but growing familiarity, respect, trust, and agreement about ways of proceeding secured a foundation for knowledge. This may be a common pattern in university-community partnerships that bring together a researcher and a community organizer. However, any two participants may represent and reconcile attachment and knowledge. Alternatively, one leader may express and balance both.

The stable core, where both attachment and knowledge were valued, made it possible to develop and use knowledge, in two ways. First, it secured space within the turbulent education field where people concerned about Southeast Baltimore schools could talk and disagree with the assurance that those assembled shared school and community interests, wanted to find common ground, and would support one another, however deliberations came out.

Second, the center's stability made it possible for the Task Force to operate as a network where those who engaged in research were only loosely coupled to, and thus buffered from, others who rode the school system's waves trying to create and manage attachments. The "umbrella" metaphor captures this condition: different people conducted projects in the Task Force name but more or less independently of one another. Some projects operated close to the center, and all Task Force members would make decisions about them—for example, what the *Southeast Community Plan on Education* or the facilities plan would recommend—but no project dominated. Some projects operated at the periphery, with involvement by one or a few persons—the safety assessment and the tutoring-mentoring project were examples; Task Force members received reports, perhaps made suggestions, but rarely gave direction. In this arrangement, research and planning proceeded alongside organizing or lobbying without direct interaction.

Parent organizing absorbed much of the field's turbulence for the Task Force—most dramatically in a handful of conflicts with principals and system administrators but also mundanely in the turnover of principals, the collapse of parent organizations, changes in parent leadership that shifted directions, and the cessation of projects when principals diverted their attention to new administrative directives. At the center, Bobby English and Ken Strong responded to school system requests or complaints, while I focused on research and planning.

University participation allowed many research and planning projects to proceed at the edge of the field. Graduate assistants analyzed student data, reviewed K–8 research, mapped the school capital budgeting process, developed a proposal for planning and developing full-service community schools, reviewed studies of attendance promotion programs, and prepared a proposal for a community fund-raising initiative. This institutional arrangement insulated researchers from the logic of action before bringing findings or recommendations to Task Force decision makers.

Although Task Force members' beliefs and preferences, as well as school system politics, shaped their use of knowledge, the stable core and loose coupling helped them develop knowledge without undue concern about preferences or politics. The quality of knowledge developed under these conditions gave it influence.

Conditions for Organizing Practice

The case points to five conditions supporting organizing practice. The first concerns participants. An effort must start out with individuals or organizations committed to forming a multi-institutional entity to address specific issues. They must be committed to developing and using knowledge to understand these issues and to identify reasonable actions. They need not know esoteric research methods or concepts but, simply, they must take seriously the idea of asking questions before deciding what to do.

Second, participants need a leader or leaders with two qualities. The leadership should value knowledge and encourage participants to use it. Though membership is largely a matter of chance—who decides to participate—a leader can recruit people who appreciate questioning as part of organizing practice. In addition, the leadership should be sufficiently stable—continuous, consistent, and able to absorb environmental turbulence—to give the entity solidity and to enable members to feel secure—*from* threat and distraction, *to* think and act.

A related third condition concerns what is commonly called "organizational culture" but is essentially a frame of mind or temperament. Organizing practice requires people who comfortably recognize their dependencies on others, want to and can join with people different from themselves, can think beyond formal intellectual and social boundaries, and are prepared to learn more before they know what to do. Leaders can foster a culture that encourages these tendencies. However, participants' actions also depend on who they are—what they want to do, what they are comfortable doing, and what they have the skill to do. Recruitment matters.

A fourth condition, on which we have focused here, is a structure that allows participants to balance attachment and knowledge, to draw back from loyal attachment to reflect, engage in research, and ponder and use the results. In one sense, this is a matter of chance, dependent on who participates. However, for any individual it is a matter of psychological positioning or strategy—regulating distance from others. And organizational design matters. A stable core that incorporates commitments to attachment and knowledge does more than just legitimate both abstractly; it provides a psychological foundation for efforts to develop and use knowledge.

In addition, loose coupling between attachment and knowledge activities provides a structural solution for the psychological problem of balancing loyalty and reflection. The loose coupling may be accomplished through a division of labor that separates people interested in attachment from others concerned with knowledge. Even if there are no strict divisions between participants, research and planning activities need to be buffered from external pressures.[1]

A fifth condition concerns resources. Any entity must have members or staff who have expertise, access to information, and, crucially, time for research. Usually these resources depend on money. In any case, getting the resources depends on strategic effort.

Psychological, social, and political interests in loyalty oppose these conditions. They make it hard to find individuals or, especially, organizations that are prepared to develop working relations with others who are independent and different from them. It is difficult to get participants that can be comfortable with a culture embracing ambiguity and uncertainty. These conditions work against organizing loosely coupled structures and, in particular, supporting and using independent, open-ended research. And funders, who want a sure, tangible thing, have little interest in spending on the development of networks among organizations that prize autonomy and see collaboration as a last resort. The challenge is to provide assurance for action.

Part 8

Lessons and Conclusions

Chapter 17

Evaluating the Southeast Education Task Force

The Southeast Education Task Force has carried out a community approach to school reform. More than 1,000 people, supported by hundreds of thousands of dollars, have participated over eight years. How should we evaluate these efforts?

A Pragmatic Path through Evaluation Predicaments

Evaluation, always difficult, is particularly problematic for community initiatives, for six reasons. First, these initiatives are complex: they aim to accomplish many goals and include multiple, often overlapping strategies. As a result, it is difficult to identify a few discrete goals or to link interventions in specific causal ways to goals. Second, the process of planning and implementing community initiatives is fluid, with participants entering and leaving and changing their thinking along the way. New perspectives, goals, and theories of change replace old, and aims and assumptions combine syncretically. It is impossible to identify single sets of goals or strategies.

Third, these initiatives include multiple interventions that not only interact with one another but also encounter a turbulent environment. Environmental reactions often oppose, reverse, or obscure an initiative's effects. As a result, it is hard to distinguish the course of planned interventions from other forces and thus to identify or collect relevant evaluation data. Fourth, the initiatives try to effect changes in social relations, family functioning, or mental conditions. Indicators of these changes are difficult to conceptualize, and relevant data are hard to collect.

Fifth, community initiatives aim to make significant changes in social institutions, living conditions, or persons, with success dependent on far-reaching contingencies and considerable time. These conditions increase the burdens and costs of evaluation, perhaps prohibitively. Finally, every community is unique. There can be no control group, and it is impossible to construct a counterfactual account of what might have happened absent the planned intervention (Annie E. Casey Foundation n.d., 1998; Connell, Kubisch, Schorr, and Weiss 1995; Fulbright-Anderson, Kubisch, and Connell 1998).

One way of working through these evaluation predicaments is pragmatic: define interventions as current participants see them. Two practical considerations argue for doing so. First, this course reduces required attention by neglecting aims and interventions that have come and gone. This is mainly an economic argument; much can be learned from analyzing the evolution of a project, if resources allow. Second, present participants care the most about an initiative and can influence its course. They can use evaluation and, in doing so, can test its validity. This is a familiar argument for formative evaluation: reflection on an ongoing intervention helps those with responsibility measure and, where appropriate, revise their course. In contrast, summative evaluation, at the end of a project, begins as a historical account only potentially useful in the future (Scriven 1967, 1991).

In this spirit, Weiss (1995, 1998) proposes engaging participants in a thought experiment. Many who work with comprehensive community initiatives have endorsed her "program theory," or "theory of change," model of evaluation (Fulbright-Anderson, Kubisch, and Connell 1998). Evaluators begin by asking participants to imagine that they (or their predecessors) set out with at least tacit plans based on assumptions about cause-and-effect relationships and that current conditions represent efforts to implement them. Evaluators ask participants to make the underlying theories explicit and then collect data that can test their validity. If participants conclude that they expected an intervention to set in motion a sequence of events culminating in certain effects on a group, then evaluators would examine whether these effects occurred in ways related to the intervention. In examining the data, evaluators and participants decide whether initial theories were realistic, whether an alternative theory fits conditions better, and whether interventions should be changed on the basis of new theoretical assumptions.

This exercise can be viewed as retrospective planning: urging people to imagine what they would have had in mind if they had planned their project, to assess conditions in terms of that plan, and in this light to reaffirm or amend the plan. Weick (1979) observes that most planning is retrospective; Weiss would formalize the process. Though community initiatives' complexity eludes precision, this approach helps define the intervention and its outcomes and identify data to be collected, appropriate measures of activity, and standards for success.[1] Definitive judgments may be difficult, but the process allows thoughtful reflection on purposes and effects.

SOUTHEAST EDUCATION TASK FORCE GOALS

Task Force participants, if asked about their goals, would say something about helping children learn. Even so, the many who were not educators recognized their limited direct influence on students. They were doing what they could to improve schools and education, and they believed that good schools were vital to the community's future. In this framework, they would describe four main purposes, each with distinct, though related, program hypotheses.

Helping Students Directly

Some activities aimed to help students in schools directly. Occasionally the Task Force planned and implemented programs in schools. Tutoring programs are an example, as are health and social services in Tench Tilghman's Family and Community Resource Center. More often, the Task Force provided human, material, or financial resources to schools for programs they managed. For example, a church helped a school rebuild its library. The University of Maryland consulted on student discipline. Organizing helped start an after-school program, and the Ad Hoc Group on Education and the Empowerment Zone stimulated extended day programs in EZ schools. Organizing was instrumental in getting an addition for William Paca, and Task Force action got the school system to repair other facilities.

The premise for these activities is that specific programs in schools have positive influences on students—by directly affecting their academic accomplishments or by helping to improve their attendance or behavior so as to contribute to academic success. The activities had program hypotheses. In some cases, Task Force members agreed on a simple postulation, as with tutoring: tutors would help students learn to read, and improved reading ability would give students the ability and confidence to master other subjects.

In other cases, connections between interventions and outcomes were more complex, and people thought and spoke about them with varying precision. Lobbying for a new school is an example. A new building would relieve overcrowding and thus reduce distractions. Particularly if it were small, it would allow greater contact between students and teachers. If the curriculum and teachers were at least as good as those students would have encountered elsewhere, students would learn more. Then they would feel more comfortable at school, attend more often, behave more appropriately there, and learn still more. These were plausible links, but they rested on a number of contingencies.

Strengthening Families' Capacity to Raise Children and Prepare Them for School

Task Force members emphasized parents' central role in education. They are children's first teachers and by raising them well prepare them for school and learning from life. Once sons and daughters are in school, parents can assist with homework and keep in touch with teachers. The Task Force wanted to help adults for whom economic strains, substance abuse, ignorance, or other problems made it hard to be good, effective caretakers. The Nurturing Program and GED classes had this focus. Organizing contributed in various ways, from getting translation and English classes for Hispanic parents to arranging mental health services for troubled families to helping parents meet teachers and administrators.

Task Force members could justify these actions in terms of their influence on students' work. The GED programs gave parents who passed the GED examination a credential that could help them get a better job that could improve their ability to support their family. In addition, the credential, as well as the parent's effort in getting it, showed a child how much the parent valued education and offered an inspiring example. The child might become more motivated to attend school, to behave well there, and to learn better. These were complicated relationships, with many steps contingent on decisions far beyond Task Force influence. Hence, Task Force members found it easier to see support for parents and other adults taking care of children as ends in themselves. English classes offered Hispanic parents opportunities to communicate better with school staff, and these results alone could be considered sufficient.

Strengthening Community Capacity to Act on Education

Community activism was the Task Force's raison d'etre, and it built community capacity to act on education in two ways. First, it conducted research and disseminated information. It invited experts, sponsored symposia, carried out studies, and prepared plans. The resultant knowledge gave community members confidence that they understood issues and had the authority to question practices and make proposals. Second, the Task Force provided means of action and skills in acting. It was itself a central vehicle, complemented by several parent and community organizations. Organizing activities motivated and trained parents, educators, and community members to meet, examine problems, and make and carry out plans.

The simplest theory that connected community activism to educational outcomes went like this: Many teachers have the potential to teach well but do not understand students' lives. Middle-class educators know little about the challenges of poverty. White teachers particularly do not recognize ways in which lower-class African-American culture influences children's lives—often prescribing failure rather than success. If parents and teachers talked, they could agree on goals for children, push and pull in common directions, and do their respective work more knowledgeably. If teachers adjusted curriculum and pedagogy to fit students' strengths and needs, and if parents and teachers together urged children to study, then students would succeed.

This theory was plausible, but there were many more steps than these. Getting parents and teachers together in anything besides ritualistic back-to-school night or report card pickup required great effort. For a teacher to meet and talk meaningfully at least once a semester with all adults responsible for their students would require a Herculean scheduling effort and extraordinary communication ability. Whether those talks led to agreement was another uncertainty, as were the effects of any agreements on children, many of whom spend much of their time with peers who do not value, or at least deeply doubt the personal possibility of, academic success.

Though many Task Force members endorsed the overall scheme, no one assumed that all of these pieces would fall into place. Hence, while they believed that community activism was strategic in promoting educational change, they valued it for its own sake. They aimed to increase individuals' and groups' abilities to establish working relations with any parts of the school system.

Developing the Community as an Asset

The Task Force cared about schools because they could educate children—and, if they could do that, then the community would hold and attract families with children. Otherwise, small parts of Southeast Baltimore would become enclaves of childless yuppies and empty nesters, while much would be home to people with few resources or choices. Task Force members emphasized to public officials and funders that improving schools made the community more viable. Pressed for details, they could elaborate program hypotheses connecting projects to changes in education. Even so, the precise links between school reform and home-buying decisions were uncertain. Hence some Task Force members took part in other Southeast Baltimore improvement efforts, including home ownership initiatives, and they saw the efforts as mutually reinforcing.

Evaluating the Southeast Education Task Force

Few Task Force programs have been formally evaluated. The scarcity, imprecision, ambiguity, and ephemerality of near-term data available for even those limit what can be learned about them. Information relevant to other initiatives is similar. With these constraints, we concentrate on major examples for each of the four purposes and emphasize conclusions that rest more or less easily on the evidence at hand. Complex judgments are difficult. Where interventions' effects are uncertain, we look at contingencies that matter.

Helping Students Directly

Facilities

Organizing got an addition built at William Paca for 250 fourth- and fifth-grade students. The building relieved overcrowding, provided physical structure, and, with its own assistant principal, contributed to a distinct identity for the upper two grades. When students first moved into the building, faculty reported a reduction in stress from the physical pressures of crowding. The climate for learning, teachers said, was better.

However, even if the new building did remove some distractions, learning depends on more than adequate space. Good teaching, well matched with students' abilities, as well as parental support, matters. In fact, two measures of student learning are, at best, inconclusive about academic accomplishments, let alone the contributions of a new building. On the MSPAP test in the spring of 1997, when overcrowding was the worst, only 3 percent of Paca fifth graders scored satisfactory on the reading test. A year later, after fifth graders had been in the new building for about six months, 8.6 percent scored satisfactory. The scores dropped to 6.1 percent in 1999, rose slightly to 6.2 percent in 2000, and climbed a little further to 7.2 percent in 2001. Scores in the other five subjects fluctuated similarly: although fifth-grade scores in all subjects except mathematics were higher in 2001 than in 1997, only writing and language usage scores were the highest in 2001 for all five years (Maryland State Department of Education 2001).

The Baltimore schools did not administer the nationally normed CTBS in 1997 but reinstated it in 1998 after a lapse of several years. Reading and mathematic scores for Paca fourth and fifth graders rose more or less continually from 1998 to 2001, with median fourth-grade readers advancing from the 15th to the 31st percentile and fourth grade mathematicians moving from the 8th to the 24th percentile, while fifth graders improved from the 12th to the 32nd percentile in reading and the 8th to the 17th percentile in mathematics. One could take these scores as a sign of improvement attributable, in part, to the addition. However, the scores of third graders, back in the crowded main building with wall-less classrooms, improved still more, from the 15th to the 36th percentile in reading and from the 7th to the 33rd percentile in mathematics ("City Test Scores on the Rise" 2001).

The evidence is not inconsistent with the possibility that the new building helped students learn, but the data do not pinpoint its contribution or suggest that any benefit was more than small. It would be reasonable to say, simply, that the Task Force succeeded in helping the school get an addition, with responsibility for its use left to others.

Materials

An organizer working with Salem United Methodist Church and Highlandtown Elementary #237 started a book drive to recreate a school library, and thousands of books came in. The school lacked dedicated space for a library, and books circulated on carts. Presumably, teachers and students made good use of the books, but it is difficult to link specific learning to their presence. As the Paca addition, the books may have been useful, but they alone were not sufficient for academic improvement.

Programs

The Task Force contributed tutors to several schools. Most were AmeriCorps reading tutors directed by the Julie Community Center to General Wolfe and City Springs Elementary schools. Both schools had phonics-based Direct Instruction reading programs. The tutors worked with approximately 300 students yearly, and Julie Center records report that children averaged one to two grade improvements in conjunction with the assistance.

The MSPAP scores showed signs of progress at City Springs over this time. In 1998, 6.5 percent of third graders scored satisfactory in reading, at the beginning of Direct Instruction, up to 10.1 percent in 1999, down to 9.3 percent in 2000, and up to 17.9 percent in 2001. At General Wolfe, in contrast, the percentage scoring satisfactory rose from zero in 1998 to 16.7 in 1999 and fell to 6.3 in 2000 and 5.6 in 2001 (Maryland State Department of Education 2001). At the same time, CTBS scores showed steady, significant improvement in reading in all grades at both schools from 1998 to 2001, though City Springs moved much further from a similar starting point. For example, General Wolfe median first grade readers rose from the 33rd to the 54th percentile, while their City Springs counterparts advanced from the 28th to the 82nd percentile; 1998 median second graders read in the 25th percentile at both schools, but City Springs second graders rose to the 63rd percentile in 2001, while General Wolfe counterparts were only in the 33rd percentile ("City Test Scores on the Rise" 2001). The test scores refer to both students who were tutored and others who were not.

Emphasizing CTBS scores, one might conclude that tutoring reinforced Direct Instruction at both schools and contributed to students' growth in reading, with likely benefits in self-confidence and gains in other subjects. However, differences between the schools in the MSPAP, as well as the CTBS, suggest, at the least, that tutoring's influence is secondary to or dependent on each school's teaching program, climate, or other elements.

The Holabird "tutoring-mentoring" program may have extended some students' horizons and motivated some to think more about academic success. However, and even if that were so, even if the presentations' effects were reinforced or at least not vitiated by other events, it will be years before the children make visible choices about work or college.

The Ad Hoc Group on Education and the Empowerment Zone moved the EZ to fund extended school day programs and, in so doing, increased the school system's investment in these programs. Some of the thirty-five Zone schools attended to children's social or cultural development in addition to academics. Some noted that even if students just took part in recreation, their being at school protected them from temptations and made the streets safer.

The quality of planning and implementation varied greatly, from schools where administrators were sophisticated about setting goals, creating programs as strategies, and organizing adults and children to implement the programs to others where principals struggled with the notion of educational goals for after-school programs. Although the Empowerment Zone collected program data, the diversity of goals and the elusiveness of relevant evidence make it difficult to draw conclusions about the programs' effects.

The broadest direct programmatic support to students at schools is the Tench Tilghman Family and Community Resource Center, working with families of about fifty students identified by staff as troubled. Activities aim to improve students' academic work by reducing stresses that interfere with attending school and participating appropriately in class. The center is collecting data on contacts, students' needs, and changes in their conditions and schoolwork.

It is premature to evaluate the center, for two reasons. First, it is new, staff are just starting to engage students and families, and any results will take time. Second, current programs are considered the beginning of a comprehensive array of supports. The incremental addition of programs is expected at some point to effect qualitative changes in the center's influence.

However, even if the center successfully links students and families to social and health services, the connections between these supports and students' schoolwork are uncertain. Services may ease burdens in students' lives without having an impact at school, if the problems solved are not directly related to learning, if students' personal changes are not reinforced by new attention from teachers, or if family members act in opposing ways. Under the best of conditions, effects in school will take time to appear. Attendance, most susceptible to short-term influence, is easiest to measure. Behavioral changes also may follow in relatively short order, but they are harder to measure. Academic improvements may come later, but it is unclear when to expect them in relation to the center's interventions and how much school performance, in any case, can be attributed to its work.

In addition to empirical difficulties isolating the effects of Task Force action, these examples frame a normative issue: how should the Task Force be judged if its efficacy depends on others' actions? It can influence neither a school's administrative policies or teaching practices, nor community conditions. It may have marginal effects on students' home lives. Thus one might conclude in some cases that the Task Force helped schools without helping students. In other instances it may have helped students without touching their academic performance. In these cases one might consider the Task Force successful at some things that were not sufficiently linked to children's learning to affect it significantly. The Task Force expected educators to teach well, while it provided community supports for families, children, and schools. In this framework, its contributions could be considered successful: it had done its part. And yet educators made no agreement to do more than they had done.

Thus conclusions are uncertain. Future analysis may show positive effects of Task Force interventions on students' academic lives. However, many activities aimed at helping students may fail to have an impact, at least because they are small, but perhaps also because countervailing forces are powerful.

Strengthening Families' Capacity to Raise Children and Prepare Them for School

Services for Parents

As part of the Task Force, the Julie Center has sponsored two programs with successful track records in assisting parents: the Nurturing Program and GED classes. The Nurturing Program's goal is for 75 percent of participating parents to master at least five strategies for managing destructive feelings and solving problems. Working with about 200 parents annually, the program has succeeded in these terms, though the center does not maintain contact with parents to know whether they use these techniques in everyday situations.

The Julie Center has conducted GED classes for approximately 125 parents annually. Its approach gives students individual attention as a way of reducing the anxiety that leads adults to leave GED classes prematurely. Fifty percent of its enrollees complete the courses, compared to a typical rate of 10 percent. Of those finishing the course and taking the GED examination, 80 percent pass the test, compared to 50 percent from other programs. The Julie Center reports that a number of its GED students go on to graduate from college.

The Julie Center's Parents Promoting Success in Schools program, designed to teach parenting skills, ran into difficulties with parents who had multiple problems, and the program was modified. Parents with troubled lives challenge parenting programs and GED instruction. It is unclear what standard of success is reasonable. Even if the programs succeed in their own terms—-parents' mastering techniques taught in class or passing a GED examination—the paths between these results and positive influence on children's learning are rocky. Parents must make and hold to decisions about nurturing and disciplining their children in the face of stresses and children's provocations. Parents with new credentials must find fitting jobs among labor market offerings. Then children must respond to their impressions of parents at work and their experiences of parents at home in ways that lead toward schooling as a means to becoming a successful worker, a good parent, and an otherwise effective adult.

Helping Parents Communicate with Schools

Organizers helped parents communicate with school staff in many ways. They trained parents to form groups, to hold an office in parent-teacher organizations, and to meet with teachers and principals. These interventions' efficacy depended on parents' time, interests, skills, and sense of security, as well as on educators' attitudes toward parents, time, interests, skills, and sense of security. The aid for Hispanic parents at General Wolfe, including interpreters for meetings, translators for school notices, and English classes, can have short- and long-term effects. They enabled parents to take part in PTO meetings and to understand what staff said. If English classes continue, those in them will be able to communicate on their own with staff and assist their children with homework. Some communication between parents and school staff is inherently helpful to children. In other cases, a series of events must intervene to affect how parents raise their children.

In Sum

Actions to strengthen families lead to uncertain conclusions. The Task Force seems to have been successful in implementing certain programs to aid parents, but influence on children is unclear. It may be unrealistic to expect the programs to show impacts on school performance, because so much time must pass before their effects register there, because these programs are such small influences in a large, turbulent field, or, simply, because so many contingent events must fall into place to have any, even small, impact. Hence, program proponents emphasize their effects on child rearing rather than on schooling. This position may be reasonable, but it gives up claims of links between parenting and children's education.

However, even if focusing on child rearing, one is left seeking evidence of a program's influence after its end. It is nearly impossible to know what goes on in homes, and, because families move often, it is hard even to keep contact. There are no data on child rearing practices that might eventually show the effects of actions aimed to influence them. This ignorance is a shaky platform for operating programs. However, the costs of evaluating these programs' effects on families would dwarf the costs of the programs themselves.

Strengthening Community Capacity to Act on Education

Gaining the Knowledge to Act

Formal educational events, as well as participation in the Task Force, contributed to community members' knowledge about education and confidence in their authority to speak about it. Through observations at schools, talks with principals or teachers, reports from parent organizers or others on school happenings, participation in planning or implementing projects, reports on progress in these projects, and ongoing discussions, Task Force members learned incrementally about schools and education and constructed increasingly explicit "shared wisdom."

Production of the *Southeast Community Plan on Education* formalized what they came to know. Preparing the plan was possible, after three years, because people came to believe that they had useful knowledge. Specific recommendations were important in codifying their conclusions about action, but most significant was just being able to make proposals after long uncertainty.

Two research efforts focused on issues about which Task Force members wanted to take positions: K–8 schools and facility needs. The K–8 research was inconclusive, suggesting that grade configuration mattered less than a school's educational program and its relations with parents and the community. When mapping showed the possibility of creating K–8 zones, Task Force members took the research as support for K–8 schools' potential influence, though they increasingly acknowledged the centrality of curricular and pedagogical details. Apart from specific findings, the research gave members confidence that they were using the best available knowledge.

The Task Force built on that research in trying to influence the system's rezoning and capital improvement plans. Members looked at enrollment projections, demographic shifts, home ownership trends, school capacities, and building conditions in developing a long-range facilities plan that set an agenda and gave them confidence in promoting it with the school system and local and state officials.

The Task Force as Umbrella and Catalyst for Action

The Task Force served as an umbrella for individuals and groups interested in Southeast Baltimore schools, and it created a critical mass of activity. People who came in initiated the tutoring-mentoring project, the student discipline consultation, church-school partnerships, parent organizing, the Paca campaign for an addition, and much of the Tench Tilghman full-service initiative, among many projects. Some under the umbrella became active education forces in their own right. For example, the Julie Center contributed resources and supported programs at several schools. When CPHA offered SECO a parent organizer grant, SECO put education on its agenda and later got its own organizing grant. SECO became the home for all parent organizers, and it added to education's salience as a community issue. The Task Force offered Ed Rutkowski information, support, and an opportunity to take leadership on K–8 schooling and facility planning, as he involved the Patterson Park Community Development Corporation in education.

Evaluating Capacity-Building

The links between most of these activities and student learning are long and intricate. For example, for community participation in creating a school facility plan to influence children's education, many intervening events must fall into place. The school board must request capital and operating funds from the city and state. Baltimore's Mayor, City Planning Commission, Board of Estimates, Board of Finance, and City Council, as well as Maryland's Governor, Inter-Agency Committee on School Construction, Board of Public Works, and General Assembly must approve the requests. Then facilities must be built or remodeled, staff must be hired and trained, equipment and materials must be purchased, staff must develop relations with parents, teachers must teach appropriately, and so forth. In this constellation, Task Force members have the most leverage with the community's city and state representatives, but these people have limited influence over school decisions. Should the Task Force, perhaps with elected officials' support, persuade the school system to accept a plan recommendation, the system normally would proceed to implement the proposal with minimal public involvement.

Accordingly, rather than hold these Task Force activities to producing educational outcomes, it is enough to evaluate them in terms of whether they add to community capacity to act on education. Three questions matter. The first is whether new activities represent an increase in community capacity. We should look for this capacity not in discrete actions, which may be a sign of it, but in the development of relationships, the accrual of human, material, and financial resources, and the formation of settings that make action possible—generally, the creation of social capital (Chaskin, Brown, Venkatesh, and Vidal 2001; Coleman 1988, 1990; Ferguson and Dickens 1999; Gittell and Vidal 1998; Putnam 2000; Saegert, Thompson, and Warren 2001).

For eight years the Task Force has been an instrument for action, and it has stimulated initiatives in several community organizations and fostered activity by partnerships of schools and parents or churches. However, communities and schools are open systems in turbulent environments. Connections—and the capacity to act—depend on personal relations. As individuals move, relationships decline or die, and little institutional memory sustains directions. Parent organizing epitomizes the challenges of building community capacity: a series of organizers had to redevelop relations with constantly changing parents and principals. Dependence on external funding jeopardizes the continuity of initiatives, partnerships, and community capacity.

These conditions frame a complicated second question, whether the Task Force acted efficiently in developing new capacity. A conclusion depends on judgments about what can realistically be expected from a largely voluntary community enterprise. The Task Force's first two years were not overtly productive but were necessary for constructing relationships, learning and building confidence, and developing a point of view. A differently focused research effort could have provided clearer information on education issues and action possibilities, but participants still needed to corroborate such information with experience. Better planning would have enabled parent organizers to accomplish more, but the fluidity of the education field resisted and undermined organization.

The Task Force could have acted more efficiently, but the personal basis of organizational relations makes capacity-building inherently "inefficient." Community capacity is entropic, requiring continual recreation. The Task Force's successes in strengthening capacity have depended on a few persons' efforts and relations. It is uncertain how much of this capacity can be transferred to others as the core group move on.

Finally, one should ask whether new capacity has been directed toward meaningful ends. This too is a matter of judgment, but the production of a community education plan, campaigns for new facilities and school reconfiguration, consultation on student discipline, development of a full-service community school, and construction of relations among community members, school staff, system administrators, churches, and universities seem meritorious.

Developing the Community as an Asset

Arguably, all of these accomplishments contributed to the value of Southeast Baltimore communities. Those familiar with educational activities feel better about the area, though their appreciation rests more on future promise than on immediate improvement. The *Baltimore Sun* touts positive signs in city schools. One article reported that "Elementaries in City Showed Marked Gains" (Bowie 2001). However, it did not mention any Southeast Baltimore schools, and, at any rate, only two of the sixteen featured elementary schools showing "significant gains" had more than 50 percent of students scoring satisfactory on the MSPAP. On the other hand, a front-page story in May 2001 highlighted Tench Tilghman's "sharp gains" in CTBS scores (Bowie and Niedowski 2001). Shortly after, an article on Direct Instruction trumpeted City Springs' CTBS gains under that program (Bowler 2001). Continuation of upward trends and publicity about them may influence parents' decisions about where to live, but Task Force activities have not reached that threshold.

Conclusions

The Southeast Education Task Force has been most effective in increasing community members' capacity to act on education. That success involves what community organizations do best—activating people, building networks, getting resources, and planning and implementing programs. Thus the Task Force put education on the community agenda, brought community voices to deliberations about schools, and contributed to a climate for change. As the first Baltimore community-based organization to focus on schools, it has stimulated other education activism and may have contributed to greater participation in school decision making.

Significantly, the Task Force conducted research that was useful not just in guiding its own efforts but also in shaping school system decision making. Part of this activity, too, was community organizations' bread and butter: identifying community views and preferences. Volunteers did some of the work, but much would have been impossible without the expertise and, particularly, the time of university partners. Still, there are limits to what community organizations can do in this respect, even with academic assistance, simply because they cannot easily raise money to pay for research.

In taking a community role, the Task Force had little direct contact with students. AmeriCorps did most of the tutoring, and university education faculty and students conducted the student discipline consultation. The main explanation is that community organizations' forte is community work. A second is the constraint of time. Few community members can volunteer regularly for classroom activity.

A consequence of this distance from schools, and a general lesson as well, is that it is far easier to start programs than to make them work—in this case, to influence children's learning. The general reason is that, while the time for necessary contingencies to fall into place runs on, contrary influences can take hold and scuttle an effort altogether (Pressman and Wildavsky 1973). The specific reason with community organizations is that they have little influence over events that impinge most closely on students' actions at school.

Unquestionably, it would be better to have more, sophisticated information about the results of Task Force activities, as well as the benefit of time, to see what becomes of them. Nevertheless, in addition to increased community action in education, there are signs of modest accomplishments that may yield educational fruit—students' positive response to tutoring and parents' efforts to learn to care for their children better, to take two examples. It is easy to suggest ways that these advances will be undermined by the riptides of everyday life. However, one can also imagine that their results, as well as the simple fact of some success, contribute in small ways to an increasingly effective effort to organize and improve the education field. Task Force projects may work their ways toward influencing children's lives, encouraging them to try harder, enabling them to achieve more, giving them confidence in their efficacy and optimism about life chances, and showing them choices that they would not have seen.

Chapter 18

Can Community Action Reform Schools or Improve Education?

The Southeast Education Task Force's community approach to reforming schools offers several lessons. First, it can be examined as a model for a new type of entity—a grassroots organization to link parents and other community members to neighborhood schools and the system administration to improve education. Second, as such, the Task Force helps understand what a community-based organization, whose members are not professional educators, can do in the education field. Third, the organization's efforts to influence the school system shed light on the system's operations and its relations with parents and community members. Fourth, the Task Force illuminates dynamics and predicaments typical of many voluntary associations and nonprofit organizations. Finally, this effort, though not as broad as many comprehensive community initiatives, offers lessons about how they should be designed and what they may accomplish. We already have explored many of these issues. In this final chapter we draw conclusions regarding the role of community action in reforming schools and improving education.

Can Community Action Reform Schools?

"School reform" refers to changes in school policies or practices that have two characteristics. They alter a school in a way that significantly improves children's learning, and they endure, institutionalized in the school as a social system. Clearly, "significantly improves" is a matter of expectation and interpretation. And because no change is permanent, institutionalization is a matter of degree and time, best judged retrospectively.

In fact, though people talk glibly of "school reform" and many would-be reformers simply assume that their designs satisfy these conditions, few give careful attention to whether, first, a specific proposed change stands a reasonable chance of being implemented as intended; whether, if that were possible, it could stay in place; and whether, if it did, the school would educate students better. Instead, the difficulty of implementing changes of any significance often leads proponents to focus on incremental progress in establishing programmatic details and to displace expectations of benefits for children onto ever-distant future completion.

In considering Task Force lessons, we can draw conclusions more easily about possibilities for community action to influence schools than about consequent effects on children, because the latter is largely outside of community control. Recognizing the importance of those questions, we focus on whether community action can significantly affect school policies or practices.

Influencing Schools

The Task Force made no effort to influence curriculum and pedagogy. In the consultation on student discipline, it got university faculty to help school staff change policies and practices, but this activity had little impact on the school. More strategic, longer-term effort with schools ready to change would have greater effect. Community members can help identify schools that are attuned to students' family and community circumstances and seem prepared to innovate, but it is impractical for a community organization to maintain a pool of educational consultants.

The Task Force has tried to change practices regarding children whose troubled family conditions hinder their learning, through the development of a full-service community school. This project adds resources that enable staff to change their responses to behavioral problems by choosing therapeutic interventions instead of, or in addition to, punitive ones. Unlike the discipline consultation, this initiative does not question basic policies and practices, and staff accept these innovations because they do not interfere with core practices. Yet that condition also sets limits to initiatives such as this. For example, conditions to which new health and social services respond might also be improved by changes in curriculum or pedagogy, staff-student relations, or discipline policies, but they lie outside of the full-service program.

Thus one lesson is that community organizations may influence schools when interventions leave basic academic policies and practices untouched. Whether changes under these conditions can be significant depends on specifics. There is an important second lesson here. Professional educators value community assistance when it addresses "community" problems—outside influences that hinder teaching and that most teachers feel they understand poorly. Whether such action is possible points to a third lesson, framed by contrasts between the discipline consultation and the full-service community school. A community organization's chances of influencing a school depend greatly on a principal's interest in having the school influenced.

The full-service project points to the area where a community organization can most easily influence a school—relations with its environment. Community organizations operate at a school's boundaries in two ways. One is by making resources available for school programs. The other is by creating relationships between school staff and outside individuals or institutions. The distinction is one of emphasis, since relationships are necessary for contributing resources, and relations can be resources. These activities can influence schools in two ways. One is by leading them to improve teaching or ancillary activities (such as attendance promotion or student guidance), either by changing policies or practices or by increasing effort. The other is by changing policies and practices vis-à-vis environmental relations.

Resources

Community organizations can bring schools resources such as time, expertise, materials, equipment, money, and programs. Whether the contributions are worthwhile depends on whether supported activities fit students' needs, whether programs are competently implemented, and whether efforts are of a magnitude to affect students significantly. Similarly, whether resources change school policies or practices depends on the specifics.

Community organizations have limited influence over these matters. Most often, they—and, more broadly, the individuals and institutions from whom they get resources for schools—do not decide which programs schools implement. Rather, a community organization has choices about which of a school's programs it may aid. The organization cannot force a school to take resources for a program that staff oppose. Moreover, community organizations have little influence over how a school uses resources. If nothing else, community members lack the time to observe and supervise. In addition, most staff would consider efforts to do so intrusive.

However resources are used, a simple increase for ongoing programs probably alters little in a school, unless that growth makes some qualitative change—for example, in the school climate or teaching methods. Helping start a new program is more likely to influence a school. Beyond this, if donors become part of school discussions or decision making, they can contribute to change within limits defined by principals' interests and staff investments in prevailing policies.

The development of the full-service community school is an example. This community initiative has introduced new programs into a school to improve its ability to reach outside of its walls to aid students and families. The idea's good sense and the community organization's readiness to raise money for it were necessary but not sufficient. The principal's interest and readiness were essential. Because the Task Force secured funding for new services and hired the coordinator, it has had considerable control over program development and operations. Because programs help students, and because the coordinator consults with the principal, teachers use it.

A community organization will have much less influence over programs when it encourages third parties, such as churches, fraternities or sororities, businesses, or social agencies, to provide resources to schools, students, or families, particularly when the activity occurs outside of the school. Whether they change school practices depends on details, but programs off site, no matter how much they may help students or families, are unlikely to affect a school directly.

Relationships

In giving something to a school, an organization or an individual forms a relationship with it, in some measure opening up the school's boundaries. Relationships can bring community organizations and community members influence in four ways. The first is a matter of quid pro quo: when someone gives the school resources, the school gives the donor something in return. It is important to note how relationships can be resources, as social capital, by offering access to others, authority, influence, or an ability to mobilize people. The Task Force gave principals information about communities and about school system studies, activities, and plans. It offered political support vis-à-vis the system administration, the school board, the mayor's office, and state decision makers. Recognizing what the Task Force could offer, two schools invited its chair to join their school improvement team. Most schools, however, do not directly trade influence for resources. Exchanges develop subtly over time.

Second, relationships are more likely to lead to influence insofar as those who donate resources—from parent volunteers to business partners to tutors and mentors—spend time around a school. They talk with staff, principals or teachers may ask their opinions, they may attend meetings, and they can make their views known to administrators. Depending on who they are and how clear their ideas are, they can shape a school's agenda by helping define problems and identify remedies. The full-service community school is an example.

Third, access to social capital influences schools by drawing staff into a larger world—of other public agencies, elected officials, nonprofit organizations, corporations, state and federal departments, foundations, and universities. Through the Ad Hoc Group on Education and the Empowerment Zone, the Task Force influenced principals by exposing them to state and federal education officials and national education experts. The resulting Empowerment Zone and Maryland Department of Education funding led schools to start new programs and helped shape them.

Fourth, community organizations can influence schools by building bonds between staff and community members to create a climate of support for a school. If parents and teachers understand and trust one another, they will regard each other with less anxiety and antagonism. They can share knowledge about children and pool authority over them. Relaxation of tension creates emotional and political space for educators to think creatively about what students need and how schools can educate them. Thus community organizations can develop new social capital. Task Force organizing had these effects at some schools with secure principals.

The Task Force partnership with the University of Maryland shows the resources and relationships that universities can offer community organizations working with schools. Faculty and students can help community organizations influence schools and school systems in three ways—by contributing to a climate of inquiry, by developing usable knowledge, and by introducing outsiders with distinct intellectual, social, or political authority.

Influencing the School System Administration

Most of this can be said as well about influencing school system administrations. Administrations differ from schools, however, in two ways. The first concerns the substance of their practice. Schools teach, while administrations manage (though schools also manage). The system administration sets formal policy on curriculum, discipline, and many other things, but schools, explicitly and in their practices, reset policy by enacting it. Teachers try to manage classrooms. System administrators try to manage principals who try to manage teachers who try to manage classrooms. Administrators deal with abstractions and try to influence teaching and learning by remote control—though decisions about abstractions can have concrete consequences.

The second difference concerns the loosely coupled dual principles of organization in school systems. Schools, because of the necessity of adapting to the diverse, variable conditions of students, grant teachers discretion in their classrooms. In contrast, central administrations are rigid bureaucracies, with tightly circumscribed roles, responsibilities, and authority. Though teachers and administrators both resist community involvement, parents have more claims and opportunities for access in schools than in the central office. Schools are defined as community institutions, and, once inside the front door, an outsider can readily find the principal's office. Inside the lobby of system headquarters, an aide and, often, a security guard confront visitors and control entry. While schools are proximate to communities and relatively accessible, the central administration is distant and nearly impenetrable.

Because contact with central administrators is harder than with school staff, because a community organization is one of many interests making requests of the system, and because a community organization is smaller than many of those interests, the resources and relationships that community organizations offer generally matter less to the administration than to schools. Further, the concrete information about neighborhood conditions that is community organizations' stock in trade is less important to central decision makers who deal with abstract policies and procedures. Thus community organizations face challenges of, first, getting system administrators' attention and, second, translating local concerns into broad policy terms.

The Task Force had little influence with the administration early on but gained influence over time. Five explanations point to lessons about community action. First, community organization is essential. System administrators resist parent and community involvement in policy making, and their attitude, combining professionalism, judgments about with whom it is reasonable and possible to talk in the face of unrealistic demands for attention and action, and paranoia, makes it difficult for the public to know what the system is doing, much less to affect it. A community organization provides a vehicle for contacting the administration and represents a constituency whose size gives it some power in asking for information and action. Thus the Task Force continually spoke for Southeast Baltimore community members.

Second, individuals matter. The superintendent in the early Task Force years had little interest in community participation. The system was under siege. Managers had little sense of direction or control. Chaos, chicanery, and incompetence kept community members out. The Task Force's efforts to get student data speak volumes. When the state forced restructuring, new top positions were filled by managers who were a little more receptive to community participation. Staff and board held more public meetings and met more with citizens.

Third, organized community pressure makes a difference. While the system was restructuring, a small but growing number of community organizations became interested in schools. They pressed the system to listen to parents and other members of the public. CPHA and four other community or educational organizations created the Baltimore Education Network (BEN) to monitor restructuring, and BEN trained parents and pushed for their involvement in system deliberations. As a result, community organizations gained some access to and legitimacy with the administration.

Fourth, information can bring community organizations influence. Task Force research on facilities gave it knowledge. It offered system administrators usable information about community conditions and trends. Its members met with officials to identify needs, to formulate problems, and to find solutions. Realistic proposals that linked to system studies and plans had some influence.

Fifth, alliances within the school system help. As the facilities story also illustrates, the Task Force gained sway with the center from associations with principals. Joining forces with principals got school board and staff attention. By bringing parties together, the community organization helped them solve problems.

The uncommon example of the Industrial Areas Foundation in Texas underlines the importance of community organization. The IAF worked for years to organize parents and to develop the power to get local and state school officials to reorganize schools, establish new ones, include parents in decision making, implement new curriculum and teaching methods, and much more. The IAF's successes are exceptional because of the funding it obtained for organizing, but the lesson is that a large parental force can change basic school system policies and practices.

Can Community Action Improve Education?

As an outcome, education involves curiosity about the world and the ability to develop and use knowledge to understand and act in it. When we consider the process that contributes to these results, we conventionally think of schooling, but we also recognize other influences on children's intellectual, political, social, and emotional development. Parents are central, as they treat their children in various ways intended to guide their growth. Relatives, friends, clergy, counselors, and others also weigh in. All tell the child who he or she is and give direction for getting ahead. The family also is the vehicle for manifold institutional influences, as what parents or siblings say, how they act, and how they are treated teach children about the larger society and their place in it. Thus children learn at home about the economy, class structure, race relations, the political culture, and social policy. They draw conclusions about whether the adult world offers them a worthwhile place, whether school takes them along a rewarding path, whether they can learn, and whether they should study. Some of these inferences from daily experience lead them toward the classroom and teachers' influence, but others lead elsewhere.

What adults say and show to children at home matters greatly. In addition, many social and economic interventions not commonly associated with "education" do a great deal by helping children develop, motivating and preparing them for schooling, and offering them rewards for school success. Reforming schools is central to improving education, but strengthening families and establishing social conditions that support children and parents also matter.

Accordingly, we extend the discussion of educational improvement beyond school reform in two ways. First, with goals, we look at how community action can contribute broadly to children's development. Although some schools aim to influence all aspects of children's growth, most restrict themselves to "academics." Second, in considering influences on these outcomes, we look outside of school, at families, communities, and social institutions. Interventions in these areas can be considered educational improvement when they aid children's development.

The connections between family or community interventions and children's education depend on many factors beyond the control of a community organization. Hence, in considering Task Force lessons, we focus on what community action can do to affect families or communities in ways that might be expected to promote children's development without insisting that those results follow. To do so is not to give community organizations a free pass but to put their potential influence in reasonable perspective. We look at what community members can do to assist children directly, provide support for family members to care for children, and create community supports for families and children.

Assisting Children

Community organizations can assist children educationally outside of schools in three ways. One is by providing resources for programs that give academic support. For example, the Task Force organized tutoring, and a church sponsored an after-school homework center. Such programs teach students or enable them to make use of and develop what they already know.

Second, community organizations can provide resources for programs that support children socially and emotionally. For example, the Task Force helped get funding for a counselor to work with children whose parents have substance abuse problems. Such programs may not change living conditions, but they can help children cope better. They will be less distracted from schoolwork, and they may feel more competent and generally in control, with regard to not just a social or an emotional problem but also the intellectual work of school.

Third, community organizations can bring children supportive relationships. Often these relationships accompany participation in a program. For example, a mentor who tutors a child offers not only academic assistance but also a tie to a caring adult who models success. Similarly, a substance abuse counselor or homework center director may encourage a child to succeed at school, offer a road map toward success, and give rewards along the way. Each relationship encourages a child to believe that he or she is part of a community that wants and will help him or her to make it.

Supporting Families

Community organizations can aid children by supporting their parents in raising them, preparing them for school, and motivating them to do well. A community organization offers families three types of support analogous to those to children. Some programs give parents academic skills. Task Force GED programs and English classes for Hispanic parents are examples. They enable parents to do better at work, to assist their children with homework, and to give their children a family example of academic success.

Other programs offer social and emotional skills. Task Force parenting courses and mental health consultations offer examples. They help parents raise children skillfully, deal with conflict constructively, and avoid problems that would prevent or discourage learning.

In addition to instrumental benefits, these types of programs extend supportive relationships to parents. Many parents with limited formal education have little contact with academically or economically successful adults, and they can easily feel excluded from the larger society. Teachers, trainers, and therapists, for example, connect them to others who are successful and provide emotional support in struggling with problems and moving ahead.

Child and family programs cover familiar territory (Crane 1998; Hamburg 1994; Schorr 1997; Schorr and Schorr 1989). Two points are affirmed here. First, community members, from individuals to neighborhood associations to churches to businesses, can set up or provide resources for these programs. Second, the effects of these interventions should be considered educational: they help children develop, and they contribute to their success at school.

Planning, implementing, and managing programs that work require skills and knowledge available to only some community organizations. Developing programs that affect a significant number of children—for example, a critical mass of students in a classroom or school—requires sophisticated expertise. In addition, it requires money that few community organizations can raise.

Strengthening Community Supports for Families

We can think of "community" in two ways. One is the people whom families encounter daily. Social relations offer friendship, emotional support, and instrumental aid. Relatives, neighbors, or other adults may give advice on raising children, look after youngsters, lend a hand at something, offer tips on finding or keeping jobs, provide examples of success, or just be reassuringly present. Those for whom a network of kin and neighbors cannot provide needed support and who cannot pay for what they lack must seek the formal services of strangers, in the social welfare system.

Community organizations can increase community support for families in several ways. First, any improvement in families or children strengthens the community of which they are a part. For instance, parents who hold good jobs and raise children well provide admirable examples and can assist other parents with child rearing and school matters. Their children are good company for other children. Students who do well at school offer models for other students and can help them learn. Thus interventions that aid students, such as a homework center, or assist parents, such as a GED program, not only help individuals but also improve those whom children in the community encounter and increase some community members' capacity to help others.

Second, a program is more than transactions between individual "providers" and "clients." Many programs represent the community to those who use them. Their existence enacts a community that supports members. Thus they offer not only aid but also reassurance that the world is caring. In turn, service agencies and programs become elements in a growing network of formal supports for community members, building a community's capacity to care for its own.

Third, community organizations can increase community members' capacity to help one another meet needs and solve problems by organizing them. Parent organizing, for example, enables parents not just to discuss issues and share knowledge but also to identify common interests and develop collective ways to serve them. Once parents collaborate on one issue, they can direct this capacity to others. Confidence about their identity and direction enables them to bring in new people and take on harder issues. In general, activities that bring community members together, even if their primary aim is not organizing, connect people and help them collaborate. Community planning is an example. Similarly, programming in which parents and teachers work together, besides benefitting parents instrumentally, creates relations from which they may get support in the future.

A second meaning of "community" is broader, including the entire social environment affecting everyday life. This community includes, for example, the labor market, the housing market, the medical system, the social welfare system, and race relations. These affect family life in more distant but consequential ways than the people and organizations that are visible nearby. Local community organizations can do little to affect this community. They can develop subsidized housing, encourage employers to hire local residents, train mothers to assess their neighbors' health needs and make referrals, and mediate racial conflicts. In such ways, they can modulate the consequences of institutional action, but they cannot change the institutions themselves.

In Conclusion

We have noted three arguments for community action in education. The logic of participation appeals to democracy: parents and other community members have a right to make decisions about children's education. The logic of research asserts from evidence that parental involvement improves children's learning and development. The logic of action holds that community alliances with other institutions increase parents' chances of getting desired educational changes. The first argument justifies community action intrinsically, on normative grounds. The second asserts, in addition, that it can be useful. The third indicates how it can succeed. This case study, assuming the normative argument, has tested the empirical ones: can community activists organize people and use knowledge to improve children's education significantly?

This question can be parsed into several. The first concerns what should be considered significant improvements in children's education. A second involves whether community activists under conditions such as they find now can accomplish something of significance. A third asks what conditions would increase the efficacy of community action in education. A fourth considers what else must be done to complement whatever community action can accomplish in improving children's education to a satisfactory level. We look at these questions in order.

What Is Significant Educational Improvement?

One way of addressing this question measures significance in terms of progress toward ideal, or at least good enough, educational conditions. Clearly, great gaps separate even modest expectations and current accomplishments. Almost any action, by communities or schools, pales into insignificance in this perspective. An alternative approach calculates significance in terms of accomplishing what is feasible. We have noted multiple influences working against children's education, from family weaknesses to school rigidity to societal institutions that create or reinforce inequality. To mix mythological analogies, even Herculean efforts can be Sisyphean.

Each perspective offers a criterion for assessing significance. An action should add to children's educational capacity or accomplishments, and it should make good use of available opportunities and resources.

Can Community Action Accomplish Something of Significance in Education?

It is easy to tick off constraints on the community approach to educational improvement or to dwell on the Southeast Education Task Force's flaws as an example. Yet school systems, too, have limited influence on education and plan and implement imperfectly. Those who work on reforming the system conclude that, though its full potential is unclear, it can make notable headway in improving children's learning. That is the proper test of community action.

The Task Force illustrates possibilities for community action in education. For example, community activists can:

- organize a community constituency for educational improvement;
- put education on local organizations' agendas;
- organize a network that can act in the local education field;
- conduct research on educational issues to increase the knowledge of parents, other community members, and school and system staff;
- develop a community education plan and priorities;
- support families' efforts to raise children and prepare them for schooling;
- enable parents to present informed, realistic expectations to schools;
- enable parents, other community members, and community institutions to work with schools;
- give schools knowledge and political support for advocating for their educational interests and getting program and facility improvements;
- insert community views and interests in school and system decision making;
- improve school and system programming by contributing local knowledge;
- increase school and system accountability to parents and the community;
- influence other institutions (e.g., the Empowerment Zone) to set policies serving parental and community interests; and
- implement, fund, or otherwise provide resources for programs that help children learn.

All of these actions can produce significant educational results.

What Conditions Would Make Community Action in Education More Efficacious?

Community action in education cannot succeed by intermittent or partial effort—some organizing for a while, then some research, some fund-raising, a little program development, perhaps a quick evaluation, some more fund-raising, a return to organizing, and so forth. All of these activities are essential, continually. Volunteers alone cannot do it. Money, a steady flow of it, is crucial to a realistic effort. (Anyone concerned about the costs of community action should note that no one is competing with community organizations to organize, inform, and involve parents in education more cheaply, efficiently, or effectively.) Occasional, episodic initiatives will fail to touch institutional practices. Moreover, if a community organization drops out of existence, not only do its efforts die, but relationships, social capital, and institutional memory dissolve. Task Force history shows what is required to create a new organization.

Public agencies and private foundations with interests in community action and education must find ways to support promising community organizations. Some have created consortia to pool resources and to increase leverage. Yet without other innovative funding arrangements, community action in education will remain rare and will have limited impact.

The premise of community action is not that community members operating alone can somehow change the education field, but that a community group may develop a network that has the collective will and capacity to improve education. Organized community members can do far more together with schools than without or against them. The schools must find a way past educators' mistaken assumption that they can improve education on their own, and they must find a cure for their resistance to outside knowledge, participation, and influence. Rather than expediently viewing a community as an occasional source of resources, schools must recognize community members as partners and create with them a culture of collective problem solving. Realistic public discussion about what can be expected of schools as part of a broad societal effort to improve education is essential.

Beyond the school system, community action could accomplish more with a larger community and more actors. For example, mayors, departments of planning, housing and community development, health, employment, and social services, and corporate leaders often are absent from school reform. Some have been rebuffed by the education establishment, but many have simply failed to imagine ways of working with schools. Few are accustomed to working with community groups, and some have avoided or resisted community involvement. All have roles in the education field and should join with community actors to organize and improve it.

What Else Must Be Done?

Many of the strongest influences on children's readiness and motivation for schooling, their academic skills and performance, and their opportunities and rewards when they leave school are beyond the influence of community groups or the schools. Poverty makes it hard to form and maintain families where at least one parent works, earns enough to support children, provides an example of educational and economic success, is present to care for children and help them with schooling and other tasks, and introduces them to the larger world.

Racial discrimination and segregation isolate minority children from social and economic opportunities and teach them to expect little of themselves. Guns, drugs, and other violence ravage families, shorten or destroy lives, and convince children that regardless of what they do in school or elsewhere, they will not live past a troubled adolescence.

Jobs are distant, and many do not pay a living wage. Medical care is inaccessible or unaffordable. Crime is an everyday event, and the police seem unconcerned or helpless. Social services are unavailable or unpublicized. Public transportation is nearly impossible. Child care is unaffordable or unreliable. Housing is crowded, dirty, dangerous, and often expensive. Neighbors and others who pass through distract, endanger, and undo parents' efforts. It would be surprising if children grew up and became educated under these conditions, though some do.

Some of these conditions can be blamed on specific culprits, but most reflect public policies. Some policy decisions concern public spending—not just how much on schooling, but how much on public safety, social welfare, housing, child care, employment, public transportation, and public health. Other decisions are non-decisions—to leave spending in many domains to the private sector. Thus in comparison to other nations, the United States has little public housing, public transportation, public health, public employment, or public welfare. The private institutions that govern these fields do only what brings a profit. The poor are not profitable. Yet alternatives in other countries show that decision makers could do a great deal to reconstruct public policy, recalibrate relations between public and private, and reassert the public responsibility of the private.

Without elaborating a full agenda, we easily can think of policies that would supplement community, school, and other local efforts in improving children's education. Many African Americans live in concentrated poverty (Massey and Denton 1993). One result is that many poor black children attend school only with other poor black children. They have no contact with, information about, or connection to college, employment, and economic success. Some school desegregation strategies have improved such children's educational, employment, and housing opportunities, not just by putting them in academically better schools but by making them part of networks that connect them to the world of success (Eaton 2001; Orfield and Eaton 1996; Rubinowitz and Rosenbaum 2000; Wells and Crain 1997). Developing practical, socially acceptable, politically feasible, and legal strategies for increasing racial contact in schools is difficult, but it is an example of social intervention that can improve schools' efficacy with children of all races.

Wilson (1987, 1996) has noted the declining pool of marriageable, gainfully employed men in poor African-American communities. The costs to children are straightforward. There is one fewer income in a family, with less for food, clothing, and shelter. There is one fewer person to take care of children. Single mothers become overextended, wear out, and fail to care for their children as they want. Boys do not see fathers who show them ways of being successful men. At the same time, while millions of men (and women) need jobs, the nation confronts another crisis in the deterioration of roads, bridges, schools and other public buildings, and urban infrastructure. A massive, long-term public employment program (the New Deal Works Progress Administration was an early example) would simultaneously put adults to work and improve the cities where they live and try to raise and educate children. This kind of policy would underpin families and give children support that is important to their growth. Arguably, such an initiative could do as much as many school reforms to improve children's education.

The needs of the poor point to various programs, including public housing construction and subsidy, public provision of and payment for health care, regional public transportation, public welfare for parents and children who lack other support, and so on. Details must be worked out, and political agreements must be crafted. Neither is easy, but a will to recognize children's needs would motivate action. No society that cared about children or families could justify present policies.

In this view, the efforts of community organizations such as the Southeast Education Task Force are small but essential, because they are central to democracy, because they assist schools and improve children's education, and because important reforms will not occur without them.

Notes

Notes to Chapter 1

1. The following data were reported in Anyon (1997) and Olson and Jerald (1998). The data come from the 1990 Census and from various surveys in the 1990s.

2. This framework draws on Meyer's and Rowan's (1983; also see Meyer 1977) distinction between technical and institutional functions of education, discussed in later chapters.

Notes to Chapter 2

1. People also participate for the social contact, but because community organizations make extraordinary time demands, those who take part usually expect action to result.

Notes to Chapter 4

1. The population dropped to 632,000 by the 2000 Census.

2. This analysis draws on Crenson (2000).

3. African Americans comprised 63 percent of Baltimore's population in 2000.

4. This section draws on Berkowitz (1997), Bowler (1991), and Orr (1999).

5. I have described this culture as "good-hearted home ownership" (Baum 1997). It is a specimen of what Gans (1988) has characterized as "middle-American individualism."

6. These data come from the Baltimore City Department of Planning (1992a, 1992b) and the Southeast Planning Council (1993).

7. On SECO, see Cassidy (1979), Clay and Hollister (1983), Crenson (1983),

Cunningham and Kotler (1983), Giloth (1993, 1994), Kuttner (1976), and Truelove (1977a, 1977b).

Notes to Chapter 10

1. The federal government gave smaller grants and lesser policy concessions to several dozen Enterprise Communities—applicants that failed to win Empowerment Zone designation.

Notes to Chapter 14

1. Alternatively, when partnerships falter, partners may unrealistically vilify one another. In either case, realism is easily displaced by imagination (Sarason 1972).

2. The funding allocation was a Planning Program decision, not a USDE requirement.

3. The Urban Community Service Program gave $1 million for five years, but the effort to support five projects allowed only four years' work on each. The Community Outreach Partnership Program supports many more university-community partnerships but gives them only $500,000 over three years.

Notes to Chapter 15

1. Saul Alinsky, a pioneering American community organizer, considered the organization of 3 percent of a community's members a success.

2. During the 2000–2001 school year, Baltimore mobility rates (proportions of students entering or withdrawing during the year) were 44 percent in elementary schools, 47 percent in middle schools, and 50 percent in high schools (Maryland State Department of Education 2001).

3. Few children in Baltimore's elite neighborhoods attend public schools. In Homeland, 16 percent of children attended public schools in 1990. In Roland Park, with one of the city's best elementary schools, 18 percent attended public schools. In economically mixed census tracts including Guilford, the number was 28 percent. In Southeast Baltimore, in contrast, 82 percent of children attended public schools, with most others in Catholic schools (Baltimore City Department of Planning 1992a).

4. In 1998, 89 percent of American children in elementary or secondary school were in public schools. This figure has fluctuated only slightly since World War II (National Center for Education Statistics 2001, table 3).

5. Surveys consistently find that the closer people are to the public schools, the more favorably they evaluate them. When the October 2000 Gallup Poll asked parents of public school students to grade their oldest (or only) child's school, 70 percent gave it an A or a B. When asked to evaluate the community's schools, 56 percent of parents gave an A or a B, in contrast to only 44 percent of adults without children currently in school. When asked to evaluate the nation's schools, only 22 percent of public school parents gave an A or a B, and only 19 percent of nonparents did so. Asked whether improvements lay in reforming the system or in finding an alternative system, similar proportions of parents (60 percent) and nonparents (59 percent) favored reform (Rose and Gallup 2000).

Although parents' assessments of their children's schools are high, only slightly more than half give their community's schools an A or a B, hardly a strong endorsement. Moreover, those without children in public schools, comprising a majority of voters and taxpayers, regard the public schools quite poorly (in fact, declining from 26 percent As and Bs in 1999 to 19 percent in 2000).

6. In Baltimore, for example, in only 40 percent of 180 schools was the fall 1995, principal still leading the school in fall 1999.

Notes to Chapter 16

1. Two common bureaucratic arrangements that hinder knowledge work illustrate the parameters for this design. In some organizations, research and planning are tightly linked to operations, with the result that knowledge workers must constantly respond to the forces with which operational staff contend; though the resultant "knowledge" is used in operations, it is neither systematic nor carefully tested. Alternatively, research and planning may be so isolated from operations that while knowledge workers can do wide-ranging research, they have little chance of getting anyone to use it.

Notes to Chapter 17

1. Still, evaluators find that participants often syncretistically draw on several theories of change, referring to different aspects of an intervention and couched at different levels of abstraction, with no clear way to distill it all into a single, complete theory. Evaluators have difficulty articulating participants' words into easily understandable theoretical formulations, and participants often find enunciated theories too complex to guide their action (Kagan 1998; Milligan, Coulton, York, and Register 1998).

References

Anderson, Elijah. 1999. *Code of the Street*. New York: W. W. Norton.

Annie E. Casey Foundation. 1998. *Evaluating Comprehensive Community Change*. Baltimore: Author.

———. n. d. *Getting Smart, Getting Real: Using Research and Evaluation Information to Improve Programs and Policies*. Baltimore: Author.

Anyon, Jean. 1997. *Ghetto Schooling*. New York: Teachers College Press.

Argyris, Chris. 1982. *Reasoning, Learning, and Action*. San Francisco: Jossey-Bass.

Argyris, Chris, and Donald A. Schön. 1974. *Theory in Practice*. San Francisco: Jossey-Bass.

———. 1978. *Organizational Learning*. Reading, Mass: Addison-Wesley.

Argyris, Chris, Robert Putnam, and Diana McLain Smith. 1985. *Action Science*. San Francisco: Jossey-Bass.

Association of Baltimore Area Grantmakers. 1996. *Member Directory*. Baltimore: Author.

Bain, Alastair, Susan Long, and Suzanne Ross. 1992. *Paper Houses: The Authority Vacuum in a Government School*. Victoria, Australia: CollinsDove.

Baltimore City Department of Planning. 1992a. Basic Social and Economic Data. *CensusNews 1990*. Baltimore: Author.

———. 1992b. *1990 Community Profiles Baltimore City*. Baltimore: Author.

Baltimore City Public Schools. 1994a. *Maryland School Performance Program Report 1994*. Baltimore: Author.

———. 1994b. *Position Statement: K–8 Schools Study Group*. Baltimore: Author.

Banks, James A., and Cherry A. McGee Banks, eds. 2000. *Multicultural Education: Issues and Perspectives*. 4th ed. New York: John Wiley and Sons.

Barber, Benjamin. 1984. *Strong Democracy*. Berkeley: University of California Press.

Bascia, Nina, and Andy Hargreaves. 2000. *The Sharp Edge of Educational Change*. London: Routledge/Falmer.

Baum, Howell S. 1987. *The Invisible Bureaucracy*. New York: Oxford University Press.

———. 1991. "How Bureaucracy Discourages Responsibility." Pp. 264–85 in *Organizations on the Couch: Handbook of Psychoanalysis and Management*, ed. Manfred F. R. Kets de Vries. San Francisco: Jossey-Bass.

———. 1997. *The Organization of Hope: Communities Planning Themselves*. Albany: State University of New York Press.

———. 2000. "Realities and Fantasies of University-Community Partnerships." *Journal of Planning Education and Research* 20:234–46.

Bennett, William J. 1999. *The Index of Leading Cultural Indicators*. Rev. ed. New York: Broadway Books.

Bennett, William J., Chester E. Finn Jr., and John T. E. Cribb Jr. 1999. *The Educated Child*. New York: Free Press.

Benson, Lee, and Ira Harkavy. 1994. *Universities and Community Schools* 4:1–2.

Berkowitz, Edward. 1997. "Baltimore's Public Schools in a Time of Transition." *Maryland Historical Magazine* (Winter): 412–32.

Bion, W. R. 1961. *Experiences in Groups*. New York: Basic Books.

Bowie, Liz. 2001. "Elementaries in City Show Marked Gains." *Baltimore Sun* (January 1), pp. 1B, 3B.

Bowie, Liz, and Erika Niedowski. 2001. "Improving Test Scores Hailed as Turnaround." *Baltimore Sun* (May 18), pp. 1A, 10A.

Bowler, Mike. 1991. *The Lessons of Change: Baltimore Schools in the Modern Era*. Baltimore: Fund for Educational Excellence.

———. 1995. "Southeast Baltimore Group Works for better Schools." *Baltimore Sun* (October 22), p. 2B.

———. 2001. "Teaching Method Makes the Grade." *Baltimore Sun* (May 27) p. 2B.

Boyte, Harry C. 1984. *Community Is Possible*. New York: Harper and Row.

———. 1989. *CommonWealth*. New York: Free Press.

Bryk, Anthony S. 1999. "Policy Lessons from Chicago's Experience with Decentralization." Pp. 67–127 in *Brookings Papers on Education Policy 1999*, ed. Diane Ravitch. Washington, D.C.: Brookings Institution.

Bryk, Anthony S., Penny Bender Sebring, David Kerbow, Sharon Rollow, and John Q. Easton. 1998. *Charting Chicago School Reform*. Boulder: Westview Press.

Cassidy, Robert. 1979. *Livable Cities*. New York: Holt, Rinehart and Winston.

Chaskin, Robert J., Prudence Brown, Sudhir Venkatesh, and Avis Vidal. 2001. *Building Community Capacity*. New York: Aldine de Gruyter.

Chubb, John E., and Terry M. Moe. 1990. *Politics, Markets, and America's Schools*. Washington, D.C.: Brookings Institution.

"City Test Scores on the Rise." 2001. *Baltimore Sun* (May 18), p. 4B.

Clay, Phillip L., and Robert M. Hollister, ed. 1983. *Neighborhood Policy and Planning.* Lexington, Mass: Lexington Books.

Clinchy, Evans, ed. 2000. *Creating New Schools.* New York: Teachers College Press.

Cnaan, Ram A. 1991. "Neighborhood-Representing Organizations: How Democratic Are They?" *Social Service Review* 65 (4): 614–34.

Cohen, James. 1995. "Initiating Participatory Planning in the Palmer Park Community of Prince George's County, Maryland." Paper presented at the 37th Annual Conference of the Association of Collegiate Schools of Planning, Detroit, Michigan.

———. 1997. "The Rhetorics of Eclectic Empowerment Planning in Palmer Park, MD." Paper presented at the 39th Annual Conference of the Association of Collegiate Schools of Planning, Fort Lauderdale, Florida.

Cohen, Michael D., James G. March, and Johan P. Olsen. 1988. "A Garbage Can Model of Organizational Choice." Pp. 294–334 in *Decisions and Organizations, ed.* James G. March. New York: Basic Blackwell.

Coleman, James S. 1988. "Social Capital in the Creation of Human Capital." *American Journal of Sociology* 94 (Supplement): S95–S120.

———. 1990. *Foundations of Social Theory.* Cambridge: The Belknap Press of Harvard University Press.

Connell, James P., Anne C. Kubisch, Lisbeth B. Schorr, and Carol H. Weiss, eds. 1995. *New Approaches to Evaluating Community Initiatives: Concepts, Methods, and Contexts.* Washington, D.C.: Aspen Institute.

Council of Urban Boards of Education, National School Boards Association. 2001. *Superintendent Tenure.* Alexandria, Va.: Author.

Crane, Jonathan, ed. 1998. *Social Programs That Work.* New York: Russell Sage Foundation.

Crenson, Matthew A. 1983. *Neighborhood Politics.* Cambridge: Harvard University Press.

———. 2000. Untitled, unpublished paper.

Cunningham, James V., and Milton Kotler. 1983. *Building Neighborhood Organizations.* Notre Dame: Notre Dame Press.

Dewar, Margaret E., and Claudia B. Isaac. 1998. "Learning from Difference: The Potentially Transforming Experience of Community/University Collaboration." *Journal of Planning Education and Research* 17 (4): 334–47.

Diamond, Michael A. 1993. *The Unconscious Life of Organizations.* Westport, Conn.: Quorum.

Dryfoos, Joy. 1994. *Full Service Schools.* San Francisco: Jossey-Bass.

Eaton, Susan E. 2001. *The Other Boston Busing Story.* New Haven: Yale University Press.

Eccles, Jacquelynne S., Sarah Lord, and Carol Midgely. 1991. "What Are We Doing to Early Adolescents? The Impact of Educational Contexts on Early Adolescents." *American Journal of Education* 99 (4): 521–42.

Edmonds, Ronald. 1979. "Effective Schools for the Urban Poor." *Educational Leadership* 37:15–24.

Emery, Fred E., and Eric L. Trist. 1965. "The Causal Texture of Organizational Environments." *Human Relations* 18:21–32.

———. 1973. *Towards a Social Ecology*. New York: Plenum Press.

Empower Baltimore Management Corporation. 1997. *Request for Proposals: Extended School Day*. Baltimore: Author.

Epstein, Joyce L. 1995. "School, Family, and Community Partnerships: Caring for the Children We Share." *Phi Delta Kappan* 76:701–12.

———. 2001. *School, Family, and Community Partnerships*. Boulder: Westview Press.

Fantini, Mario D. 1973. *Public Schools of Choice*. New York: Simon and Schuster.

Federal Register. 1994. 59 (April 4): 64.

———. 1997. 62 (March 20):54.

Feld, Marcia Marker. 1998. "Introduction." *Journal of Planning Education and Research* 17 (4): 285–90.

Ferguson, Ronald F., and William T. Dickens, eds. 1999. *Urban Problems and Community Development*. Washington, D.C.: Brookings Institution.

Finn, Chester E., Jr., Bruno V. Manno, and Gregg Vanourek. 2000. *Charter Schools in Action*. Princeton: Princeton University Press.

Fisher, Robert. 1984. *Let the People Decide*. Boston: Twayne.

Forester, John. 1989. *Planning in the Face of Power*. Berkeley: University of California Press.

———. 1999. *The Deliberative Practitioner*. Cambridge: MIT Press.

Fowler, Robert Booth. 1991. *The Dance with Community*. Lawrence: University Press of Kansas.

Friend, John K., John M. Power, and Christopher J. L. Yewlett. 1974. *Public Planning: The Inter-corporate Dimension*. London: Tavistock.

Fulbright-Anderson, Karen, Anne C. Kubisch, and James P. Connell, eds. 1998. *New Approaches to Evaluating Community Initiatives, Vol. 2, Theory, Measurement, and Analysis*. Washington, D.C.: Aspen Institute.

Gans, Herbert J. 1988. *Middle American Individualism*. New York: Free Press.

Giloth, Robert P. 1993. "From Cannery Row to Gold Coast in Baltimore: Is This 'Development'?" Pp. 103–17 in *Comparative Studies in Local Economic Development*, ed. Peter B. Meyer. Westport, Conn.: Greenwood Press.

———. 1994. "In Search of Collaboration: Community Planning in Baltimore 1988–1994." Unpublished manuscript.

Gittell, Marilyn. 1994. "School Reform in New York and Chicago: Revisiting the Ecology of Local Games." *Urban Affairs Quarterly* 30:136–51.

Gittell, Marilyn, and Kathe Newman. 1998. *Empowerment Zone Implementation: Community Participation and Community Capacity*. New York: City University of New York, Graduate School and University Center.

Gittell, Ross, and Avis Vidal. 1998. *Community Organizing*. Thousand Oaks, Calif.: Sage.

Gollnick, Donna M., and Philip C. Chinn. 1997. *Multicultural Education in a Pluralistic Society*. 5th ed. Old Tappan, N.J.: Prentice Hall.

Gould, Laurence J., Robert Ebers, and Ross Clinchy. N. d. "The Systems Psychodynamics of a Joint Venture: Anxiety, Social Defenses, and the Management of Mutual Dependence." Unpublished paper.

Gray, Barbara. 1985. "Conditions Facilitating Interorganizational Collaboration." *Human Relations* 38:911–36.

———. 1989. *Collaborating: Finding Common Ground in Multiparty Problems*. San Francisco: Jossey-Bass.

Greenwood, Davydd J., and Morten Levin. 1998. *Introduction to Action Research*. Thousand Oaks, Calif.: Sage.

Greenwood, Davydd, William Foote Whyte, and Ira Harkavy. 1993. "Participatory Action Research as a Process and as a Goal." *Human Relations* 46 (2): 175–92.

Hamburg, David A. 1994. *Today's Children*. New York: Times Books.

Harkavy, Ira, and John L. Pickett. 1991. "The Role of Mediating Structures in University and Community Revitalization: The University of Pennsylvania and West Philadelphia as a Case Study." *Journal of Research and Development in Education* 25 (1): 10–25.

Hartman, Chester. 2002. "High Classroom Turnover: How Children Get Left Behind." Pp. 227–44 in *Rights at Risk*, ed. Dianne M. Piche, William L. Taylor, and Robin A. Reed. Washington, D.C.: Citizens Commission on Civil Rights.

Henderson, Anne T., and Nancy Berla. 1994. *A New Generation of Evidence: the Family Is Critical to Student Achievement*. Washington, D.C.: Center for Law and Education.

Henig, Jeffrey R. 1994. *Rethinking School Choice*. Princeton: Princeton University Press.

Henig, Jeffrey, R., Richard C. Hula, Marion Orr, and Desiree Pedescleaux. 1999. *Race, Politics and School Reform: Atlanta, Baltimore, Detroit, and Washington, D.C.* Princeton: Princeton University Press.

Herman, Rebecca, et al. 1999. *An Educators' Guide to Schoolwide Reform*. Arlington, Va.: Educational Research Service.

Hirsch, E. D., Jr. 1996. *The Schools We Need and Why We Don't Have Them*. New York: Doubleday.

Hirsch, E. D., Jr., Joseph Kett, and James Trefil. 1988. *Cultural Literacy*. New York: Vintage.

Hirschhorn, Larry. 1988. *The Workplace Within*. Cambridge: MIT Press.

———. 1991. *Managing in the New Team Environment*. Reading, Mass.: Addison-Wesley.

Hodgson, Richard C., Daniel J. Levinson, and Abraham Zaleznik. 1974. *The Executive Role Constellation*. Boston: Harvard University, The Graduate School of Business Administration.

Honig, Meredith I., Joseph Kahne, and Milbrey W. McLaughlin. 2001. "School-Community Connections: Strengthening Opportunity to Learn and Opportunity to Teach." Pp. 998–1028 in *Handbook of Research on Teaching*, 4th ed., ed. Virginia Richardson. Washington, D.C.: American Educational Research Association.

Hrabowski, Freeman A., III, Kenneth I. Maton, and Geoffrey L. Greif. 1998. *Beating the Odds*. New York: Oxford University Press.

Hunter, James Davison. 1991. *Culture Wars*. New York: Basic Books.

Janis, Irving L. 1982. *Groupthink*. 2nd ed. Boston: Houghton Mifflin.

Janowitz, Morris. 1952. *The Community Press in an Urban Setting*. Glencoe, Ill.: Free Press.

Kagan, Sharon L. 1998. "Using a Theory of Change Approach in a National Evaluation of Family Support Programs." Pp. 113–21 in *New Approaches to Evaluating Community Initiatives, Vol. 2, Theory, Measurement, and Analysis*, ed. Karen Fulbright-Anderson, Anne C. Kubisch, and James P. Connell. Washington, D.C.: Aspen Institute.

Katz, Michael B. 1975. *Class, Bureaucracy, and Schools: The Illusion of Educational Change in America.* Expanded ed. New York: Praeger.

Kets de Vries, Manfred F. R., and Associates. 1991. *Organizations on the Couch*. San Francisco: Jossey-Bass.

Kets de Vries, Manfred F. R., and Danny Miller. 1984. *The Neurotic Organization*. San Francisco: Jossey-Bass.

Kettner, Peter M., Robert M. Moroney, and Lawrence L. Martin. 1990. *Designing and Managing Programs*. Newbury Park, Calif.: Sage.

Klein, Stephen P., Laura S. Hamilton, Daniel F. McCaffrey, and Brian M. Stecher. 2000. *What Do Test Scores in Texas Tell Us?* Santa Monica, Calif: RAND Corporation.

Kretzmann, John P., and John L. McKnight. 1993. *Building Communities from the Inside Out*. Evanston, Ill.: Northwestern University, Center for Urban Affairs and Policy Research.

Kuttner, Bob. 1976. "Ethnic Renewal: How Ordinary People in East Baltimore Have Created a Model Answer to Inner-City Blight." *The New York Times Magazine* (May 9), pp. 18–19.

Lambert, Christopher S., and Jennean Everett Reynolds. 1997. *The State of Baltimore's Schools: Data and Information on the Current Status of Baltimore City Public Schools.* 3 vols. Baltimore: Advocates for Children and Youth.

LeGates, Richard, and Gib Robinson. 1998. "Institutionalizing University/Community Partnerships." *Journal of Planning Education and Research* 17 (4): 312–22.

Levin, Benjamin, and J. Anthony Riffel. 2000. "Changing Schools in a Changing World." Pp. 178–94 in *The Sharp Edge of Educational Change*, ed. Nina Bascia and Andy Hargreaves. London: RoutledgeFalmer.

Lewin, Kurt. 1951. *Field Theory in Social Science.* Edited by Dorwin Cartwright. New York: Harper and Brothers.

Lewis, Helen Block. 1974. *Shame and Guilt in Neurosis.* New York: International Universities Press.

Lindblom, Charles E. 1965. *The Intelligence of Democracy.* New York: Free Press.

Long, Norton E. 1958. "The Local Community as an Ecology of Games." *American Journal of Sociology* 44:251–61.

Lynd, Helen Merrell. 1958. *On Shame and the Search for Identity.* New York: Harcourt, Brace, and World.

Mandelbaum, Seymour J. 2000. *Open Moral Communities.* Cambridge: MIT Press.

Marris, Peter, and Martin Rein. 1982. *Dilemmas of Social Reform: Poverty and Community Action in the United States.* 2nd ed. Chicago: University of Chicago Press.

Maryland State Department of Education. 1994. *Maryland School Performance Report 1994: State and School Systems.* Baltimore: Author.

———. 2001. *Maryland School Performance Report: Report Card 2001.* Http://msp.msde.state.md.us/MSPAP.ASP.

Massey, Douglas S., and Nancy A. Denton. 1993. *American Apartheid.* Cambridge: Harvard University Press.

Maton, Kenneth I., Monica L. Greene, Freeman A Hrabowski, III, and Geoffrey Greif. 2002 *Overcoming the Odds: Raising Academically Successful African American Young Women.* New York: Oxford University Press.

Maurrasse, David J. 2001. *Beyond the Campus.* New York: Routledge.

Mayfield, Loomis, Maureen Hellwig, and Brian Banks. 1998. *The Chicago Response to Urban Problems: Building University/Community Collaborations.* Chicago: University of Illinois at Chicago, Great Cities Institute, College of Urban Planning and Public Affairs.

McCall, Robert B., Christina J. Groark, Mark S. Strauss, and C. N. Johnson. 1998. "Challenges of University-Community Outreach to Traditional Universities: The University of Pittsburgh Office of Child Development Experience." Pp 203–30 in *University-Community Collaborations for the Twenty-First Century*, ed. Richard M. Lerner and Lou Anna K. Simon. New York: Garland.

McDonald, Joseph P. 1992. *Steps in Planning Backwards: Early Lessons from the Schools.* Coalition of Essentials Schools Fieldbook. Http://www.essentialschools.org/pubs/exhib_schdes/steps.html.

———. 1993. *Dilemmas of Planning Backwards: Rescuing a Good Idea.* Coalition of Essential Schools Fieldbook. Http://www.essentialschools.org/pubs/exhib_schdes/dilemmas.html.

McMillan, David W., and David M. Chavis. 1986. "Sense of Community: A Definition and Theory." *Journal of Community Psychology* 14:6–23.

Medoff, Peter, and Holly Sklar. 1994. *Streets of Hope: the Fall and Rise of an Urban Neighborhood.* Boston: South End Press.

Meier, Deborah. 1995. *The Power of Their Ideas.* Boston: Beacon Press.

Meyer, John W. 1977. "The Effects of Education as an Institution." *American Journal of Sociology* 83:55–77.

Meyer, John, and Brian Rowan. 1983. "The Structure of Educational Organizations." Pp. 60–87 in *The Dynamics of Organizational Change in Education*, ed. J. Victor Baldridge and Terrence Deal. Berkeley: McCutchan.

Meyer, John W., William R. Scott, and David Strang. 1994. "Centralization, Fragmentation, and School District Complexity." Pp. 160–78 in *Institutional Environments and Organizations: Structural Complexity and Individualism*, ed. William R. Scott, John W. Meyer, and Associates. Thousand Oaks, Calif.: Sage.

Milligan, Sharon, Claudia Coulton, Peter York, and Ronald Register. 1998. "Implementing a Theory of Change Evaluation in the Cleveland Community-Building Initiative: A Case Study." Pp. 45–85 in *New Approaches to Evaluating Community Initiatives, Vol. 2, Theory, Measurement, and Analysis*, ed. Karen Fulbright-Anderson, Anne C. Kubisch, and James P. Connell. Washington, D.C.: Aspen Institute.

Moynihan, Daniel Patrick. 1970. *Maximum Feasible Misunderstanding: Community Action in the War on Poverty.* New York: Free Press.

Murnane, Richard J., and Frank Levy. 1996. *Teaching the New Basic Skills.* New York: Free Press.

National Center for Education Statistics, Office of Educational Research and Improvement, U. S. Department of Education. 1999. *Digest of Education Statistics 1998.* Washington, D.C.: U. S. Government Printing Office.

———. 2001. *Digest of Education Statistics 2000.* Washington, D.C.: U. S. Government Printing Office.

National Commission on Excellence in Education. 1983. *A Nation at Risk.* Washington, D.C.: U. S. Government Printing Office.

National Diffusion Network. 1994. *Educational Programs That Work.* 20th ed. Longmont, Colo.: Sopris West.

Nettles, Saundra Murray, and Joseph H. Pleck. 1994. "Risk, Resilience, and Development: The Multiple Ecologies of Black Adolescents." Pp. 147–81 in *Stress, Risk, and Resilience in Children and Adolescents*, ed. Robert J. Haggerty, Lonnie R. Sherrod, Norman Garmezy, and Michael Rutter. Cambridge: Cambridge University Press.

Nyden, Philip, Anne Figert, Mark Shibley, and Darryl Burrows, eds. 1997. *Building Community: Social Science in Action.* Thousand Oaks, Calif.: Pine Forge Press.

Office of the Mayor, City of Baltimore. 1994. Application for Empowerment Zone Designation. Baltimore: Author.

Olsen, Johan P. 1976. "Choice in an Organized Anarchy." Pp. 82–139 in *Ambiguity and Choice in Organizations*, ed. James G. March and Johan P. Olsen. Bergen: Universitetsforlaget.

Olson, Lynn, and Craig D. Jerald. 1998. "Barriers to Success." *Quality Counts, Education Week* 17 (17): 9–23.

Orfield, Gary, and Susan E. Eaton. 1996. *Dismantling Desegregation.* New York: The New Press.

Orr, Marion. 1999. *Black Social Capital: The Politics of School Reform in Baltimore, 1986–1998.* Lawrence: University Press of Kansas.

Perrucci, Robert, and Marc Pilisuk. 1970. "Leaders and Ruling Elites: The Interorganizational Bases of Community Power." *American Sociological Review* 35:1040–56.

Peterson, Paul E., and Bryan C. Hassel, eds. 1998. *Learning from School Choice.* Washington, D.C.: Brookings Institution.

Piers, Gerhart. 1971. "Shame and Guilt." Pp. 15–55 in *Shame and Guilt*, ed. Gerhart Piers and Milton B. Singer. New York: W. W. Norton.

Podl, Jody Brown, Steven H. Godowsky, Maryan Scarbrough, Carolyn Steinwedel, Marianne Devine, Cathy Katz, Susan Lukas, and Julie Gainsburg. 1992. *The Process of Planning Backwards: Stories from Three Schools.* Coalition of Essential Schools Fieldbook. Http://www.essentialschools.org/pubs/exhib_schdes/proback.html.

Pollock, Marcus, and Ed Rutkowski. 1998. *The Urban Transition Zone: A Place Worth a Fight.* Baltimore: Patterson Park Community Development Corporation.

Portz, John, Lana Stein, and Robin R. Jones. 1999. *City Schools and City Politics.* Lawrence: University Press of Kansas.

Pressman, Jeffrey L., and Aaron B. Wildavsky. 1973. *Implementation.* Berkeley: University of California Press.

Purkey, Stewart C., and Marshall S. Smith. 1983. "Effective Schools: A Review." *Elementary School Journal* 83 (4): 427–452.

Putnam, Robert D. 2000. *Bowling Alone.* New York: Simon and Schuster.

Rainwater, Lee, and William L. Yancey, eds. 1967. *The Moynihan Report and the Politics of Controversy.* Cambridge: MIT Press.

Rasell, Edith, and Richard Rothstein. 1993. *School Choice*. Washington, D.C.: Economic Policy Institute.

Reardon, Kenneth M. 1995. "Creating a Community/University Partnership That Works: The Case of the East St. Louis Action Research Project." *Metropolitan Universities: An International Forum* 6 (2): 47–59.

———. 1998. "Enhancing the Development Capacity of East St. Louis' Community Organizations." *Journal of Planning Education and Research* 17 (4): 323–33.

———. 1999. "Promoting Community Development through Empowerment Planning in East St. Louis, Illinois." Pp. 124–39 in *America's Poorest Urban Neighborhoods Urban Policy and Planning,* ed. W. Dennis Keating and Norman Krumholz. Thousand Oaks, Calif.: Sage Publications.

———. 2000. "An Experiential Approach to Creating a Community/University Partnership That Works: The East St. Louis Action Research Project." *Cityscape: A Journal of Policy Development and Research* 5 (1): 59–74.

Rose, Lowell C., and Alec M. Gallup. 1999. "The 31st Annual Phi Delta Kappan/Gallup Poll of the Public's Attitudes toward the Public Schools." *Phi Delta Kappan* 81:41-56.

———. 2000. "The 32nd Annual Phi Delta Kappan/Gallup Poll of the Public's Attitudes toward the Public Schools. *Phi Delta Kappan* 82:41–57.

Rosenfield, Sylvia, and Barbara Ann English. 1996. Education in the Baltimore Empowerment Zone: A Report. College Park, Md.: Author.

Rosenfield, Sylvia A., and Todd A. Gravois. 1996. *Instructional Consultation Teams*. New York: Guilford Press.

Rubin, Victor. 1998. "The Role of Universities in Community-Building Initiatives." *Journal of Planning Education and Research* 17 (4): 302–11.

Rubinowitz, Leonard S., and James E. Rosenbaum. 2000. *Crossing the Class and Color Lines*. Chicago: University of Chicago Press.

Saegert, Susan, J. Phillip Thompson, and Mark R. Warren, eds. 2001. *Social Capital and Poor Communities*. New York: Russell Sage Foundation.

Sarason, Seymour B. 1972. *The Creation of Settings and the Future Societies*. San Francisco: Jossey-Bass.

———. 1990. *The Predictable Failure of Educational Reform*. San Francisco: Jossey-Bass.

———. 1998. *Charter Schools: Another Flawed Educational Reform?* New York: Teachers College Press.

Sarason, Seymour B., Charles F. Carroll, Kenneth Maton, Saul Cohen, and Elizabeth Lorentz. 1977. *Human Services and Resource Networks*. San Francisco: Jossey-Bass.

Sarason, Seymour B., and Elizabeth Lorentz. 1979. *The Challenge of the Resource Exchange Network*. San Francisco: Jossey-Bass.

Sarason, Seymour B., and Elizabeth M. Lorentz. 1998. *Crossing Boundaries: Collaboration, Coordination, and the Redefinition of Resources*. San Francisco: Jossey-Bass.

Schön, Donald A. 1971. *Beyond the Stable State.* New York: W. W. Norton.

———. 1983. *The Reflective Practitioner.* New York: Basic Books.

Schön, Donald A., and Martin Rein. 1994. *Frame Reflection.* New York: Basic Books.

Schorr, Lisbeth B. 1997. *Common Purpose.* New York: Anchor.

Schorr, Lisbeth B., with Daniel Schorr. 1989. *Within Our Reach.* New York: Anchor.

Schwartz, Howard S. 1990. *Narcissistic Process and Corporate Decay.* New York: New York University Press.

Scriven, Michael. 1967. "The Methodology of Evaluation." Pp. 39–83 in *Perspectives of Curriculum Evaluation*, AERA Monograph Series on Curriculum Evaluation, vol. 1, ed. Ralph W. Tyler, Robert M. Gagne, and Michael Scriven. Chicago: Rand McNally.

———. 1991. *Evaluation Thesaurus.* 4th ed. Newbury Park, Calif.: Sage.

Sennett, Richard. 1980. *Authority.* New York: Alfred A. Knopf.

Shirley, Dennis. 1997. *Community Organizing for Urban School Reform.* Austin: University of Texas Press.

Siegel, Eric. 1997. "City Schools Must Tackle Special Ed." *Baltimore Sun* (February 9), pp. 1B, 2B.

Simon, David, and Edward Burns. 1997. *The Corner: A Year in the Life of an Inner-City Neighborhood.* New York: Broadway Books.

Smith, Stephen Samuel. 1997. "Hugh Governs? Regime and Education Policy in Charlotte, North Carolina." *Journal of Urban Affairs* 19:247–74.

Southeast Education Task Force. 1997. *K–8 Schools: What the Research Shows.* Baltimore: Author.

———. 1999. *Southeast Community Plan on Education.* Baltimore: Author.

———. 2000. *Report of the Southeast Education Task Force: Critical Need for Capital Improvements in Southeast Schools.* Baltimore: Author.

Southeast Planning Council. 1993. *Southeast Community Plan.* Baltimore: Author.

Stein, Howard F. 1994. *Listening Deeply.* Boulder: Westview Press.

Stone, Clarence N. 1993. "Urban Regimes and the Capacity to Govern: A Political Economy Approach." *Journal of Urban Affairs* 15:1–28.

Stone, Clarence N., ed. 1998. *Changing Urban Education.* Lawrence: University Press of Kansas.

Stone, Clarence N., Jeffrey R. Henig, Bryan D. Jones, and Carol Pierannunzi. 2001. *Building Civic Capacity.* Lawrence: University Press of Kansas.

Strauss, Jessica. 1996. *Education Agenda—Community Input Process. Report to the Economic Opportunities, Education, and Community Development Committee, Empower Baltimore Management Corporation.* Draft. Baltimore: Author.

Thompson, Jean. 1995. "Amprey May Lose Special Ed Duties." *Baltimore Sun* (April 9), pp. 1B, 5B.

3D/International. 1998. *Comprehensive Facilities Assessments: Final Report for Baltimore City Public Schools: Summary Report.* Baltimore: Author.

Towers Perrin/Cresap. 1992. *A Report of a Management Study of the Baltimore City Public Schools.* Baltimore: Associated Black Charities.

Trist, Eric L. 1977. "Organizational Ecology." *Australian Journal of Management* 2: 162–75.

———. 1983. "Referent Organizations and the Development of Inter-organizational Domains." *Human Relations* 36: 269–94.

———. 1985. "Intervention Strategies for Interorganizational Domains." Pp. 167–97 in *Human Systems Development,* ed. Robert Tannenbaum, Newton Margulies, Fred Massarik, and Associates. San Francisco: Jossey-Bass.

Truelove, Lee. 1977a. *The Director Wears Blue Jeans: The Story of SECO.* Draft manuscript. Baltimore: South East Community Organization.

———. 1977b. *SECO History.* Baltimore: South East Community Organization.

Tuckman, Bruce W. 1965. "Developmental Sequence in Small Groups." *Psychological Bulletin* 63:384–99.

Tuckman, Bruce W., and Mary Ann C. Jensen. 1977. "Stages of Small-Group Development Revisited." *Group & Organization Studies* 2 (4): 419–27.

Tyack, David D. 1974. *The One Best System: a History of American Urban Education.* Cambridge: Harvard University Press.

Tyack, David, and Elisabeth Hansot. 1982. *Managers of Virtue: Public School Leadership in America, 1820–1980.* New York: Basic Books.

U. S. Department of Education, Urban Community Service Program. 1997. *FY 1997 Project Abstracts.* Washington, D.C.: Author.

U. S. Department of Housing and Urban Development. 1994. "Statement of Henry Cisneros on the Announcement of Empowerment Zones and Enterprise Communities." News Release HUD #94-212. Washington, D.C.: Author.

———. 1997. *SuperNOFA 1.* Washington, D.C.: Author.

U. S. Department of Housing and Urban Development, Office of University Partnerships, Office of Policy Development and Research, Community Outreach Partnership Centers Program. 1995. *University-Community Partnerships: Current Practices.* Rockville, Md.: HUDUser.

———. 1996. *University-Community Partnerships: Current Practices.* Vol. 2. Rockville, Md.: HUDUser.

———. 1999. *University-Community Partnerships in America: Current Practices.* Vol. 3. Rockville, Md.: HUDUser.

Warren, Mark R. 2001. *Dry Bones Rattling: Community Building to Revitalize American Democracy.* Princeton: Princeton University Press.

Warren, Roland L. 1967. "The Interorganizational Field as a Focus for Investigation." *Administrative Science Quarterly* 12:396–419.

———. 1971. *Truth, Love, and Social Change.* Chicago: Rand McNally.

Warren, Roland L., Stephen M. Rose, and Ann F. Bergunder. 1971. *The Structure of Urban Reform.* Lexington, Mass.: D. C. Heath.

Weber, Max. 1967. *From Max Weber.* Edited and translated by Hans H. Gerth and C. Wright Mills. New York: Oxford University Press.

Weick, Karl. 1979. *The Social Psychology of Organizing.* Reading, Penn.: Addison-Wesley.

Weiss, Carol H. 1995. "Nothing as Practical as Good Theory: Exploring Theory-Based Evaluation for Comprehensive Community Initiatives for Children and Families." Pp. 65–92 in *New Approaches to Evaluating Community Initiatives: Concepts, Methods, and Contexts,* ed. James P. Connell, Anne C. Kubisch, Lisbeth B. Schorr, and Carol H. Weiss. Washington, D.C.: Aspen Institute.

———. 1998. *Evaluation.* 2nd ed. Upper Saddle River, N.J.: Prentice Hall.

Wellman, Barry. 1999. "From Little Boxes to Loosely-Bounded Networks: The Privatization and Domestication of Community." Pp. 94–114 in *Sociology for the Twenty-First Century: Continuities and Cutting Edges,* ed. Janet Abu-Lughod. Chicago: University of Chicago Press.

Wells, Amy Stuart, and Robert L. Crain. 1997. *Stepping Over the Color Line.* New Haven: Yale University Press.

White, Sammis B. 1999. "The Case for Parent Education." Paper presented at the American Collegiate Schools of Planning Conference, Chicago.

Whyte, William Foote, ed. 1991. *Participatory Action Research.* Newbury Park, Calif.: Sage.

Wiewel, Wim, and Michael Lieber. 1998. "Goal Achievement versus Relationship Building: The Challenges of University-Community Partnership." *Journal of Planning Education and Research* 17 (4): 291–301.

Wilson, William Julius. 1987. *The Truly Disadvantaged.* Chicago: University of Chicago Press.

———. 1996. *When Work Disappears.* New York: Vintage Books.

Index